FORCED TO ABANDON OUR FIELDS

FORCED TO ABANDON OUR FIELDS

The 1914 Clay Southworth Gila River Pima Interviews

David H. DeJong

University of Utah Press | Salt Lake City

The Defiance House Man colophon is a registered trademark of the University of Utah Press. It is based upon a four-foot-tall, Ancient Puebloan pictograph (late PIII) near Glen Canyon, Utah.

Library of Congress Cataloging-in-Publication Data

DeJong, David H.
Forced to abandon our fields : the 1914 Clay Southworth Gila River
Pima interviews/David H. DeJong.
    p.   cm.
Includes bibliographical references and index.
ISBN 978-1-60781-095-7 (pbk. : alk. paper)
1. Pima Indians—History. 2. Pima Indians—Agriculture—History. 3. Pima Indians—
Interviews. 4. Water-supply—Gila River Region (N.M. and Ariz.)—History. 5. Water
rights—Gila River Region (N.M. and Ariz.)—History. 6. Gila River (N.M. and
Ariz.)—Water rights—History. 7. Human ecology—Gila River Region (N.M. and
Ariz.) 8. Nature—Effect of human beings on—Gila River Region (N.M. and Ariz.) I. Title.
E99.P6.D448 2011
979.1004'9745529—dc22   2010044190

Frontispiece courtesy of the Arizona Historical Society.

Errata and further information on this and other titles available online at UofUpress.com

Printed and bound in the United States of America.

CONTENTS

ILLUSTRATIONS AND TABLES

PREFACE

My interest in the Gila River (Pima) Survey interviews is a by-product of my doctoral work at the University of Arizona on Pima water rights and agricultural history between 1848 and 1921. In the spring of 2004 Wendy Bigler (then a Ph.D. student in Geography at Arizona State University, analyzing riverine geomorphology) and I spent several days rummaging through the dank and dusty basement of the San Carlos Irrigation Project in Coolidge, Arizona. In the midst of hundreds of maps, engineering drawings, and blueprints, we came across the original hand-drawn maps of U.S. Indian Irrigation Service engineer Clay "Charles" Southworth (while born Clay, he went by Charles or Buzz for most of his adult life), who oversaw the Gila River Survey in 1914 in anticipation of the federal government's litigation of Pima water rights. After I had secured permission from Carl Christensen of the San Carlos Irrigation Project to remove the maps, Wendy (through her contacts at the Salt River Project in Tempe, Arizona) digitally scanned them. The maps proved to be extremely beneficial to both Wendy's dissertation and mine. The interviews were in the Arizona State Museum Library Archives in Tucson. I later found a copy of the interviews at the National Archives repository in Laguna Niguel, California.

Once we had completed our respective dissertations, Wendy and I talked about "doing something" with the maps and the interviews that Southworth conducted with the Pima elders. We recognized that the maps and interviews were largely inaccessible to the broader academic world and the Gila River Indian Community. For several years we discussed jointly publishing the material. Due to a busy research and teaching schedule at the University of Illinois, Carbondale, Wendy could not commit to the project, so I progressed alone. Without her enthusiasm about the interviews, I might not have pursued publishing them. I am indebted to Wendy and acknowledge her commitment to and support for making these interviews accessible to the public.

Several others are worthy of acknowledgment. Carl Christensen was the chief engineer for the San Carlos Irrigation Project for nearly two decades and had an encyclopedic knowledge of the project from its inception in 1924. Without Carl's support in digitizing the plane table maps and providing access to the paper archives of the San Carlos Irrigation Project, the Pima interviews might have remained inconspicuous in their absence from the broader academic world. I am also indebted to Henrietta Lopez. Henrietta is an Akimel O'otham (Pima) from the Gila River Indian Community and is fluent in the O'otham language. I have known Henrietta for nine years and appreciate her deep sense of respect for the history and *himdag* (way of life) of the Huhugam (meaning those who walked before). Henrietta provided valuable assistance in translating antiquated and misspelled O'otham words from the nearly 100-year-old Southworth interviews and letters.

I also appreciate the support of J. Andrew Darling and M. Kyle Woodson. In addition to their expertise in Hohokam and O'otham history and Kyle's proficiency in prehistoric and historic irrigation practices, Andy and Kyle were supportive of my efforts. Both of these scholars directed me to pertinent public domain maps that the Cultural Resource Management Program prepared as part of its overall treatment plans for mitigating work by the Pima-Maricopa Irrigation Project as it constructs and rehabilitates the irrigation delivery system for the Gila River Indian Community.

Finally, I recognize the Gila River Indian Community. I am humbled that the Community has provided me with the opportunity and responsibility of overseeing a historic irrigation construction project. The Pima-Maricopa Irrigation Project is poised to restore the agricultural economy to the Pima and Maricopa. It has been a blessing to work with the Community for the past thirteen years. I dedicate the reproduction of these Pima interviews to the Akimel O'otham and Pee Posh of the Gila River Indian Community.

I also offer a word on several of the irrigation ditches referenced in the interviews. Some of the ditches have multiple names and this can cause confusion. To clarify this, it is helpful to remember that the Sweetwater Ditch [#23] was also known as the Stotonic Ditch. In a similar manner, the Ancient Sweetwater Ditch [#25] was also known as the Ancient Stotonic Ditch. Finally, the Sranuka ditch [#15] is often misspelled as Sranaka by Southworth and his interpreters. The Sranuka ditch was also known as the Old Snaketown ditch or simply as the Old Ditch.

INTRODUCTION

"Indians Starving to Death"

In June 1900 the *Chicago Tribune* reported what many people in Arizona Territory already knew: the Pima Indians on the Gila River Indian Reservation faced harsh economic times. In an article entitled "Indians Starving to Death," the *Tribune* reported that thousands of Pima were "perishing" due to "failure of crops."[1] Newspapers across the nation followed the *Tribune*'s lead and printed a series of articles on the socioeconomic conditions facing the Pima.[2] For the Pima, an eight-year-long drought combined with more than thirty years of upstream diversions had left the Gila River dry through the reservation and their fields dusty. Many proud Pima starved rather than seek government charity.[3] Pima village chief Joseph Head remarked on these difficult times in 1914: "White people have no idea how the Pima Indian has suffered by the diversions of their water."[4]

A chorus of Pima farmers and leaders joined Head's lamentation. "We have suffered much loss," 49-year-old John Rhodes explained.[5] Farming on the reservation "got uncertain," 84-year-old Jose Enis recalled, with the Pima "forced . . . to do the best we can for subsistence. [We] never suffered so before the white man came."[6] Numerous ditches "are now lying idle and covered with brush," 53-year-old village leader James Hollen explained.[7] As villages and fields disappeared, the Pima's "pride as a self-supporting and independent people was forever taken from us."[8]

Despite difficult times, optimism for a brighter future remained. "I hope that some day all these once cultivated land[s] may bring to the coming children abundant harvests again," 70-year-old Ho-ke Wilson told Southworth in 1914.[9] As 65-year-old George Pablo recalled, there was once a "time when water in the river was plentiful and the Pimas irrigated their lands," but upstream diversions had taken their toll.[10] With construction of the upstream Florence Canal in 1886 (and its completion in 1889), Pima fields were left short of water. Indians living in the lower villages felt the water loss first, 48-year-old Juan Lagons explained, "as we were the last to take out our water from the river."[11]

In the midst of these difficult times, the U.S. Indian Irrigation Service assigned 33-year-old engineer Charles Southworth to oversee the Gila River Survey in 1914. This survey was part of a broader effort by the federal government to restore some measure of prosperity to the Pima, who for decades had requested protection and restoration of their water taken by upstream settlers along the Gila River. In addition to surveying currently cultivated lands, Southworth surveyed all lands and fields showing evidence of previous irrigation and cultivation by the Pima and Maricopa. As a result of this effort, the U.S. government published "The History of Irrigation along the Gila River" in 1919.[12]

As part of the survey, Southworth interviewed thirty-four Pima farmers, elders, and leaders. These interviews, which did not include any women or any Maricopa, put a face on the depth of economic hardships faced by the Pima in the late nineteenth and early twentieth centuries. While Southworth noted the interviews in "The History of Irrigation," he never published them and later regretted that he did not make them known to a wider audience. In 1931 Phoenix archaeologist Odd S. Halseth of the Pueblo Grande Museum approached Southworth about publishing the interviews and received an enthusiastic response.[13] Unfortunately, Halseth never published them.

For many years the only extant copies of the interviews were the copy in the hands of the Southworth family and the copy that Halseth filed in the Pueblo Grande Museum in Phoenix.[14] Anthropologist Robert A. Hackenberg, then working for the U.S. Justice Department on Pima claims before the Indian Claims Commission, discovered the interviews in 1958 and submitted a copy of the original field notes to the University of Arizona's Bureau of Ethnic Research four years later.[15] Hackenberg commended Southworth's efforts and said that he "was a much better ethnographer than [Frank] Russell," whose 1901–2 research on the Pima was posthumously published by the U.S. Bureau of Ethnic Research in 1908.[16] Hackenberg considered Southworth's work "superior in every respect," because Southworth "attempted to reconstruct practises [*sic*] as they existed in 1850," prior to sustained American contact.[17]

The interviews cover decades of history and demonstrate the nexus between upstream diversions and the Pima economy, agriculture, water use, and water rights. They provide firsthand accounts of the impact that federal land and resource policies had on the Pima economy and agriculture during a crucial era of American and American Indian history in the late nineteenth century when the federal government opened the West to homesteading and facilitated development of the region's vast resources.

As an agricultural people, the Pima did not passively accept these policies and events. They proved to be adaptive, demonstrating their resourcefulness in important ways. In response to water deprivation and infringement of their water rights, they reduced the amount of land they cultivated but nonetheless continued to farm. "Although the water supply is small," James Hollen explained to Southworth, "we manage to distribute it equally among us, thereby getting a crop of some kind each year."[18] While the Pima had increased their cultivated acreage and expanded their trade networks before 1870, in later years they creatively found ways to keep land in production despite water shortages. As the water crisis deepened, the Pima abandoned their least productive lands. In the midst of great hardship, they relocated (or abandoned) a number of villages and scores of fields in an attempt to maintain an agricultural economy against great odds.

Deciphering the interviews provides a window into an important time in Pima history, offering firsthand descriptions of both the pinnacle of the Pima agricultural economy and the depth to which it had descended by the twentieth century. As the interviews reveal, the success of American Indian agrarian economies a century ago rarely matched the rhetoric of federal policymakers. Federal policies toward American Indians were inconsistent, entirely failing to protect the cornerstone of western Indian agricultural economies: the water upon which such economies depended.

The federal government opened the West to settlement by employing a socioeconomic and political philosophy of economic liberalism. The application of this philosophy had several consequences for the Pima. Initially it fostered an economic boom (1846–68) that resulted in greater material prosperity, expansion of the Pima economy, and an increase in Pima acreage under irrigation (an estimated 15,000 acres by 1859). Extending new ditches above

TABLE 0.1. Estimated Pima Irrigated Acreage: Selected
Years, 1850–1911

Year	Acres
1850	12,500
1859	15,000
1860	14,582
1876	7,000–8,000
1893	< 5,000
1896	< 4,000
1900	< 3,600
1911	4,500

Source: Annual Reports of the Commissioner of Indian Affairs,
1850–1912; and Willis T. Lee, The Underground Waters of Gila
Valley, Arizona.

the villages and away from the Gila River led to a period of unprecedented
economic growth. This era represents the peak of Pima agriculture and economic activity.

With Pima agriculture providing a food source for emigrants and miners,
homesteading above the reservation took root and expanded after the Civil
War. This initiated a second stage in the application of economic liberalism
and resulted in water deprivation among the Pima (1869–90). The Pima share
of river water declined year by year, resulting in widespread famine throughout the villages. The final stage of economic liberalism culminated in the
complete capitulation of the Pima economy (1891–1905). During this period
the Pima faced starvation, near-complete water deprivation, and extreme
poverty.

In the end, lack of federal restraint despoiled the Pima agricultural
economy and pushed the Indians to the periphery of the national economy.[19]
Federal lawmakers exhibited no "interest in the welfare of Native Americans"
and manipulated a dynamic federal resource policy for the purpose of con-
trolling and directing the land and its resources for the benefit of themselves
or their constituents.[20] Rather than promoting yeoman Indian agriculture in
the West, federal land and resource policies diminished it.[21] Economic and
social policies designed to foster indigenous farming instead fractionated the
land and deprived the Pima of their water, making economic enhancement of
tribal lands difficult.

As the interviews show, the Pima desired to remain agriculturalists, despite water shortages and economic hardships. The Pima might have continued their adaptation to a market economy and might have maintained parity with local farmers and remained part of the national economy had they not been deprived of the waters of the Gila River and its tributaries. Handicapped by federal land and resource policies, the once-prosperous Pima descended into poverty as their overall irrigated acreage precipitously declined (table 0.1).

The Pima, once "rich in harvests," abandoned their ditches, fields, homes, and, in some cases, villages.[22] "Poverty began to stare us in the face," 66-year-old Juna Osif remembered, and "we did not know how to take it. Some Indians are now in the begging business."[23] As upstream farmers cultivated more land, "the less land the Indian is able to cultivate," 51-year-old Oliver Sanderson lamented, "and [the] more land he is forced to abandon."[24]

The Pima interviews provide important insight into the effects of federal land and resource policies and offer a broader picture of the application of federal Indian policies in the late nineteenth century. As they suggest, it was not the triumph of Western civilization that displaced the Pima agricultural economy but the application of the philosophy of economic liberalism, which prevented the Pima from building on their previous successes.

One

"HIGH AND DRY"

The Akimel O'otham (River People) or Pima have lived in the middle Gila River Valley for centuries, irrigating and cultivating the land much as their Huhugam ancestors did for millennia.[1] This history of agriculture is part of the social, economic, and cultural fabric of the Pima and their Pee Posh (the People) or Maricopa neighbors. The Pima benefited from sufficient and fertile land, a steady and reliable supply of water, and favorable physiographic conditions to produce an abundance of food and fiber crops in the late eighteenth century and much of the nineteenth century. These conditions continued until the introduction of upstream diversions from the Gila River and its tributaries by non-Indian settlers in the late 1860s.

A HISTORY OF IRRIGATED FARMING

The Pima have a long history of irrigated agriculture, going back at least 2,000 years to their Huhugam ancestors, who irrigated lands in the Gila, Salt, and Santa Cruz river valleys in south-central Arizona. From the seventeenth to the nineteenth century, the Pima exhibited a pattern of ecologic and economic adaptation to their environment. By the time Jesuit priest Eusebio Francisco Kino arrived in their villages in 1694, the Pima had already demonstrated propitious agricultural production.[2] A stable agriculture-based economy ensured a dependable food supply, enabling them to maintain a thriving trade with Indian, Spanish, Mexican, and later American communities.

The Pima enjoyed a variety of cultivated and natural food sources. Corn, tepary beans, squashes, and cotton served as staple food and fiber crops. As early as 1680 the Pima traded their corn with New Mexican settlements near Santa Fe. Grown in sixty days, small-eared Pima corn required minimal amounts of water beyond its preplanting irrigation and could be planted, cultivated, and harvested three times a year. Its yield, while not extravagant, was ten to twelve bushels per acre.[3]

The Pima did not grow food as a commercial crop until the late eighteenth century, instead producing sufficient crops for subsistence, limited trade, and seed. Their adaptation to Spanish wheat altered this pattern and served as the basis for Pima prosperity in the late eighteenth and early nineteenth centuries. Planted in the fall and harvested in late spring when winter stores were at their lowest, wheat was planted off-season as a complement to the traditional crops of corn, beans, and squash. Because it could be stored for long periods, wheat provided the people with a balanced food supply and helped ensure a stable economy. While it did not immediately modify their economy, within decades it would join corn as a principal Pima crop.[4]

Wheat modified the Pima economy in a variety of ways, one of which was the expansion of their irrigation system. Although Kino observed abandoned Huhugam canals at Casa Grande and chronicled Pima agricultural production, he never specifically mentioned irrigation farming on the Gila in any of his journals. Nonetheless, the Pima probably engaged in some level of irrigated agriculture. While they utilized irrigation prior to the introduction of wheat, they may have had little need or economic incentive to irrigate away from the river: the fields planted in the floodplains and on the islands within the Gila satisfied their needs.[5]

By the 1740s the Pima were growing a surplus of cultivated foods. So extensive were their crops that their relatives the Tohono O'odham (Papago) began assisting them with the harvest in return for a share of the crop. While the Pima had a limited supply of food crops to trade, they bartered grain in Tucson in time of famine on the upper reaches of the Santa Cruz River. When Jacobo Sedelmayr visited the Pima villages in 1744, he observed the cultivation of wheat and noted that the Pima irrigated "on either bank of the river and on the islands." The Pima enjoyed "broad acres for cultivation of crops," growing large quantities of food and fiber crops by means of "trenches which, the country being level, are easily carried from the Gila." By 1760 Pima lands

were "fruitful and suitable for wheat, Indian corn, etc." Their cotton production was so successful that their Sonoran neighbors coveted their excess.
"[A]fter the crop is gathered in, more remains in the fields, than is to be had
for a harvest here in Sonora."[6]

Although the Pima already engaged in intertribal trade, adaptation to
wheat shifted their economic focus from a more barter-based farming to a
commercial-based economy. Once having bartered simple manufactured
goods, such as cotton blankets, woven baskets, and pottery, by the late eighteenth century the Pima were exporting agricultural commodities. In the process, they were metamorphosing into a more commercial economy. While
they had made their own woven and cotton blankets, trade with Spanish
settlements or Indian villages that had access to Spanish trade goods allowed
them to acquire both *bayeta* (flannel) and *sayal* (woolen) cloth. The integration of wheat into their economy made it possible to improve their standard
of living and acquire additional technology, such as metal tools. Having
always used the river to their advantage, the Pima now combined their agricultural expertise and the Gila River with a new crop—wheat—to expand
trade networks. Visiting the Pima villages in May 1774, Fray Juan Díaz noted
that the Pima were well dressed and attributed this to their superior agricultural production and trade networks with Spanish and Indian communities
to the south.[7]

By the waning years of the eighteenth century, the Pima were well on
the road to economic prosperity. Passing through the Pima villages in the
spring of 1774, Juan Bautista de Anza described "fields of wheat . . . so large
that, standing in the middle of them, one cannot see the ends, because of
their length. They are very wide, too, embracing the whole width of the valley on both sides [of the river]." Pima cornfields were "of similar propor-
tions." De Anza described fields planted with "from sixty to eighty fanegas of
wheat, marvelously fine and about ready to harvest." This particular field, he
marveled, was "the smallest one they have." Díaz admired how each village
planted large fields of wheat, corn, and other crops, in spite of the drought
and famine plaguing other Piman tribes farther south.[8]

The Pima villages were not immune to the periodic drought that could
grip the Pimería Alta. Franciscan priest Pedro Font, traveling with de Anza
in the fall of 1775, observed that the lack of rain affected the Pima as well.
While they were not without food, Font noted that "only in the time of floods

is [the river] useful for the grain fields and corn fields of the Indians." Pima crops required "much water" to ensure a bountiful harvest. Franciscan priest Francisco Garcés, who accompanied de Anza and Font, was more patronizing. In spite of drought conditions, he wrote, the Pima still "raise large crops of wheat, some of corn, cotton, calabashes, etc." To grow such crops the Pima "constructed good irrigating canals, surrounding the fields in one circuit common [to all] and divided those of different owners by particular circuits." De Anza, no stranger to the Pima, concurred with Garcés, opining that their vast cultivated and irrigated fields made their villages an ideal location for both missions and a presidio. Their fields were not as extensive as they might have been because the river was "so short of water." But Pima farmers, having managed their irrigation system within the confines of such environmental realities for centuries, assured de Anza that the winter rains would soon arrive and they would plant their crops as usual.[9]

The Pima also modified their mode of agriculture in the late eighteenth century. They extended their irrigation canals (mostly to lands on the south bank), increased the size of their log and brush dams, probably used for centuries to direct water, and used them to raise the water surface elevation and ensure a sufficient head to reach fields farther from the river. Pima farmers fastened together "many logs in the middle of the river" and then used brush to raise the water into long canals that watered individual fields. Intensive agriculture meant that fields were flooded before planting and nearly the entire flow of the river was "drained off." Pima farmers turned back excess water into the river so that downstream villagers could make use of it (map 1.1). Increased and widespread flood irrigation helped flush the salts out of the soil and keep the land productive.[10]

The Pima continued to make adaptations to their environment. They dug wells in areas south of the Gila, where it flowed beneath the surface. Garcés noted a large well south of the villages and found several more thirty miles farther south at the Papago village of Pozos Salados. By the mid-eighteenth century Pima farmers were constructing fences around their irrigated lands. Font described farms that were "fenced in with poles and laid off in divisions." Garcés was the first to note fences in 1770, when he observed that "their sowings of wheat [are] large, well set off and fenced." While reporting fence building as a communal event, Garcés noted that individual Pima farmers had "their lands within divided" into rectangles about two hundred by three

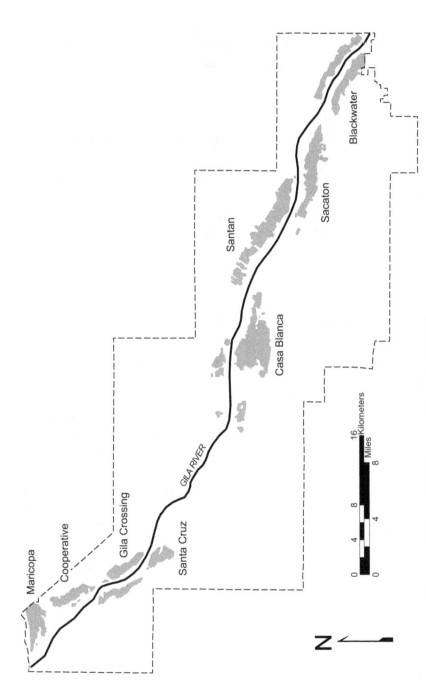

MAP 1.1. Pima and Maricopa Villages and Fields, ca. 1900. (*Source:* Author's file)

hundred feet for "convenience of irrigating." By the close of the eighteenth century, "each proprietor fenced his sowed fields."[11]

The Pima economy depended on the waters of the Gila River and its tributaries. Following the *himdag* of their Huhugam ancestors, the Pima exercised sovereignty over all their land, enabling them to remain economically and politically independent for generations. As 65-year-old Pima farmer George Pablo recalled in 1914, they were "self supporting people" who raised crops "in abundance."[12] This independence metamorphosed to dependence in the 1870s when the United States government encouraged emigrants to settle in the Gila River Valley. The settlers then diverted the limited water supplies from the Gila River upstream from the Pima villages, leaving the Indians "high and dry," in the words of 71-year-old Pima elder Frank Hayes.[13]

PIMA AND MARICOPA IRRIGATION DELIVERY SYSTEMS

The Huhugam built the earliest canals along the Gila River in the central portion of the modern-day Gila River Indian Reservation. Many of the historic canals constructed by the Pima and Maricopa followed these prehistoric alignments.[14] Located in the center of the reservation, these canals irrigated lands in the historic breadbasket of the Pima and Maricopa villages (centered in the Casa Blanca area). The Pima, and the Maricopa after they immigrated to Pima country beginning in the late eighteenth century, had continuously cultivated these lands since before the arrival of Spanish conquistadors in the seventeenth century.

The Pima and Maricopa constructed or used forty-two canals (excluding three waste ditches and one seepage ditch) over the course of the nineteenth and early twentieth centuries (table 1.1). The oldest historic canals included the Ancient Maricopa, Old Santa Cruz, Old Bridlestood, Old Snaketown (Sratuka), Old Sranuka, Bapchil (Ooist), Old Mount Top, and Ancient Stotonic (Sweetwater). All of these ditches were located within the historic breadbasket of the Pima and Maricopa villages. This period from the late 1700s until the 1860s reflects the pinnacle of Pima agriculture before water deprivation affected their agricultural economy.

As upstream diversions altered Indian economics in the 1870s and Apache hostilities ended, the Pima and Maricopa constructed new canals corresponding with the establishment of dispersed settlements upstream and downstream from the main corridor of the Indian villages. Some Pima and Maricopa relocated to the Salt River Valley. The Pima reestablished upstream settlements near Blackwater in the 1860s, resulting in new irrigation canals (the North Blackwater [#43] and Blackwater Island [#44] ditches) on both sides of the Gila River. In the 1870s the Pima established the village of Hashan Keik and constructed the Sacaton Flats canal (#36), North Sacaton Flats ditch (#35), Cottonwood ditch (#32), and Yaqui ditch (#38).

On the north side of the river, the Pima established the Santan village fields in 1879, utilizing water from the newly constructed Lower Santan Canal (extension canal #45), which they integrated into the Santan Indian Canal (#27) in 1883. With old canals abandoned due to water loss in the Casa Blanca and Sweetwater district, the Pima constructed new canals or reconstructed existing ones, including the Snaketown (#18) and the Bridlestood (#16). Concurrently, the Maricopa moved downstream to the Gila Crossing and Maricopa areas between 1873 and 1886 and established the Maricopa Canal. The Pima also constructed new canals in the Gila Crossing District, including the Oscar Walker (#2), John Thomas (#4), John Hoover (#5), and Hollen ditches (#7) (map 1.2).

To irrigate their fields, the Pima and Maricopa used multiple sources of water, including water from the Gila, Little Gila, Salt, and Santa Cruz rivers, McClellan Wash, and Blackwater slough. Twenty-seven canals headed on the Gila River or bifurcated from canals heading on the Gila. An additional seven ditches headed on or bifurcated from canals on the Little Gila River. One ditch headed on the Santa Cruz River, one utilized the intermittent flow from McClellan Wash, one received water from Blackwater slough, fed by a natural spring, and four received water from other ditches. The Maricopa constructed one canal to divert water from the Salt River.

LAND POLICIES AND PIMA AGRICULTURE
IN THE NINETEENTH CENTURY

In the early nineteenth century a remarkable although ephemeral economic transformation occurred among the Pima. Continuing the irrigated agricultural economy bequeathed to them by their Huhugam ancestors, the Pima

TABLE 1.1. Historic Pima and Maricopa Canals, 1800–1914 (West to East)

Canal No.	Canal Name	Dates of Use	Source	Length (miles)
1	Maricopa	Pre-1894–1914*	Salt River	2.98
2	Oscar Walker	1903–14*	Gila River	4.71
3	Cooperative	1900–1914*	Gila River	5.33
4	John Thomas	1876–1914*	Gila River	4.65
5	John Hoover	1873–1914*	Gila River	7.07
6	Joseph Head	1886–1905	Gila River	2.48
7	Hollen (Simon Webb)	1877–1914*	Gila River	4.90
8	Breckenridge	1902–14*	Santa Cruz River	1.00
9	Ancient Maricopa	1830s–80s	Gila River	3.29
10	Waste ditch	n/a	n/a	n/a
11	Old Santa Cruz	1854–75	Gila River	3.47
12	Old Sranuka Laterals	1840–80s	Old Sranuka Canal	1.24
13	Old Sranuka/Alkali Camp	1914*	Gila River	5.39
14	Waste ditch	n/a	n/a	n/a
15	Old Sranuka (Old Ditch)	1840–80s	Gila River	0.50
16	Bridlestood	1880s–early 1900s	Gila River	2.11
17	Old Bridlestood (Palinkirk)	early 1800s–1889	Gila River	1.24
18	Snaketown	early 1800s–1914*	Gila River	5.64
19	Palomas Branch	1906–7	Gila to Bridlestood	1.74
20	Waste ditch	n/a	n/a	n/a
21	Old Snaketown (Sratuka)	early 1800s–1905	Gila River	1.36
22	Bapchil (Ooist)	early 1800s–present	Gila River	5.70
23	Stotonic (Sweetwater)	early 1800s–present	Gila River	6.39
24	Ancient Ditch	early 1800s–1866	Extension of Old Mount Top	2.48
25	Ancient Stotonic (Sweetwater)	early 1700s–1880	Little Gila River	6.39

(and to a lesser extent the Maricopa) leveraged a favorable geopolitical setting into a viable and sustainable agricultural economy that resulted in economic prosperity. Accordingly, they sought inclusion in the emerging American economy of the Southwest and became an economic force in the middle Gila River Valley by the late 1840s. Parlaying their economic shrewdness stimulated by Spanish, Mexican, and American citizens in the late eighteenth and first decades of the nineteenth centuries, the Pima enjoyed economic success for less than five decades, producing food and fiber crops for emigrant trains and military expeditions alike. Moreover, crops from their fields provided a

TABLE 1.1. Continued

Canal No.	Canal Name	Dates of Use	Source	Length (miles)
26	Old Mount Top	early 1800s–1866	Old Stotonic	1.86
27	Santan (Indian)	1869/1883–1914*	Gila River	14.88
28	Old Maricopa	1849–70	Little Gila River	2.67
29	Old Stotonic Branch	1848–70	Old Maricopa	0.68
30	Old Santan	1865–present	Little Gila River	4.96
31	New Mount Top	1866–69	Little Gila River	2.29
32	Cottonwood	1872–1914	Old Connecting	2.98
33	Old Connecting (Morago)	1882–84	Gila River	2.42
34	Hendricks	1904–14*	Little Gila River	0.87
35	North Sacaton Flats	1872–present	Little Gila via Sacaton Flats ditch	2.36
36	Sacaton Flats (Upper Stotonic)	1872–present	Little Gila River	3.72
37	Seepage	pre-1904	McClellan Wash	2.11
38	Yaqui	1891–1914*	Blackwater slough	2.67
39	Cayah (Cayau)	1869–80	Gila River	2.11
40	Diversion	pre-1914	Gila to Little Gila	1.24
41	Old Woman's Mouth	1881–1905	Gila River	1.80
42	Old Indian/Upper Blackwater	1884	Gila River	6.70
43	North Blackwater (Cholla)	1866–present	Gila River	7.56
44	Blackwater (Island)	1862–present	Gila River	9.73
45	Extension of (Lower) Santan Indian	1879–83	Gila River	?
46	Padilla	1910–14	Gila River	?

Source: Adapted from M. Kyle Woodson, "A Research Design for the Study of Prehistoric and Historic Irrigation Systems in the Middle Gila Valley, Arizona" (2003).
* Still in use in 1914.

source of food for the Mexican presidio in Tucson as well as the American mining districts near Prescott.

Emigrant settlement above the villages eventually deprived the Pima and Maricopa of their water, which undermined their agricultural economy. By the 1890s they faced the pangs of hunger and poverty and grew dependent on the U.S. government for subsistence. The demise of their economy, however, resulted from complex and complicated issues. American settlers and federal policies sought to "bring Indian resources, land and labor into the market" but did not encourage Indian participation in the national economy.[15]

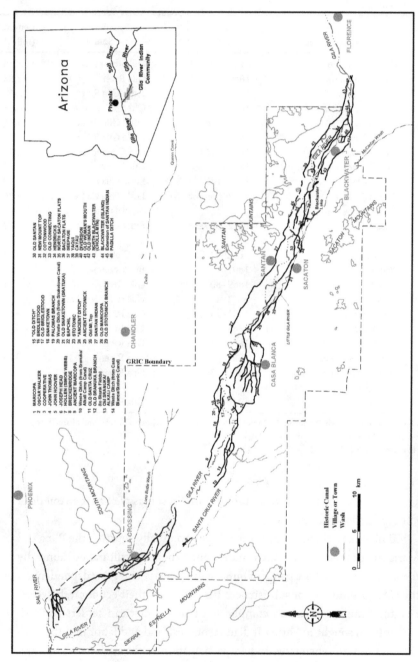

MAP 1.2. Historic Pima and Maricopa Canals, 1800–1914. (*Source:* Author's file)

Despite federal policies that promoted Indian agriculture, political rhetoric rarely matched reality in Indian Country, even in environments where indigenous economies were based on agriculture. The result was Pima dependence on the American market rather than participation in that market.

ECONOMIC LIBERALISM

In the American West, water undergirds economic sustainability. While our understanding of the West historically has been predicated on the theory that the federal government took a laissez-faire approach to settlement and the utilization of water resources, the federal government played a major role.[16] Employing liberal land and resource policies, the U.S. government directed both the development and exploitation of the West and its resources. These policies facilitated settlement and represented a strong federal presence in shaping not only the culture of the West but its very growth. These policies represent economic liberalism.[17]

Born in the age of enlightenment, the philosophy of economic liberalism became the guiding principle for national expansion in the nineteenth century. By the 1880s scientific racism supported and bolstered lawyer/anthropologist Lewis Henry Morgan's development of the seven stages on the "civilization"–"savagery" continuum. Morgan relegated American Indians to the low end of barbarism (eastern tribes) and upper end of savagery (western tribes) in 1877.[18] The American scientific community institutionalized this Darwinian transformation of the American Indian in the late nineteenth century, as poignantly exhibited at the 1915 Panama Pacific International Exposition in San Francisco. James Earle Fraser's *The End of the Trail* served as a not so subtle metaphor for American Indians.[19]

Federal policies in the nineteenth century did not support yeoman Pima or Maricopa agriculture but focused on promoting non-Indian settlement and agriculture in central Arizona to the disadvantage of Indian agriculturalists.[20] The broader settlement of the American West and the concomitant displacement of American Indians from the land resulted from this government action. Social and scientific theory influenced the federal policies that shaped social thought and action, dispossessing tribal nations such as the Pima of most of their water resources.

With the founding of the United States, national policies toward tribal nations centered on socially and culturally molding American Indians into self-sufficient farmers in the Euro-American model.[21] Treaties with tribal nations frequently contained provisions for agricultural goods and equipment. In the 1790 Creek Nation treaty, for instance, the United States encouraged the Creeks "to become herdsmen and cultivators" and agreed "from time to time [to] furnish gratuitously . . . useful domestic animals and implements of husbandry."[22] Furthermore, in the 1825 Osage treaty the United States agreed to provide "farming utensils . . . and shall employ such persons to aid the [Osage] in their agricultural pursuits."[23] The yeoman Jeffersonian farmer exemplified American agrarian idealism. Inherent in this was the belief that hunting or gathering was the basis of *all* tribal economies. While this was generally true of western tribes, the Pima and Maricopa enjoyed a successful agricultural economy before the effects of economic liberalism crippled it.

American agricultural idealism finds its roots in the ancient Greeks and Romans and is traced to the biblical command to subdue and cultivate the earth.[24] European theorists such as Swiss jurist Emmerich de Vattel adopted this idealism and represented agriculture as "the most useful and necessary" of the arts in which civilized nations were obliged to engage.[25] Following de Vattel's reasoning, societies naturally progressed from transient herding (barbarism) to gathering to hunting before advancing to cultivation of the soil, which marked a society's entrance into the realm of civilization.

In North America, the yeoman landowning farmer symbolized political and economic independence and decency. Colonial agricultural clubs spread this gospel of yeoman farming, viewing those who cultivated the soil as "heroic figure[s] of the idealized frontier . . . armed with that supreme agrarian weapon, the sacred plow."[26] Thomas Jefferson opined that those who tilled the soil were "the chosen people of God" and "wedded to [a nation's] liberty and interests, by the most lasting bonds."[27] Jefferson's views, influenced by natural law theory, found fertile soil in agrarian idealism and revolutionary egalitarianism and helped canonize the social theory that American Indians had to "advance toward civilization" through agrarian social development in order to survive. Congress seeded these theories by appropriating $15,000 to encourage Indian agriculture in the Trade and Intercourse Act (1802).[28] These funds became permanent with the enactment of the "Civilization Act" (1819).[29] The theory that American Indian civilization could not "exist without cultivation of the soil" was the basis of federal Indian policy by 1830.[30]

The most far-reaching aspect of federal action in the West was the Homestead Act (1862), which, along with companion legislation in the Timber Culture Act (1873) and Desert Land Act (1877), influenced how and where the West was settled. Social reformers envisioned that these acts would support a "Jeffersonian utopia of small farming."[31] The intent was to carve the West into parcels of land, sell them for a nominal fee, and enable settlers to develop the nation's resources. In short, these laws provided a framework and vehicle for populating the West by opening it for settlement. While shaped by American social thought and action and serving as a safety valve for an overpopulated East, liberal policies nonetheless stimulated fraudulent and dummy land entries in Arizona that left large blocs of public domain in the hands of land speculators.[32] Rather than facilitating individual landownership, these federal land laws frequently "promoted monopoly and corruption," especially in and around the river valleys of the mountain West.[33]

As settlers quickly discovered, the real wealth of the West was its life-giving streams. While the Homestead Act and the Desert Land Act were part of the larger social experiment of transforming the West into a series of yeoman farms, the lack of precipitation necessitated an alternative source of water for the land. Westerners, led by Francis Newlands (D-NV), advocated federal support for reclamation projects. The U.S. Geological Survey (USGS), then surveying potential Western water development, advocated "single use resources [with] many potential uses," including reclamation. The older, more established Army Corps of Engineers, however, placed responsibility for reclamation "upon private landowners," holding to a more conservative orthodoxy of water use and development.[34]

By the closing years of the nineteenth century, the federal government's control of western water was independent of state law. The Corps of Engineers controlled the construction of dams on navigable rivers, and in 1898 Congress affirmed federal authority over all water passing through national forests if it could be used for "domestic, mining, milling or irrigation" purposes. The following year, the U.S. Supreme Court opined in *United States v. Rio Grande Dam and Irrigation Company* that if any part of a river (including its tributaries) was used for transportation it fell under federal auspices.[35]

Just as importantly, in the Desert Land Act Congress subjected all public land titles to prior appropriation as long as such rights did not include "surplus waters over and above such actual use."[36] States might distribute water, but the federal government retained all of its rights.[37] By the turn of the twentieth century, Congress was primed for a national reclamation policy that facilitated land development. With the ascendancy of Theodore Roosevelt to the presidency, a progressive leader occupied the White House. Despite tepid eastern support, backing for reclamation was assured: on June 30, 1902, Congress enacted the National Reclamation Act.

The Reclamation Act was one of the most decisive laws in the history of the American West, initiating an era of federally subsidized reclamation projects. While these projects were ostensibly designed to complement land laws and foster yeoman settlement of the West, powerful and politically well-heeled speculators, government bureaucrats, and congressional allies asserted control over the region's water resources and manipulated the act to their benefit. In the initial years of the twentieth century, western water advocates strengthened their position by forming political alliances to determine and manipulate water policy in the West.[38] This alliance consisted of key congressional committee members and legislators, executive agencies (the Reclamation Service and the Army Corps of Engineers), and special-interest groups (water users in the West). This "iron triangle" influenced public policy to its own advantage. Rather than benefiting yeoman farmers, the Reclamation Act became part of an overall "incongruous land system" that encouraged speculation.[39] Although it affected the economy of the West, the Reclamation Act did not fulfill its purpose of fostering yeoman farming.[40]

While iron triangles influenced the development of Western land and resource policies, Congress used its constitutional authority specifically to direct federal Indian affairs.[41] The 1790 Trade and Intercourse Act authorized the United States to interact lawfully with tribal nations by asserting federal authority to regulate Indian trade. Federal treaties with tribes further advanced the goal of pastoralizing American Indians.[42] The geographical expansion of the United States resulted in amendments to the Trade and Intercourse Act. In 1851 and again in 1856 an amended act extended federal authority over the Pima and Maricopa villages.

After the Civil War, Congress enacted policies designed to assimilate American Indians. The 1887 General Allotment Act provided statutory authority for the U.S. Indian Service to divide tribal land by allotting it in severalty to American Indians. This era of land severalty represented an extraordinary attack on tribal nations and is another example of economic liberalism. The United States Supreme Court supported such policies. The

Lone Wolf v. Hitchcock (1903) ruling upheld federal authority to dispose of unallotted or "surplus" lands without tribal consent.[13] Nonetheless, the same court recognized tribal resource rights in *United States v. Winans* (1904) and *Winters v. United States* (1908). The 1908 decision upheld tribal rights to water resources.[44]

Federal land and resource policies became more extraneous with the passage of a western water policy and allotment of Indian lands that placed great demands on tribal lands and resources. Under intense pressure by land-hungry settlers and government agents to part with their land and resources, tribal nations faced a juggernaut of continental imperialism, resulting in the loss of more than 86,000,000 tribal acres between 1887 and 1934.[45]

The philosophy of economic liberalism inspired federal land and Indian policies in the West and enabled speculators, settlers, and politicians to undermine Indian economies and access resources, which led to the economic dependence of American Indians rather than their participation in the national market. By misunderstanding the West and misapplying land and resource policies beyond the 100th meridian, the political philosophy of economic liberalism weakened the Pima economy and favored non-Indian settlement and economic development over American Indians. The enforcement of western land and resource policies and the application of economic liberalism had an element of racial privileging and ignored the planning and foresight advocated by John Wesley Powell. Had government officials heeded Powell's advice, they might have mitigated some of economic liberalism's malevolent impacts (such as monopolization of water) on tribal nations.[46] Lack of federal foresight and adequate planning compounded federal liberality, with aggressive settlers usurping Pima water and marginalizing the Indians in the national market.

THE GILA RIVER PIMA AND MARICOPA

Congress established the Gila River Indian Reservation by a legislative act in 1859, with seven presidential executive orders expanding the reservation to 371,792 acres by 1915. The reservation varies from three to thirteen miles in width and has a low western gradient of 579 feet. It is composed of a mosaic of agro-environments shaped by precipitation, soil types, geology, drainage patterns, and slope gradients. The area is surrounded by low-lying mountains that provided rain runoff that the Pima used to their agricultural advantage for centuries. Sedimentary alluvial fans, which emanate from the foothills and coalesce with the lower-lying floodplain along the Gila River, surround the mountains. These physiographic features, including temperature and precipitation, influenced cultural attitudes toward the land for centuries. With a mean annual rainfall on the reservation of just 8.37 inches, evapo-transpiration exceeds annual precipitation, necessitating a supplemental water supply to yield adequate harvests.

At the end of the eighteenth century, Pima intercourse with Spain diminished. By the time of Mexican independence in 1821, the Pima and Maricopa had little commerce with Hispanic towns to the south, although they did engage in trade with American fur trappers in the 1820s. The Pima remained "willing to share their food and shelter" with emigrants.[47] The advent of the Mexican War in 1846 gave the Pima cause to extend this hospitality. That fall, two U.S. military detachments descended upon the Pima and Maricopa villages. General Stephen Watts Kearny led U.S. troops down the Gila and through the Pima villages in November, en route to San Diego. Henry Smith Turner, one of 120 dragoons forming the column, welcomed the "hospitality and friendship" of the Pima and considered them "more industrious than I have ever found Indians—they have all the necessaries of life in sufficient abundance, & all produced by their own industry."[48]

The Army of the West camped eight or nine miles above the Pima villages. Once word had been dispatched to the villages regarding the friendly nature of the visit, it was only a matter of hours before the camp was filled "with Pimos loaded with corn, beans, honey and zandias [watermelons]" and a "brisk trade was at once opened." When Army scout Kit Carson asked to purchase bread to sustain the dragoons, he was informed that "bread is to eat, not to sell; take what you want."[49]

The American troops were struck by the nature of agriculture in the villages, including the draining of the water from the land. "We were at once impressed with the beauty, order and disposition of the arrangements for irrigating and draining the land," topographical engineer William H. Emory noted. "All the crops have been gathered in, and the stubbles show they have been luxuriant." Large fields were divided by earthen borders into smaller fields for convenience of irrigating. For fifteen miles downstream, the troops passed over a luxuriantly rich, cultivated land. "The plain," Emory estimated, extended "in every direction 15 or 20 miles." The farmers drew off the "whole water" of the Gila for irrigation, taking care to return the unused water to the river "with little apparent diminution in its volume."[50]

Emory concluded that the Pima "surpass[ed] many of the Christian nations in agriculture" and were "little behind them in the useful arts."[51] When 340 tired Mormon troops arrived from the south six weeks later, a cadre of mounted Pima men met them eight miles from the villages. They came with "sacks of corn, flour, beans, etc.," Henry Standage recalled, and were "glad to see us, running and taking us by the hand." Colonel Philip St. George Cooke traded "every spare article for corn," mustering twelve quarts per animal for the trip to California. The "wonderfully honest and friendly" Pima eagerly traded and sold food crops "for bleached domestics, summer clothing of all sorts, showy handkerchiefs, and white beads." Sergeant Daniel Tyler opined that the Pima were so industrious that "our American and European cities would do well to take lessons in virtue and morality from these native tribes."[52]

By the time the California 49ers passed through the villages, the Pima and Maricopa recognized the advantages of participating in the national economy. The establishment of the Southern Trail through their villages in 1849 proved to be an economic boon. Tens of thousands of emigrants passed through the villages, purchasing or trading for food and forage crops. While the Pima and Maricopa initially traded material goods for food crops, by 1850 they demanded silver and gold coin, using it to purchase goods directly from merchants in Tucson.[53] Having seen modern American and Mexican farm tools, the Pima sought to acquire such implements so they could more efficiently and effectively cultivate their fields and expand production.[54]

The opening of the national road through the Pima villages in 1858 further expanded their economy. While the Pima sold 2,400 bushels of grain in 1858, they constructed new canals upstream of their villages and produced more than 171,180 bushels of grain and 222,895 bushels of corn by 1860.[55] They sought to purchase oxen, mules, and other draft animals, indicating that their mode of agriculture was changing from manpower to animal power. The Pima and Maricopa irrigation system "comprise[d] nearly five hundred miles of well-defined acequias and extend[ed] over a tract of land eighteen miles in length."[56]

In the first half of the 1860s the Pima and Maricopa grew and sold most of the wheat and corn for the newly established Arizona Territory. Wheat sold

FIG. 1.1. Pima men threshing wheat in Sacaton, ca. 1900. (Courtesy of the National Archives and Records Service)

for $2.00 a bushel to military contractors, miners in Prescott, and emigrants passing through the villages. The Pima and Maricopa supply of grain was "ample for all the citizens and a portion of the troops at present in Arizona." Their surplus grain and corn, Pima farmer Henry Austin recalled in 1914, "used to fill up all [the trader's] store houses."[57] They used the proceeds to purchase clothing and other "articles as they require" in Tucson or from local traders.[58] When Joseph P. Allyn visited the villages in the summer of 1864, he estimated that Pima and Maricopa grain production had quadrupled since 1859 (fig. 1.1).[59]

The Pima were so prosperous by 1866 that they informed Indian agent M. O. Davidson that they "want[ed] no aid at the hands of the Government, except such as will promote their education . . . in the mechanic arts, and agriculture."[60] When C. H. Lord, deputy agent in Tucson, visited Pima chief Antonio Azul and the village chiefs in May, he distributed agricultural implements and observed "many well-to-do farmers." Lord estimated that the Indians would have more than 1,500,000 pounds of grain to sell in the spring.[61] The Pima expanded their area of cultivation again, reclaiming previously irrigated land above the reservation in the Blackwater area. In 1866 they sold over 2,000,000 pounds of wheat, in addition to corn and beans.[62]

The first sign of trouble came in 1863, when Arizona superintendent of Indian affairs Charles Poston notified federal officials of the three most important considerations facing the Pima and Maricopa: "Water! Water!! Water!" Emigrants were arriving in the Gila Valley and settling on the land under the provisions of the Homestead Act. This was problematic to Poston, who recognized that trouble would result if settlement above the villages occurred without protecting Indian water.[63] By 1868 forty-two individuals had filed Homestead entries for 160 acres, all directly above the reservation. Florence soon boasted of a population of 268, and nearby Adamsville was home to more than 400.[64] A year later, settlers in Florence intentionally diverted and wasted river water in order to deprive the Pima of the water needed to irrigate their crops.[65] The Pima reciprocated by threatening to drive the settlers out of the valley.[66]

Lieutenant Colonel Roger Jones, assistant inspector general for the U.S. Army, raised the specter of war if Pima water concerns remained unaddressed. More settlers arrived each year, and Jones predicted that in a low-flow year Pima and Maricopa crops "would be ruined for want of water." The continued waste of river water above the villages by settlers would "inevitably result in a collision."[67] In June 1869 interior secretary Jacob Cox asked the U.S. Army to remove intruders from the reservation and "protect [the Indians] in their occupancy of the land, and in the right to the waters of the Gila for purposes of irrigation."[68] While the military protected Pima and Maricopa land and water from encroachment, the federal government continued to encourage settlement, in complete disregard of Pima rights.

The trouble predicted by Poston arrived in the fall of 1869. Following a disastrous flood that destroyed three Pima villages, the Sacaton and Casa Blanca trading posts, and the Casa Blanca flour mill and a poor crop in 1869, the Pima openly resisted the settlers who encroached on their ancestral land above the reservation. A detachment of troops from Camp McDowell was sent to "quell the disturbance." Four hundred Indians, mainly Pima, left the reservation in the fall and claimed the fields of upstream Mexican settlers near Adamsville.[69] Another group of Pima took up land above the reservation in an attempt to protect the headwaters of the Little Gila River, and a third group clashed with settlers in October. Diminished rainfall left Pima crops in ruin, with Chief Antonio Azul publicly admitting that he could no longer preserve order among the Pima.[70] Settlement of the Upper Gila Valley beginning in

1872 added to the water users above the villages, leading the federal government to seek removal of the Pima and Maricopa to Indian Territory.[71]

Diminished rainfall in 1875 continued until 1883, adding to Pima and Maricopa hardships. In virgin flow conditions, they dealt with drought by utilizing the low water flow to irrigate their crops. As upstream agriculture increased, this flow diminished and made the Pima and Maricopa irrigation system ineffective. By 1877 five hundred Pima and Maricopa supported themselves off the reservation on "good land and plenty of water" in the Salt River Valley, with an additional two hundred families living above the reservation on the Gila River. Alarmed residents petitioned the Indian Office and Congress to return all the Indians to the Gila River Reservation. When commissioner of Indian affairs Ezra Hayt urged Pima agent John Stout to comply, the agent objected that to do so would cause "great suffering." By the winter of 1878, the Pima and Maricopa irrigated less than one-quarter of their fields, with no harvest projected below Sacaton.[72]

By 1880 the Pima and Maricopa could no longer sustain their economy, as the surface flow of the Gila River was insufficient. Some Indian families lacked even domestic water. For the first time the U.S. government purchased wheat for "destitute Indians."[73] Pima elder Chir-purtke described how his people "were prosperous and contended [sic]" before "white people began to take water from the river." The first diversions of water for irrigation purposes were so small, Chir-purtke continued, that "we hardly noticed it, but they gradually took more out each year till we noticed our loss by not being able to irrigate all our fields. We were forced to abandon them little by little, until some twenty years ago [1894] when we were left high and dry." Pima farmer Juan Lagons was more forthwith, lamenting that "civilization did us more harm than good."[74] The Pima had "ample lands" but lacked water and feared the destruction of their "pride as independent and self-supporting people."[75]

Between 1889 and 1901 upstream settlers added 13,458 acres of new irrigated farmland, representing 86.4 percent of the new land developed along the Gila River. The Pima put 2,116 acres of new (downstream) lands into production after the failure of upstream water on traditional Pima and Maricopa lands in the Casa Blanca district (table 1.2). The water that remained in the river increasingly failed to reach the reservation or arrived in short, ephemeral flows. More low water flow was absorbed into the sandy alluvium than arrived on the reservation.[76] Summer crops failed eleven times between 1892

TABLE 1.2. New Acres with Priority Rights to Water, 1889–1901

Year	Florence–Casa Grande	Safford/Solomonville	Pima Reservation
1889	205	1,016	130
1890	143	1,065	233
1891	974	888	110
1892	400	604	105
1893	326	372	105
1894	192	246	105
1895	740	568	473
1896	310	993	90
1897	0	1,110	90
1898	38	790	90
1899	5	690	90
1900	0	1,075	340
1901	40	668	155
Total	3,373	10,085	2,116

Source: "Gila River Priority of Irrigated Acres, Water Distribution Chart #1 and #2."

and 1904 and winter crops failed five times between 1899 and 1904, marking the period between 1892 and 1904 as the years of starvation. While the Pima and Maricopa grew 8,640,000 pounds (144,000 bushels) of winter grain in 1889, they grew just 720,000 pounds (12,000 bushels) in 1904 (table 1.3). Conditions were so serious that Indian inspector William Junkin recommended the purchase of flour and bacon for "destitute Indians."[77]

As farming failed, many Pima and Maricopa turned to wage labor in the surrounding towns and cities. Scores of Indians began cutting thousands of acres of mesquite to sell as fuel wood in local towns for cash. Hundreds of Pima went to work as laborers for the Southern Pacific Railroad (or local mining railroads).[78] More Indians served as field laborers in the Florence–Casa Grande Valley to the south and east and in the Salt River Valley to the north. Pima women, especially young women, hired out as local domestics, worked in the fields alongside the men, or found work in government Indian schools. Many of the elderly were too proud to accept government charity (rations); some starved to death rather than accept assistance.[79] Others became dependent on government assistance. While these economic adaptations were significant, the adaptations made in Pima agricultural practices were remarkable: the Pima demonstrated the lengths to which they were willing to go to continue their centuries-old agrarian economy and *himdag*.

TABLE 1.3. Pima and Maricopa Grain Production, 1887–1904

Year	Grain (bushels)	Corn (bushels)
1887	105,000	5,000
1888	110,000	2,700
1889	144,000	3,600
1890	114,000	3,000
1891	50,000	—
1892	110,000	5,500
1893	76,000	3,000
1894	62,000	0
1895	70,950	500
1896	51,250	0
1897	51,250	0
1898	117,819	0
1899	34,488	1,072
1900	12,980	180
1901	25,417	36
1902	16,955	18
1903	42,051	18
1904	12,000	500

Source: Annual Reports of the Pima Agency, 1888–1905, in *Annual Reports of the Commissioner of Indian Affairs,* 1888–1905.

Every year between 1892 and 1904, the Pima grew insufficient crops to sustain themselves. Agent Cornelius Crouse estimated that one thousand Indians would raise no grain at all in 1893 and asked for departmental authority to purchase 300,000 pounds of wheat for subsistence and seed. The Pima prepared an additional 5,000 acres of land in 1895 but could not irrigate their crops because of the "scarcity of water."[80] They not only "abandon[ed their] old farms and homes" but also reduced their irrigated crops.[81] Conditions on the reservation were such that agent J. Roe Young requested permission from the commissioner of Indian affairs to purchase an additional 225,000 pounds of wheat "to prevent starvation."[82] In 1894 settlers improved an additional 2,100 acres above the reservation in Florence, bringing the total acreage of improved land in Florence to 26,343.[83] At that time, 6,520 acres in Florence and 19,239 acres in the Upper Gila Valley were being irrigated, totaling 25,759 irrigated acres above the reservation.[84] Having farmed 15,000 acres in 1859, the Pima and Maricopa now farmed fewer than 4,000.[85]

TABLE 1.4. Use of Gila River Natural and Flood Water Flow: Selected Years, 1866–1918 (percentages)

Year	Pima Reservation*	Florence–Casa Grande	Safford/Solomonville
1866	100	0	0
1878	73.60	11.23	13.57
1892	48.27	9.79	35.38
1901	42.69	10.90	36.56
1910	37.99	10.50	41.30
1914	36.38	13.00	40.71
1918	29.50	28.64	33.62

Source: "Gila River Priority of Irrigated Acres, Water Distribution Chart #3."
Note: Percentages do not total 100 percent because smaller users have been omitted.
* Percentage calculated by default by subtracting Florence–Casa Grande, Safford/Solomonville, and smaller users. This represents the total available flow (natural and flood), not the amount that actually reached the reservation boundary.

Federal policies sanctioned settlement and diversion of water upstream from the reservation. Following federal mandates spelled out in the Desert Land Act, settlers were required to apply water to their land or risk losing it and any improvements thereon. To comply with federal law, settlers in 1886 constructed the Florence Canal above the reservation, which further deprived the Pima of their legal rights to Gila River water.[86] By 1900 upstream settlers had largely appropriated the natural flow of the Gila River.[87] The geomorphologic features of the river channel forced the Pima to abandon most of their traditional irrigation system: with many ditches "lying idle and covered with brush."[88] The irrigation of Pima fields now required a costly conveyance system that headed upstream. They need "water for irrigation or [they will] starve," agent Frank C. Armstrong informed interior secretary Ethan Allen Hitchcock in 1901.[89] The Maricopa, however, continued to irrigate nearly a thousand acres of land, with Salt River water protected under the Haggard Decree.[90] As a result of continued non-Indian diversions, the Pima share of the river declined to less than 30 percent of the total flow in 1918 (table 1.4).

The passage of the National Reclamation Act set off the final showdown over control of Indian land and resources in central Arizona.[91] North of the reservation was Maricopa County's Salt River Valley, which increased in population from 20,487 in 1900 to 34,488 in 1910. With the completion of the Salt River project (Roosevelt Dam), the number of farms within the county

TABLE 1.5. Mean Field Size of Pima Cultivated Lands and Lands Abandoned Due to Water Loss, 1914

Category	Cultivated	Abandoned Due to Water Loss
Fields	2,112	1,066
Acres	12,069	6,998
Mean Field Size	5.16	6.57

Source: Author analysis of the 1914 Southworth Maps (from SCIP Archives).

more than doubled to 2,229, with the value of farm property increasing by 312 percent to $33,879,281, more than twice the territorial average increase of 150 percent. Further development above the reservation in Graham and Pinal counties influenced Pima access to water and agricultural development. Over 58 percent of the farms in Arizona were in the three counties upstream from and north of the reservation.[92]

Settlers living in these areas near the reservation cultivated 142,322 acres in the Salt River Valley, 35,000 acres in the Gila River Valley, and 18,000 acres in the Casa Grande Valley.[93] Federal legislation assisted these settlers in acquiring and developing the land and required them to make bona fide application of water in order to perfect their land titles. These federal requirements put settlers in direct competition with the Pima over control and use of the waters of the Salt and Gila rivers.

The loss of water created a domino effect that reduced Pima irrigated acres and field size. By 1900 the Pima farmed fewer than 3,600 acres. The amount of Indian land statewide irrigated under the Indian Irrigation Service in 1919 plummeted from 19,386 acres to 8,733 acres. Non-Indian irrigated acreage, however, increased by 46.1 percent to 467,565 acres, with 247,260 acres north of the Pima Reservation in the Salt River Valley.[94] Upstream settlers irrigated another 76,982 acres along the Gila River above (east of) the reservation, with 33,019 acres irrigated upstream from the Pima along the Santa Cruz River. Just as significantly, capital improvements along the Gila River and its tributaries (including the Salt River) increased by 509.1 percent between 1902 and 1919, jumping to $25,165,814. Reclamation Service improvements totaled $20,277,919, while Indian Irrigation Service improvements totaled just $585,029.[95]

TABLE 1.6. Comparison of Pima-Maricopa and Arizona-Wide Crop Selection, 1914

Crop	Reservation Acreage	Percent of Total	Arizona Acreage	Percent of Total
Corn	920	8	18,878	6
Grain	9,911	82	96,723	31
Hay	1,001	8	124,922	41
Cotton	164	1	53,151	17
Other	73	1	14,197	5

Source: The Pima/Maricopa figures are based on author's analysis of the 1914 Southworth maps; the Arizona figures are an average of 1910 and 1920 U.S. Census data.

Due to insufficient water, the Pima abandoned fields across the reservation, mostly in the traditional breadbasket along the river in the central region of the reservation. These abandoned fields had greater mean field sizes (21 percent larger than the 1914 cultivated acres), indicating that the effects of federal policy reduced both the aggregate acreage in production and the mean size of the fields that remained in production (table 1.5).

Upstream irrigated agriculture related proportionally to Pima agriculture. While settlers diversified their agricultural production, the Pima and Maricopa, having limited water resources and needing to feed their families, did not (table 1.6). Overall, non-Indian farmers sowed 31 percent of their acres to grain, while Pima and Maricopa farmers sowed 82 percent to grain, lending credence to the hypothesis that the philosophy of economic liberalism had a deleterious impact on Pima agriculture. Indian Irrigation Service chief engineer Wendell Reed supported this assertion in 1919 when he acknowledged in congressional testimony that the lack of water related directly to the disproportionate acreage sown to grain.[96]

Once able to feed all who visited their villages, the Pima and Maricopa no longer enjoyed uncontested use of the river after 1866 and could no longer irrigate all of their food and fiber crops by the 1880s. Within three decades, the prosperous Indians were reduced to penury and want as their share of river water decreased to less than a third of the natural and flood flow of the river. Upstream farmers in the Florence–Casa Grande (29 percent), Safford/Solomonville (34 percent), and Duncan (5 percent) valleys appropriated more than two-thirds of the annual flow for their own use.[97]

Two

"FORCED TO ABANDON OUR FIELDS"

In 1913 the United States Indian Irrigation Service initiated the Gila River adjudication survey in an attempt to protect Pima rights to the remaining waters of the Gila River. To accomplish this, the Indian Irrigation Service determined historic and active Pima and Maricopa agricultural lands by surveying the reservation and its agricultural fields. This theoretically would encourage passage of federal legislation to restore water to the Indians. The work of conducting this survey fell to engineer Clay Southworth.

In surveying the extent of Pima agriculture, Southworth interviewed thirty-four Pima elders and leading men intimately familiar with Pima agriculture, water use, and water rights. From this survey, Southworth concluded that the "total agricultural yield" of the Pima over the four previous decades had greatly diminished "and this one time proud and powerful race has been forced since the advent of the whites to depend at least partly upon the bounties of the government."[1] While Southworth is remembered for the government publication "The History of Irrigation along the Gila River," his heretofore-unpublished interviews with the Pima elders and leading men are first-person accounts of the depths to which the Pima agricultural economy tumbled.

C. H. SOUTHWORTH

Clay "Charles" Southworth was born on September 4, 1881, in Brockville, Ontario, Canada, to U.S. citizens Stoddard and Ella Louise (Perrington) Southworth.[2] When he was three years of age, his father moved his family to

Carson City, Nevada. Clay attended elementary school there before graduating from high school in Genoa, Nevada, in 1898.[3] He entered Nevada State University at Reno at the age of seventeen that fall and earned a bachelor of science degree in civil engineering from the School of Mines four years later. Upon graduation, Southworth joined the U.S. Geological Survey, conducting irrigation surveys in Nevada. A year later he became a member of the newly established U.S. Reclamation Service, serving as instrument man and party chief on Nevada's Truckee-Carson Project. He remained with the Reclamation Service for five years then entered private practice as a civil engineer in a series of Nevada mining boomtowns, including Goldfield, Rhyolite, and Beatty.

In 1912 Southworth joined the Richardson Construction Company of Los Angeles and supervised topographical, canal, and dam site crews along the Yaqui River in Sonora, Mexico, as part of the Yaqui River Irrigation Project. A year later, following political unrest in Mexico, Southworth returned to the United States when President William Howard Taft ordered the U.S. Marines and the U.S.S. *Beaufort* to evacuate all American citizens from south of the border. Southworth then accepted a position with the United States Indian Irrigation Service, a newly established office within the U.S. Indian Service. Assigned to District 4 of the Indian Irrigation Service, he worked under the direction of superintendent of irrigation Charles Real Olberg in Los Angeles.[4] Olberg immediately assigned survey and data collection responsibility for the Gila River survey to Southworth, who remained intimately involved in planning, designing, and constructing irrigation works on the Gila River Indian Reservation until 1917, when he was promoted to the position of superintendent of construction for the Fort Hall (Idaho) Indian Irrigation Project.[5]

Southworth spent three years working on the Fort Hall Project, a joint Indian/non-Indian irrigation system that served the Shoshone and Bannock tribes as well as non-Indian farmers in the valley.[6] In 1918 he applied to the U.S. Army's Engineer Training Corps in Salt Lake City with the intent of volunteering for service in World War I. The Indian Service, however, "did not feel justified in grating [*sic*] a release." In September the Water User's Association of Pocatello adopted a resolution recommending that Southworth not be released for military service because his engineering "services were necessary to the maintenance of the [Fort Hall] Project and production of [wartime] food-stuffs." The War Department canceled Southworth's call for duty.[7]

On March 4, 1920, Southworth resigned as engineer in charge of the Fort Hall Project and moved to Tonopah, Nevada, where he engaged in nonengineering work for two years.[8]

In 1922 Southworth returned to Arizona—and the Indian Irrigation Service—to oversee construction of the Florence–Casa Grande Project (FCGP), which was authorized in part because of the Gila River survey.[9] He married Mabel Hall in Prescott on August 5, 1925, and became the resident construction engineer for Coolidge Dam on the Gila River three years later.[10] With completion of the dam and the Pima Canal above the Gila River Indian Reservation in 1929, Southworth resigned from government employment and accepted an offer to organize and establish the San Carlos Irrigation and Drainage District (SCIDD) in Florence. As the first district engineer for SCIDD, he was responsible for the off-reservation portion of the joint-works San Carlos Irrigation Project.[11] He remained in Florence overseeing SCIDD until September 22, 1936, when he resigned after directing the development and organization of the district, the utilization of groundwater wells by district farmers, and the expansion of the rural electrification component of the San Carlos Irrigation Project. Southworth's advocacy of groundwater pumping by SCIDD threatened the very Pima rights for which he had advocated in the Gila River survey. On October 1, 1936, he returned to government work, serving seven years as assistant to the director of the Indian Irrigation Service (fig. 2.1).[12]

In 1943 the Indian Service promoted Southworth to director of the Indian Irrigation Service in Washington, D.C., where he remained one year before voluntarily reassigning (and demoting) himself as district engineer in Los Angeles.[13] Two years later, the Indian Irrigation Service moved its district offices from Los Angeles to Phoenix, where Southworth remained until he retired from government employment on September 30, 1951.[14] For the next six years, he served as a civil engineering consultant covering Indian water claims in the pending Arizona v. California decision.[15] He died in 1962 at the age of eighty-one. In 1966 the Southworth family donated the Clay Southworth Papers to the University of Wyoming's Western History Research Center Library in Laramie, Wyoming.[16]

Southworth's work on the Gila River adjudication survey had important and enduring impacts on Arizona water history. "The History of Irrigation along the Gila River" was an authoritative documentary of irrigation along the Gila River and served as the basis of the Bureau of Indian Affairs film

FIG. 2.1. Clay Southworth (far right) and other dignitaries at Coolidge Dam, ca. 1926.
(Courtesy of San Carlos Irrigation Project)

The River People (1946).[17] His effort to document the historic and prehistoric
canals both on and off the Gila River Indian Reservation has served histori-
ans and archaeologists for over ninety years. It also laid important ground-
work for the 1935 Gila River (Globe Equity 59) Decree (*United States v. Gila
Valley Irrigation District*) and served a role in the modern legal framework for
the Central Arizona Project Indian Distribution Division, including the portion on the Gila River Indian Reservation that is known today as the Pima-
Maricopa Irrigation Project.

Southworth's crowning achievement was the San Carlos Irrigation Project, for which the Gila River survey and interviews were instrumental. When
the Indian Irrigation Service assigned Southworth to lead the survey in 1913,
little did it know that his comprehensive analysis would affect the course
of irrigation history on the Gila River for decades. In reporting his survey
findings to chief irrigation engineer Wendell Reed in Washington, D.C.,
Southworth articulated the challenges facing Pima farmers: "The Indians

during former years had a larger area under cultivation than they have at present." The reason for the reduction in acreage was the depletion of their "low-water surface supply," which relegated Pima farmers to using ephemeral stream flows or irrigation return flows. Geological features beneath the bed of the Gila River forced these seepage flows to the surface.[18]

THE FEDERAL FOOTPRINT

When the Indian Irrigation Service assigned Southworth to conduct the Gila River survey, Congress contemplated the Florence–Casa Grande Project as a means of safeguarding Pima rights "to the use of the [Gila River] water." The project was envisioned by its political supporters as an integral component of the larger, long-hoped-for San Carlos Irrigation Project (and Coolidge Dam). The FCGP proposed constructing a joint-use irrigation system designed to integrate the economy of the reservation with that of Pinal County by emphasizing fiscal economy and efficient utilization of the declining natural flow water of the river.[19]

At the same time, the Indian Service prepared to allot the Gila River Reservation in severalty. Following contemporary political sentiments, Pima reserved water rights—as defined in the Supreme Court's 1908 *Winters v. United States* decision—would have little relevance after land severalty. The federal consensus supported the theory that Indian water rights followed the doctrine of prior appropriation upon the completion of land severalty. Until such time, the federal government would reserve water rights on behalf of the Pima and Maricopa.[20]

While settlers could acquire up to 320 acres of land under the Desert Land Act and secure rights to available water, the Indian Service proposed five-acre allotments on the reservation, a proposal rejected by the Pima.[21] Indian Service irrigation engineer William Code initially proposed an allotment of three acres (with water) to each adult Pima and Maricopa, with the potential for another two acres with water later. Code questioned the wisdom of allotting land to each tribal member (including children) for fear "a family should receive 30 or 40 acres and the head of the family could only take care of 10 acres."[22] Many Indian farmers cultivated more land than this, although scarcity of water reduced the number of such farms.[23]

The Pima and Maricopa opposed land severalty on multiple grounds, not the least of which was their desire to protect their water rights first. To allot land without appurtenant rights to the water made little sense. Lacking water, tribal farmers faced devastating circumstances. In 1901 the Presbyterian Church commissioned a report on Pima conditions in the Gila River Valley by ministers Sheldon Jackson and George L. Spining. Distributed to churches, charities, philanthropists, and members of Congress, the report painted an austere picture of the severity of the crisis. "Of 586 families recently visited," the Presbyterians wrote, "of whose number 1,428 are males and 1,425 are females, only 7 families have been able to get a full crop; 17 have raised three-fourths of a crop; 39 have secured about half the regular crop; 91 have got only one-sixth to one-fourth of a crop, and 432 families of industrious Indians eager to work have not been able to raise any crop at all for lack of water."[24]

Three years later, J. R. Meskimons, superintendent of irrigation for the Pima Agency, initiated efforts that he believed would enable half of the Pima farmers dependent on the Gila River to become self-supporting by utilizing seepage water forced to the surface.[25] In August 1904 Meskimons released a report with a corresponding map illustrating the state of agriculture on the reservation. Dissecting the reservation into thirty tracts of Pima and Maricopa farmland, Meskimons estimated that the Pima and Maricopa had abandoned 13,648.8 acres of land "within the last 15 or 20 years on account of lack of water" (see table 2.1).[26]

Meskimons estimated that 13,365.4 acres were then being irrigated, nearly four times the 3,600 acres reported in production by the USGS in 1901.[27] While Meskimons mapped all acres previously and then being irrigated, he assumed that all these acres were in fact currently being cultivated. This is not the case, however, as the Pima interviews indicate. The acres being irrigated that Meskimons reported were actually lands prepared for cultivation but not necessarily irrigated. Moreover, irrigated acres often did not produce a crop or produced only a partial crop. As the Presbyterian report demonstrated, some fields lacked water and others received water at inopportune times.

The Pima frequently planted crops at multiple locations but generally harvested little, failing at times to provide for their families. Had the Pima cultivated 13,365.4 acres as Meskimons claimed, they would have been more than able to feed themselves and their families and would have had excess

TABLE 2.1. Irrigated Acres per Meskimons Report, 1904

District	Canal	Being Irrigated	Abandoned
Maricopa	Maricopa	1,322.9	—
Gila Crossing	Oscar Walker	9.8	—
		10.3	—
		8.4	—
	Cooperative	294.8	—
		19.9	—
	John Thomas/Joseph Head	786.4	—
	John Hoover	827.1	—
	Simon Webb	588.8	—
	Webb branch	311.6	—
Mass Acumult		—	168.7
Sranuka		—	210.6
		—	393.2
		—	448.2
Stotonic	directly from river	—	742.7
	directly from river	—	666.3
	directly from river	—	2,090.1
Casa Blanca/Sweetwater			7,711.0
Lower Santan	Old Santan	215	299.8
		51.6	—
Santan	Santan	4,178.8	—
Sacaton	Old Santan	114	918.2
Cottonwood	Cottonwood	439.6	—
Sacaton Flats	Sacaton Flats	1,105.2	—
	Yaqui	48.8	—
Blackwater	North Blackwater	1,456.1	—
	Blackwater	1,506.1	—
		23.1	—
		46.0	—
TOTALS		13,364.3	13,648.8

Source: "J. R. Meskimons, Superintendent of Irrigation, to The Honorable Commissioner of Indian Affairs, dated August 15, 1904," Phoenix, Arizona, RG 75, Records of the Bureau of Indian Affairs, Records of the Irrigation Division, Reports and Related Records, 1891–1946, Gila River Project, National Archives and Records Administration.

* Lands prepared for cultivation but not necessarily irrigated.

crops to sell. As it was, government charity supported many Indians, and hundreds of Pima and Maricopa fields were left with partial or failed crops. As table 1.3 indicates, the Pima and Maricopa grew only 12,000 bushels of grain and 500 bushels of corn in 1904, the bleakest harvest ever documented on the reservation.

The Maricopa continued to grow a good article (crop) of grain, largely due to the 1903 Haggard Decree, in which the Territorial Court ruled that the Maricopa were entitled to 5,900 acre-feet of Salt River water for their 1,480 acres of farmland.[28] In 1903 the Maricopa planted 1,000 acres of wheat (harvesting 16,000 bushels) and 450 acres of corn.[29] In the Gila Crossing District, Pima farmers irrigated with seepage water. With sufficient water, the six ditches in the district could irrigate 2,857 acres, although irrigation engineer William Code estimated closer to 1,035 acres.[30] Seepage water, combined with water from Mass Acumult (a spring-fed slough east of Gila Crossing), limited the irrigated acreage to less than 40 percent of what it could have been.

Most of the Pima farmers east of the Maricopa and Phoenix Railroad no longer received water from the Gila River. By 1904 many of the Pima had abandoned their traditional villages and fields in the Casa Blanca District and moved downstream to Gila Crossing, to Santan on the north side of the river, into the Salt River Valley, or upstream to the Blackwater District. Pima farmers in the Sacaton and Casa Blanca districts grew no crops in 1904, while those in Sacaton Flats managed a meager crop. The USGS reported that the Pima upstream from the railroad had insufficient water to grow crops and that for the past thirteen years most Pima farmers had "ceased to prepare their fields due to no water." Farmers in Blackwater depended entirely on floodwater in the Gila or on the limited seepage water available.[31]

While the Pima attempted to cultivate their land, partial or complete crop failure was the norm in 1904. Although considerable land (perhaps the 13,365 acres that Meskimons reported) could be productive if supplied with water, in reality the water system nearly failed. Restoration of Pima prosperity could occur only with the return of their water.

In 1911 Chief Antonito Azul penned the "Appeal for Justice," a plea to the American people (particularly the United States Congress) to come to the defense of the Pima and restore their water. In February 1912 Representative John H. Stephens (D-TX), moved by the appeal, introduced a bill authorizing federal action on Pima water rights.[32] A number of eastern friends of the

Indians assigned to the House Committee on Indian Affairs who could expend political capital on Indian causes without fear of voter insurgency supported the bill. Some members of Congress, including Stephens and Senator Joseph Robinson (D-AR) and Senator Carroll Page (R-VT), were knowledgeable about Pima water needs and their long-standing grievances. Western politicians, who had voting constituents competing with tribes for federal reclamation, opposed Indian irrigation projects. Carl Hayden (D-AZ), a member of the House Committee on Indian Affairs, was no exception. Hayden, a first-year congressman and son of a former trader on the reservation, argued that litigation would not provide the reservation with "as much moisture as was to be found in the ink of the signature of the judge who would sign such a decree."[33]

Hayden convinced the committee to kill the bill and instead worked to gain support for a reclamation project on the Gila River that would rival the Salt River project (Roosevelt Dam). Such a project would aid the Pima as well as their non-Indian neighbors in the Florence–Casa Grande Valley. When the bill died in committee, Hayden secured legislation authorizing the U.S. Army Corps of Engineers to conduct a feasibility study of the San Carlos site, further encouraging his resolve to bring another federally supported reclamation project to Arizona.

Heavy flooding along the Gila River in the spring of 1912 destroyed the Pima's brush diversion dams used to direct the limited natural flow remaining in the river to their fields. By the time the Indians made the necessary repairs, the floodwaters had receded and they again lacked water. Indian agent Charles E. Ellis recommended to commissioner of Indian affairs Robert Valentine that an inexpensive diversion dam be constructed on the east end of the reservation to harness seepage and floodwater. Graves Moore, supervisor in charge of the Pima Agency, reminded Valentine that the Pima benefited less each year from the floodwaters as upstream diversions increased. "It has nearly demoralized them," he explained, "and should another series of delays be forced upon them it is a grave question as to whether or not they would ever regain their past confidence."[34] Chief engineer Charles Olberg informed Valentine that upstream diversions in Safford, Solomonville, and Florence continued to "materially diminish" the river flow and that without protection of their water the Pima would not "cultivate as much land as they formerly did."[35]

After 1912 well-publicized Indian water cases from the Ft. Belknap Gros Ventre and Assiniboine in Montana, Pyramid Lake Paiute in Nevada, Yakima

in Washington, Uintah and Ouray Ute in Utah, and Gila River Pima dominated both the U.S. Justice Department and congressional Indian affairs
committees. Challenges remained, however, in prosecuting these cases.
Wendell Reed complained to commissioner Cato Sells in 1913 that the Justice
Department litigated Indian cases but did not "get out and secure the evidence" needed to prosecute such claims successfully. It "simply fights with the
ammunition that is brought to [it]." Opponents of the Indians, in contrast,
hire "good lawyers" and "leave no stone unturned" in gathering the evidence
to support their position. While the Justice Department assigned two water-
rights attorneys to handle Indian cases, it failed to provide any resources to
research Indian water claims.[36]

This unresponsiveness forced the Indian Service to adopt a new para-
digm. To protect Pima water rights and provide them with an equal chance
to succeed in the American economy, the Indian Service needed data that
would substantiate Pima and Maricopa claims. This increased in importance
as severalty occurred on reservations in Arizona. Initiating a meaningful
severalty program that included rights to water forced the Indian Service to
reorient its thinking away from random allotments to a planned severalty program. To protect the limited water that remained, the Indian Service sought
to determine when and where irrigation and cultivation on the reservation
occurred. This was vital not only for prosecuting Indian water claims but also
for completion of land severalty at Gila River.

Olberg informed Sells of the importance of survey data in documenting
the extent of Pima and Maricopa land previously and currently cultivated.
With the support of Sells, Olberg proposed putting four men in the field to
conduct surveys. He then assigned John S. Layne to examine land records
in Pinal, Pima, and Graham counties, regarding "water appropriations that
might have some bearing" on legal proceedings. Without this information,
Olberg could not "guess within a couple thousand acres" how much Pima and
Maricopa land was or might be irrigated.[37]

By 1915 some members of Congress, including Senator Henry F. Ashurst
(D-AZ), agreed on the propriety of a reclamation project on the Gila River if
it benefited Pima farmers.[38] Hayden and Ashurst sought to use this sentiment
to the advantage of all Pinal County farmers and advocated a joint-use system that would enable the Pima and Maricopa, as well as their upstream non-
Indian neighbors, to put their water to beneficial use and thereby protect it
under state prior appropriation laws. Distributing the benefits of reclamation

through a joint-use project was socially and politically more palatable than reallocating water, leading Hayden to support the more conservative and expedient action.[39]

In June Hayden and Ashurst co-introduced legislation calling for construction of a San Carlos dam and a joint-use irrigation project. Facing opposition from western congressmen who believed that Arizona already had its share of federal reclamation (the Salt River Project), Hayden and Ashurst initiated a public relations campaign designed to shape opinion for the San Carlos project. "Our best, and in fact our only avenue of approach is by reason of the fact that the Pima Indians will be benefited," Hayden noted.[40] The Pima instituted their own public relations blitz, stressing their moral rights to the water of the Gila. The Pima First Presbyterian Church in Sacaton wrote members of Congress seeking support for a reclamation project on the Gila for their benefit.[41] John Truesdell, assistant U.S. attorney assigned to represent the Pima, pushed for an "early adjustment" of Gila River water rights by court decree.[42]

Ashurst, chairman of the Senate Indian Affairs Committee, asked interior secretary Franklin Lane to prepare a position paper outlining the views of the Indian Service regarding a smaller joint-use diversion dam above Florence, which was considered more feasible after the winter floods of 1914–15. Flooding in December was not extensive; but when rain again fell in January, it "ripped things wide open" in the valley below. "Certain it is," assistant engineer Nicolas W. Irsfeld wrote Southworth from Sacaton, that "more acres of [reservation] land went downstream with the last flood." The torrent left several canals on the reservation in "very bad condition." While upstream farmers might be able to build a permanent diversion dam above Florence to protect them from flooding and better utilize the water, Lane told Ashurst, the government would have to oppose them "in order to protect the water right now claimed by the Indians." Lane gave his blessing to the proposed FCGP, but only if it would "give the Indians an advantage of location that they have not heretofore enjoyed."[43]

Reed proceeded cautiously, seeking to protect Pima water through the politically conservative beneficial-use approach. Writing to Sells, Reed stressed the desirability of increasing Indian irrigation as a means of self-support and for "the preservation of undisputed legal rights to the water." Showing his deference to prior appropriation, he informed Sells that such use of the water was more in accordance with the "law in arid states" and that "cooperation with state officials is encouraged by acting in harmony with this plan."[44] At the same time, Reed had to justify to a parsimonious Congress the expense of constructing a reservation irrigation system mandated by the deprivation experienced by the Pima and Maricopa and the need to facilitate land severalty. Congress demanded evidence that the Indians would farm their allotments before authorizing the expenditure for an irrigation system.

Reed dispatched a letter to Olberg, stressing the importance of demonstrating the actual number of acres cultivated by the Indians. "I find that Congressmen simply go up in the air when they question [me] and find that a considerable amount [of money] has been expended in irrigation projects and [I am] unable to show any tangible beneficial results."[45] Olberg responded to Reed's request, describing the difficulty of gathering such data without surveying the land, which required money that Congress was hesitant to authorize. The "amount of land irrigated changes from year to year," Olberg reasoned, depending on water availability. With completion of the survey, he promised Reed, "I can tell you to a fraction of an acre."[46]

In the meantime Senator Harry Lane (D-OR) badgered Hayden on the quantity of irrigable Pima land should Congress approve the FCGP. It was essential for the allocation of the water to demonstrate acres under ditch (irrigated) and potentially irrigated acres. Hayden, desperately wanting approval of the project, played his Indian card. The Pima's current diversion of water was "below the white diversion," but passage of the FCGP would "carry the Indian diversion up the river so that he will get an equal chance to obtain his share of the water."[47] To do this the United States would have to purchase the Florence Canal. Any lateral extension to the reservation would cross private and public lands. While the 1890 Canal Act allowed such latitude, Hayden preferred an exchange for existing rights-of-way, with the government allowing non-Indian farmers to divert water from the same canal. If the government built and controlled the diversion dam on the Gila River and operated the distribution and lateral canals, the Pima would receive their water. Despite a lack of consensus on the meaning of Indian water rights, the House and Senate agreed that the most expedient means of resolving the Pima water dispute was to build a joint-use irrigation system that distributed the benefits and costs of the project. While the Senate Indian Affairs Committee recommended an appropriation not to exceed $175,000 to initiate the project, a House filibuster at the close of the Sixty-third Congress prevented its passage.

THE GILA RIVER SURVEY BEGINS

To clarify rights and priorities in regard to the waters of the Gila, the U.S. Corps of Engineers recommended adjudication as a precursor to any irrigation project. Litigation, however, made Hayden and Florence–Casa Grande area farmers uneasy, especially if Congress authorized federal action. Desiring to restore water to the Pima and provide for his voting constituents, Hayden encouraged Pinal County water leaders to settle any water dispute in a friendly manner rather than "quarrel over the meager supply." Water going to waste in times of flood, Hayden reasoned, made little sense when all farmers in the Gila Valley could benefit from it by harnessing such flows.[48]

In anticipation of legal proceedings, Sells approved Olberg's request to survey the reservation and precisely determine the extent of Pima agriculture. F. M. Schanck suggested that Olberg survey the reservation and the upstream lands to "limit and define the quantity of water" being used above the reservation.[49] Assistant Indian commissioner Edgar Merritt authorized $3,000 to install and maintain gauging stations on the Gila to quantify the flow of water and effects of upstream diversions. At Olberg's request, six of these stations were placed on the Gila River, one on the Santa Cruz River, and one on the San Pedro River. In an attempt to keep water hearings out of federal court, Pinal County water users initiated a friendly complaint in Florence on December 9, 1913. Olberg immediately begged Reed to do all he could to "stave off the adjudication a few months longer [so] we will be in a position to present the claims of the Indians."[50]

Reed delayed hearings in the *Lobb v. Avenente* complaint until June 10, 1914, when Cochise County judge A. C. Lockwood commenced hearings on the rights of water users in Pinal County. As noncitizen wards of the government, the Pima were not present in the Florence courthouse and their interests were not represented. Hayden convinced Lockwood to limit the proceedings to Pinal County, believing that keeping Upper Valley users in Gila County out of court best served all parties.[51]

Reed agreed with Olberg's request to survey all the middle Gila River Valley in order to quantify the current and formerly irrigated lands of the Pima and Maricopa as well as their non-Indian neighbors both above and below the reservation. Olberg then assigned Southworth to conduct the surveys. Southworth and a crew of Pima instrument men went about surveying and mapping all irrigated and previously irrigated lands within the reservation, producing a set of thirteen plane table maps. In the process, the Indian Service produced a graphic representation of the historic parameters of agriculture on the reservation. The maps illustrate in detail "the land at present irrigated, that previously irrigated, and that susceptible of irrigation" as well as the "various kinds of crops to which the land was planted." The survey clearly showed the abandonment of scores of Pima and Maricopa farms due to water loss, with entire villages shifting location or being deserted. It found 3,766.19 acres not in cultivation and an additional 3,231.81 previously irrigated acres, leaving a total of 6,998 acres (36.7 percent of the irrigated land) abandoned due to water deprivation.[52]

Southworth's interviews with Pima elders substantiate this quantitative analysis. Pima farmer George Pablo complained that many of his people "had to leave our farms there and move further up the river" where seepage water was available. James Hollen added: "Our fathers were forced to leave their old fields in the District of Sacaton Siding (Sranuka) where they built their homes and cultivated land. We felt the decrease of water first as we were the last to take out our water from the river." Whole villages, including Pablo's Mount Top Village, simply disappeared as the water dried up.[53] Furthermore, several villages abandoned canals after the first upstream diversions of water, including Blackwater, Sacaton, and Casa Blanca, all older, established communities. Blackwater, Sacaton, and Casa Blanca had the largest percentage of abandoned acres (38 percent, 36 percent, and 37 percent, respectively).[54]

Sixty-seven-year-old Antonito Azul of Sacaton lamented the abandonment of 123 acres of land that he and his late father had cultivated under the Cottonwood ditch "because there is no water to irrigate with." George Pablo explained how he abandoned thirty of his forty-five acres of land due to lack of water.[55] Juan Lagons told Southworth that crops under the Hollen (Simon Webb) ditch in Santa Cruz fared poorly because of seepage water. Reliance on episodic floodwater maintained the fields; "otherwise they would have been useless long ago."[56] Marginalized from the growing Arizona economy, Pima farmers struggled to cultivate a fraction of the land they formerly farmed.

The interviews clearly support the notion that multiple villages and scores of farms shifted location, as whole groups of Pima and Maricopa farmers and families abandoned one location and reestablished themselves in another. Overall prospects for water to irrigate crops were unpredictable at

TABLE 2.2. Proportion of Fields Sown to Grain by Acres, 1914

Village*	Acres of Grain	Total Acres	Percent of Total
Blackwater	1,495.38	1,619.68	92.3
Sacaton	853.40	1,396.36	61.1
Santan	2,114.61	2,670.98	79.2
Casa Blanca	2,747.92	3,092.45	88.9
Santa Cruz	472.38	581.39	81.3
Gila Crossing	953.27	1,140.76	83.6
Cooperative	317.42	451.37	70.3
Maricopa	956.10	1,114.95	85.8
Totals	9,910.48	12,067.94	82.1
Arizona	96,722.50	307,869.50	31.4

Source: Author analysis of the Southworth maps (1914) and the 1920 U.S. Census.
* From east to west.

best, leading farmers to abandon their fields or plant fewer acres. Many families left their villages and moved to places where seepage water was available, limiting such farmers to one crop per year.[57] Some farmers were no longer able to grow sufficient food for their needs. Many left their fields to cut mesquite wood to sell off-reservation in order to provide for their families.[58]

The type of crops grown is indicative of the severity of water loss. The overall proportion of acres sown to grain was 258 percent higher than the statewide proportion (table 2.2). "Wheat and barley are the staple crops," Wendell Reed informed the House Committee on Indian Affairs. "While the grains are the least profitable . . . they require the least water for irrigation and this consideration is responsible for the selection of these particular crops." Reed further noted that the Pima grew some corn and garden produce, but such crops were "not a safe proposition under the [existing] gravity [irrigation] system" due to the inability to get water on the crops at the right time.[59]

Moreover, the Pima interviews support the hypothesis of reduced field sizes due to water deprivation. Larger mean field sizes are found on the eastern half of the reservation. Water was the primary limiting factor, so it might be assumed that larger cultivated fields would have been located in areas where seepage water was more likely to be available or in newly established villages, such as those on the western (downstream) portion of the reservation. However, this is not the case. The largest cultivated mean field sizes (6.92

acres in Santan and 6.86 in Casa Blanca) were in areas where the river was dry. In areas where the river still contained water, mean field sizes were the smallest (3.36 acres in Santa Cruz, 3.93 in Gila Crossing, and 4.07 in Cooperative). While the river was generally dry in Blackwater (mean field size 6.75 acres), seepage water allowed crops—especially grain (92.3 percent of all Blackwater acres)—to grow.

In an analysis of all fields, including those abandoned due to water loss and those cultivated in 1914, traditional farming areas retained the largest mean field sizes: Blackwater (7.67 acres), Casa Blanca (7.26 acres), and Sacaton (5.78 acres). Santan, established in 1877, had a mean field size of 6.82 acres. Newly established villages such as Santa Cruz (3.21 acres), Gila Crossing (3.74 acres), Cooperative (4.75 acres), and Maricopa (5.73 acres) all had smaller mean field sizes. As water deprivation increased, not only did villages move downstream nearer the confluence of the Santa Cruz, Gila, and Salt rivers but Pima and Maricopa farmers established smaller fields. The larger mean field sizes of Casa Blanca, Sacaton, and Blackwater were in older villages, reflecting the pinnacle of Pima agriculture, when they annually sold millions of pounds of surplus grain, corn, and vegetables to military expeditions, government contractors, and tens of thousands of emigrants. The interviews substantiate this and tell the story of village farmers constructing canals downstream in new districts to irrigate smaller fields with the limited seepage or natural flow waters available. With little time to build ditches and little expectation of planting larger fields, heads of families reestablished their farms and villages downstream in areas where they believed limited amounts of water would sustain them.[60]

Three

THE SOUTHWORTH INTERVIEWS

In March 1931 Southworth penned an introduction to the "Statements on Irrigation of the Pima Indians." Writing to archaeologist Odd S. Halseth, who considered publishing the interviews, Southworth explained that their purpose was to "support Pima rights to the waters of the Gila River." He also spoke fondly of the men he interviewed and specifically recognized the work of Lewis Nelson, a graduate of Albuquerque Indian School and former teacher at the Pima Day School; John Enis; and Rudolph Johnson, the Pima interpreters who accompanied him.[1]

The Pima interviews were part of a larger investigation "conducted for the purpose of protecting [Pima] water rights." In each interview, Southworth accompanied the leading Pima men to the specific area in which each man farmed or had firsthand knowledge of the events described. More often than not, the Pima men (no women or Maricopa men were interviewed) preferred to "ride their horses or if need be to walk" to these areas rather than drive in the engineer's automobile, fearing "some evil spirit or something they could not understand furnished the motor power." Typically, the men required a week or ten days' notice to collect their thoughts before talking with Southworth.[2]

Southworth later regretted that the interviews "did not cover a wider and perhaps more interesting field" of study. Irrigation, he noted, was "a vital factor" in the lives of the Pima, "as their welfare depended entirely upon it." The interviews reflect these "innermost thoughts and view-points."[3] "Always in these talks," Southworth explained, "a certain bitterness was disclosed [by the chiefs and elders] at living in the knowledge that the white man far up the river was stealing his water which had once given life to fields and had established a land of plenty for hundreds of happy Indian families who were now scattered and left to shift for a meager livelihood on a semi-barren desert."[4] Pima elder Oliver Sanderson epitomized this sentiment when he lamented to Southworth that the Pima was forced "by his white brother" to be "on the road continually" selling wood or looking for work.[5]

Despite such feelings, the elderly Pima "were quite talkative and gave us much useful information." The men always made everything ready for Southworth by spreading a blanket "in the shade of a tree." He conducted the interviews between May and October 1914, generally in an upstream to downstream fashion. He later organized them in upstream districts (Blackwater) to downstream districts (Cooperative), although he did not sequence them in chronological order. The engineer understood from the interviews that irrigation was "a vital factor in their lives as their welfare depended entirely upon it."[6]

While the record is silent as to the exact way in which Southworth edited the interviews, we do know that he transcribed them, in his words, "almost verbatim" as Nelson, Enis, and Johnson interpreted them into English. To what extent Southworth took editorial license is unknown, although he likely took some measures to edit them. In 1931 he lamented that a "wider circle of the friends of the Pimas" did not have access to the detailed accounts. This book presents these firsthand accounts to that wider circle.[7]

The interviews appear exactly as they were in the typed copies in the National Archives, including all typographical errors and omissions. Where clarification is needed, I bracketed the inserted language. I also added bracketed reference numbers to correspond to the map depicting the canals and ditches that each interviewee described so that the reader can more easily identify the locations. Numerous endnotes provide additional information. Each note referring to the interviewee comes from Southworth's original manuscript, although I edited these notes for clarity. Within the interviews, I combined some paragraphs. Southworth had numerous one-sentence paragraphs that did not warrant standing alone. These are the only portions of the interviews that I have edited. The interviews are in the same sequence in which Southworth presented them. All parenthetical statements are Southworth's editorial comments.

INTRODUCTION TO THE STATEMENTS ON IRRIGATION OF
THE PIMA INDIANS BY CHARLES H. SOUTHWORTH, 1931[8]

Interviews with a number of the oldest members of the Pima Indian tribe on the Gila River Reservation were obtained in 1914 during the course of what was officially called the Gila River Survey, of which the writer was engineer in charge. The Indian Service made these surveys and intended to use them to obtain information to support Pima rights to the waters of the Gila River. This work was extended and enlarged to permit of an investigation of the San Carlos irrigation project. The report of this survey, and investigation some ten years afterwards, formed the basis of the legislation under which the Coolidge Dam and San Carlos project was constructed.

The report itself without any supplemental matter was published in the Hearings before the Committee on Indian Affairs, House of Representatives, Sixty-sixth Congress, First Session, and while it gives brief historical analysis of irrigation on the Reservation, only reference mention was made to the interviews with the Indians. With the view that they be more readily available than possible from the few copies on file, and that they may be preserved for future reference, they are herewith most gladly submitted.

As will be noted the statements given were taken down almost verbatim as interpreted into English. In each instance an educated Pima Indian was employed as an interpreter and to Louis [Lewis] Nelson, John Enis, and Rudolph Johnson, all full-blooded Pima Indians, much credit is due for their efforts and keen interest in the work.

In each instance, an effort was made to have our informant accompany us over the locality, which happened to be the subject of the interview. Automobiles were then comparatively scarce and it was only in rare instance that we were able to induce the old Indians to ride in them. They feared that possibly some evil spirit or something they could not understand furnished the motor power and they accordingly much preferred to ride their horses or if need be to walk.

The older Indian also is not in the habit of exercising his mental faculties in an impromptu fashion[;] for a while all the Indians were anxious to assist in our efforts yet in practically every instance the old Indian required a week or ten days to think things over before he would consent to talk. In some instance even after appointments had been made we were told to come back later as sufficient time had not transpired to permit of the mental effort necessary to recall the earlier historical events.

Exception in this respect was made in the case of two of the old Indians who were the proud possessors of calendar sticks.[9] By the use of these sticks they could readily recall the important event of each year as recorded by the little character indentation on the stick. In many instances direct irrigation or ditch construction history was recorded and it was possible through correlation to establish accurately the dates and other information desired. The Indians were induced to interpret for us the entire chronological events on each stick, and these records are included with the statements of the Indians. These calendar sticks resembled and are some time[s] used as walking canes. On them the yearly events are recorded in a series of indentations cut into the stick and these little markings serve to stimulate the memory of the maker. As a rule these markings have no significance or are unintelligible to other Indians, so that when the possessor dies the records are lost. It was the custom, we were told, that the calendar sticks were invariably buried with their owner.

No attempt has been made to arrange the statements in chronological order or otherwise. Each one is independent of the others and is given in the order as it relates to the irrigation districts on the reservation. The uppermost on the river, or the Blackwater district, [were] put down first and the other districts [follow] in their order proceeding down stream.

It is to be regretted that the interviews with these old Indians, nearly all of whom have since passed away, did not cover a wider and perhaps more interesting field. However, in accordance with our objective we were intent on irrigation history and confined our inquir[i]es largely to that matter. Irrigation to the Pima Indians has always been a vital factor in their lives as their welfare depended entirely upon it, so their statements in connection with it offered not only valuable information, but also furnished an outlet to their innermost thought and view-points.

The collection is gladly furnished in appreciation of having them preserved in published form and in the hope that they may prove of interest to a wider circle of the friends of the Pimas.

STATEMENT OF JUAN THOMAS (BLACKWATER DISTRICT)[10]

That the general history of irrigating in this particular district is that the ditch known as Cholla Mt. Ditch [#43] was already constructed and being used as an irrigating ditch when I came to this district, thirty-eight years ago [ca. 1876]. About two-thirds of the present cultivated land was under cultivation and irrigated from said Cholla Mt. Ditch.[11]

From the record I keep, I know that this Cholla Mt. Ditch was constructed forty-nine years ago [actual date 1866]. Also from said record, I know that the ditch known as Island Ditch Blackwater [#44] was constructed and finished fifty-two years ago [1862].[12]

When I first came to this district, both the Cholla Mt. and Island Ditches were carrying big heads of water all the year round, and the Indians were prosperous and independent, getting two crops a year. But as white settlers increased above the reservation and diverted water from the Gila River, the water gradually decreased. Indians were then forced to abandon some of their fields for lack of water. When Florence Canal was constructed, the Indians' water was no more, except flood water, which only runs on the average of two months a year.[13]

STATEMENT OF HAVELENA (BLACKWATER DISTRICT)[14]

That the ditch known as Cholla Mt. [#43] was constructed and completed forty-nine years ago [actual date 1866]; was in course of construction for less than a year, as there were several Indians working together.[15] *I did not do any of the work myself as I was serving as a scout for the United States at the time. Coming home for a visit once in a while when not needed.*[16] *When said ditch was first completed, the Indians brushed, cleaned and put under cultivation about one-third of the present cultivated land [about 320 acres].*

Year after year they brought more land under cultivation and were making a good living and were independent of the Government. They continuously made beneficial use of the water of the Gila River, getting two crops a year.

The ditch known as Island Ditch Blackwater [#44] on the plat was under construction for at least two years before it was finished now about fifty-two years ago [1862].[17] *We Indians on both sides of the river were getting all the water we wanted for irrigation and were self-supporting people. But when white people began to take the water above, we were reduced to poverty and sought aid from the Government. The Florence Canal was the ditch which took all the water from the Indians.*[18] *At least three ditches in this district were abandoned: viz: Cayah [#39][,] on the north side of the river[; and] Old Woman's Mouth Ditch [#41] and Old Indian Ditch [#42], on the south side.*[19]

STATEMENT OF WILLIAM WALLACE (BLACKWATER DISTRICT)[20]

The ditch known as Island Ditch Blackwater [#44], and marked on the plat as No. 2, was constructed by myself, fifty-two or fifty-three years ago [ca. 1862].[21] Myself and another man by the name of Pal-hau-dae were the ones who called a meeting and made suggestion of digging the ditch. Plans were at once made to do the work. We were at it two years before we finished it. Corn, melons and pumpkins were at once planted, as we did some clearing on some claims on the way to the work and on the way back from work on the ditch.

Land was rough and it took some time to level it. We gradually increased our fields, and wheat, cotton, tobacco and plants were planted. Said ditch, when first constructed, was about three feet bottom. About five or six years after the main ditch was constructed, three main branches were dug, and nearly all of the present cultivated land was then cultivated. The main ditch, above where said branches were connected, was enlarged to about five feet wide.

Water in the river flowed all the year round and the Indians used it continuously and were self-supporting and independent. We were not beggars then as we are now, always asking the Government to help us. But when white people began to come in and take up land above us and began to take our water out of the river, we were forced to reduce our cultivated fields.

When Florence Canal was constructed, there was no more water left for us in the river to irrigate our fields.[22] We were forced to abandon our ditches and fields. Our pride as independent and self-supporting people was forever destroyed. We have floodwater, but it only runs a short time, just long enough to make a fair crop, nothing like what we used to get before our water was taken. Sometimes, we do not get any crop at all.

STATEMENT OF FRANK HAYES (BLACKWATER DISTRICT)[23]

The general history of irrigation in this particular district, as best I can recall it now, is that the ditch known as Island Ditch Blackwater [#44] was begun to be constructed about fifty-four years ago [ca. 1860; actual date 1862].[24] It was in the course of construction for two years before it was finished, as we worked on it about two or three months each year, then we would go back to Casa Blanca to harvest our fields. Half of it was finished the first year.

After we had harvested our wheat fields and stored it away, we would come up again and dig the rest of it. Then we planted corn, melons and pumpkins. For the first two or three years, we drifted back and forth to Casa Blanca and Blackwater, tending to our fields there and here. Finally some of us made permanent homes and did not go back to Casa Blanca any more. We then put all our time in our fields except when going to war with the Apaches, or when called upon to protect some white people, as they had then begun to come into the country. We steadily increased our farms each year, and within four or five years, all the land that could be cultivated was put under cultivation. This was done by adding or connecting three main branches. The connection to the main ditch was enlarged from its original size of about three feet wide to about four or five feet wide.

The Cholla Mt. Ditch [#43] was built about four or five years after the Island Ditch was constructed.²⁵ The Indians had an abundant crop of everything the first few years and the people became anxious to take land here, and therefore, the Cholla Mt. Ditch was built.

Both sides of the river now being settled and having all kinds of water in the ditch, the whole year round, to irrigate with, this district began to catch the envious eye of the white land invader. Consequently, the waters of the Gila River, which belongs to us, was [sic] taken out above our reservation. It gradually decreased in the river until finally when the Florence Canal was constructed [1886–89], we were left high and dry. We protested to our Agents, but no one knows whether any of them did anything towards establishing our water rights or not.

We were forced to abandon some of our ditches and cultivated fields. Starvation drove us with shame downhearted to seek the aid of the Government. Our pride as self-supporting and independent people was forever taken from us.

STATEMENT OF SAMUEL SCOFFER (BLACKWATER DISTRICT)²⁶

The general history of irrigating in this particular district, as best I remember, is that the ditch known as the Island Ditch Blackwater [#44], and the ditch known as Cholla Mt. Ditch [#43], were already constructed and were in operation and used as an irrigating ditch when I came to this district forty-seven years ago [1867]. Fields were also all under cultivation as at present and were irrigated as such with the water of the Gila River.

After peace was made with the Apaches, the Pimas began to spread out digging ditches and taking up more land away from the villages.²⁷ The most important of these are the three as follows: Cayah, or Wood's Ditch, in 1869; Old Woman's Mouth, in 1881; Old Indian Ditch, in 1884.

Cayah Ditch [#39] irrigated about two or three hundred acres.[28] *Old Woman's Mouth Ditch [#41] irrigated about like amount as Cayah.*[29] *Old Indian Ditch [#42] was completed and water turned into it for trial and it worked all right.*[30] *Just then, water in the river was pretty low and in vain the Indians tried to get water for the new ditch, but alas, the Florence Canal was then finished and took all the water regardless of our ditches.*

Our irrigating water having been stolen from us, we have fallen back to want and despair. We were compelled to abandon the Cayah, Old Woman's Mouth and Old Indian ditches and all the cultivated land under them. Instead of being successful agriculturists and irrigators, we were forced to face for the first time, poverty and hardships.

STATEMENT OF JOSE PABLO (YAQUI DITCH)[31]

I remember the time that I and five other Indians went to Agent Crouse to let him know that we had planned to make a ditch [Yaqui] for the purpose of diverting the water from the Little Gila River for the irrigation of certain areas south of said river, and by doing this, we not only wished to let the Agent know, but at the same time, we wanted permission so we could have our plans perfected.[32]

C. W. Crouse told us that we could make the ditch as planned by us. While we were making this ditch, one Miguel Artez, a Yaqui Indian, voluntarily helped on this ditch work. Miguel Artez had no land anywhere under this ditch, but nevertheless he did the work.

There was one other Yaqui man, Nacho, who had lived among the Pimas some years prior to the coming of Miguel Artez and who had been always friendly to the Pimas, was given a piece of land under this new ditch. Miguel Artez lived with Nacho for a length of time until he had obtained this plot of land of Nacho's somehow, still unknown.

About a year or two later, after the completion of this ditch, this man, Miguel Artez, hired a number of Yaquis who were then on the reservation, and made a ditch [Yaqui ditch] [#38] from Blackwater Lake for the purpose of using this lake water for irrigation. This lake is about ninety feet wide and about one-half mile in length, containing a small spring.[33]

Miguel Artez had not always been very liberal in allowing other Indians to irrigate their crops with this water coming from the lake. The impossibility of securing a steady flow of river water to supplement this spring water from the lake made it discouraging and all the more favorable to Miguel Artez.

The case was brought to the Agent J. Roe Young (who succeeded C. W. Crouse) by several Indians on the Island,[34] who stated that years ago, before Sacaton Flats was a settled territory, a number of Indians from Stotonic villages made a ditch from this Blackwater Lake to empty the water into the river for use by the Indians in Stotonic and vicinity, and by this they had as much right to use the water from the Lake, they said.

Nothing very much was done in our favor after that until Elwood Headly [Hadley] came in as Agent, when J. R. Meskimens [Meskimons] was detailed to look into the matter, and finally a ditch was made by the Government from this particular lake to the river, thereby giving water to the Pimas on the Island, as well as the Yaquis.[35]

STATEMENT OF JUAN ENAS (BLACKWATER DISTRICT)[36]

John D. Walker, according to his own story, came first to the Pima settlement at Casa Blanca with the California Column from Ft. Yuma, in 1861 or 1862.[37] When he was discharged, he came back again and lived among the Indians. He later lived with my sister, Juana (deceased), as man and wife. He was then made Sergeant over a company of Pima scouts who enlisted at Maricopa Wells.[38] After serving with the Pimas, he went to Blackwater and took up land, about forty-two years ago [1872]. He did not do anything towards cultivation till after he had put up an adobe house.

It was about two years before he did any irrigating on said lands. He irrigated for the last time in the year 1886. The place began to run down then. It was later abandoned and remained abandoned until Price & Powell took it up and dug the ditch known as Price & Powell Ditch, about four or five years ago.[39]

What is now known as Steinfeld Ranch was also put under cultivation about the same time as did John D. Walker, as Juan Largo, the man who first owned and cultivated said land, was an intimate friend of Mr. Walker; so they dug and irrigated these two ranches from the same ditch.[40] The latter, however, was abandoned much earlier than the former until Padilla leased or rented it about four years ago. He then dug the ditch known as Padilla Ditch [#46].[41]

During the summer seasons, when water gets very low, we had to go up the river and dig in places where there is a sign of seepage water in order to get more water for our crops. Although our own experience showed us that we could not grow anything like beans and other plants, which are sensitive to alkaline, such as seepage water contained, we felt obliged to use it anyway in order to keep our families alive.

STATEMENT OF JOHN HAYES (SACATON FLATS DISTRICT)[42]

That the general history of irrigating in this particular district, as far as I know and remember, is that the ditch known as Sacaton Flats Ditch [#36] began to be constructed forty-two years ago [1872].[43] The construction was in progress for one year before it was finished. Corn, melons and pumpkins were planted, as these seeds can be planted in almost any kind of ground. Land was pretty rough and it required time to put it in a condition for wheat and other seed. It took at least five years to make it look as it is at present.

There was plenty of water in the river all the year round; we, therefore, had a constant flow in our ditches, we used it continually for irrigating our land, and were prosperous and independent. We never asked for help from the Government until the Government, through its officials, failed to protect our water rights, and the subsequent users took it all. We were then forced to fall back on the seepage water, which is very small and alkaline.

STATEMENT OF HAS MAKIL (SACATON FLATS)[44]

The ditch known as Sacaton Flats [#36] was built and used as an irrigation ditch before I came to live here.[45] All the good land under said ditch was under cultivation, except the spots where there was alkali. We Pimas, however, knowing how to deal with alkali by long experience, soon made these spots fertile farms.

Indians always had plenty of water to irrigate their fields with until whites took it above the reservation. The ditch known as Yaqui [#38] was constructed eighteen years ago [ca. 1896; actually constructed in 1891].[46] It gets its water from Blackwater Lake, when there is no water in the river.

STATEMENT OF ANTONITTE [ANTONITO] AZUL (SACATON FLATS)[47]

I was born and raised in Sweetwater District; lived in said district until 1871, when I and my father borrowed five hundred dollars from William Bichard, who was then trading at Sweetwater.[48] *My father and I came up to Cottonwoods and put men to work in constructing a ditch now known as Cottonwood Ditch [#32][,] paying said men with the five hundred dollars borrowed.*[49] *We finished said ditch the same year, but did not get any water into the ditch, as our money was exhausted. In 1872, we made an agreement with several Indians who were to take land under said ditch and pay us $15.00 each, which $15.00 would go to pay for the $500.00 borrowed.*

In the latter part of 1872, some of the Indians were able to clear and plant a little of melons, corn and other plants. In 1873, much more land was put under cultivation. In 1874, all land was cultivated except high places. About this time, Florence District began to be cultivated in small patches. It was at least two or three years after this particular district was put under cultivation, a battle took place at Old Santan between Blackwater and Casa Blanca Indians.[50]

We had to abandon about thirty-four acres in one place on account of water getting low, as Florence settlement increased. I, however, stuck to one field which is about 50 acres. Although I never did put it all under cultivation, as cultivation of land is very uncertain all over the reservation. In rainy seasons, we put more land under cultivation; when there is no rain, we cultivate only what we can.

This uncertainty continued for years until the Florence Canal was constructed [in 1889], when all of our water was taken. We then had to fall back on the seepage water, which is small; we were also forced to abandon several acres of our land, which is now covered with brush. As for my father and myself, we abandoned about 123 acres. The claims which we were clearing at the time the water went down had to be abandoned and now remains [sic] under brush. Not because we cannot work, but because there is no water to irrigate with. This is not only so with this particular district, but it is so with all other districts on the reservation.

Mescal was one of the main foods of the Pimas, as well as their farm products, so every winter they go out into the mountains to gather said mescal.[51] *It was in one of these mescal gathering seasons that the Pimas, who owned and inhabited this particular district, went to a place somewhere east of the present town of Tucson, and there, while all the men folks were away on a deer hunt, the Apaches came to the camp and took all the women and children away. When they came back to the camp, they saw what had happened, and instead of following up the Apaches to fight them and get back their wives and children, they came home, burned up everything they had in the way of houses and shelters. They tried to keep up their farms but grave and sorrows were too much for them; they finally burned their dam and what shelters they had built, left the place, each going to their nearest relatives in other districts.*

I do not recall when the construction of the next ditch was begun to reclaim this district. But I remember that land was being cultivated at [the] same time when [Ammi] White was captured by Texas Volunteers in 1862.[52]

In 1864 or 1865, all of the land under this new ditch was cultivated. There was plenty of water in the river the whole year round to irrigate with. There was [sic] no Mexicans or whites cultivating any land above us. The Indians had bountiful crops that they gathered the best for themselves and left the poorest ones for their horses and other animals.

About 1866, the [New] Mt. Top Ditch [#31] was constructed and land laying on the south bank of Little Gila was irrigated.[53] *The ditch known as Old Maricopa Ditch [#28] was constructed in 1849.*[54] *It was built by Maricopas and Pimas. When finished, water was turned into it, as it was mescal gathering season, so instead of getting water, they went to a mountain now known as Pecacho [Picacho] Mountain. While in camp, they were attacked by a war party of Apaches and were murdered. Few who escaped and those who remained at home kept up the new ditch, cultivating and irrigating land under it.*[55]

STATEMENT OF JOHN MANUAL (SANTAN)[56]

The ditch known as Santan Ditch [#27] was surveyed by Rev. Charles H. Cook in 1877.[57] *I rodded for him. The construction of said ditch was commenced right away after his survey was finished. At the intake of this ditch, the cut was nine feet deep and about ten feet wide at the bottom. The cut gradually reduced to three feet. The work on said ditch continued for years. Land being cultivated and irrigated as the ditch was extended, until 1883, the whole construction work was finished. A ditch known as Lower Santan Ditch [#27] was also constructed in 1879.*[58] *It was used to irrigate the Lower Santan District until flood water washed out the head of said ditch. Then they connected to the Santan Ditch and used the Santan Ditch ever since. Water had then begun to decrease in the river gradually until we have nothing left except flood waters.*

STATEMENT OF APACHOES
(ANCIENT SWEETWATER AND OLD MARICOPA)[59]

The Sweetwater District, as well as the ditches that are now being used, were the same at the time of my earliest remembrance. The old ditch above the present

Sweetwater Ditch [#23], and which you have called the Ancient Sweetwater [#25], was about six feet wide at the bottom, twenty feet wide on top and several feet deep.[60] *The irrigation under this old ditch began about three-quarters of a mile below the heading, and the land just above this old ancient ditch was irrigated by the Old Maricopa Ditch [#28].*[61] *The Santan Indians, in the early days, lived in and cultivated lands near the end of this old Maricopa ditch. They later moved to where the old Preacher [Charles H.] Cook had his school,*[62] *and then after that, they moved over to the north of the river and built the present Santan Canal.*[63]

The Old Maricopa Ditch was a much younger ditch than the Old Stotonic [Ancient Sweetwater], and I think the Old Maricopa was built when I was very young. I remember when a branch ditch was built running to the south of the Old Maricopa and out on the alkali flats. Shortly afterwards, it was abandoned because the Indians found that the alkaline was too strong for their plants. The Maricopa fields were abandoned, as near as I can remember, about forty or fifty years ago [map 3.1].

As to the ridge which you have asked me about, and which has been reported to be an old ancient canal, I do not believe that any of the land has been irrigated near this old ridge. These lands have always been alkali flats, and while some of the Indians lived on them, they never could cultivate them, and they have always been known by the Indians as hur-churl-jurk, *or "bare places" [open space or by itself].*

STATEMENT OF JOHN MAKIL (CASA BLANCA DITCH)[64]

The early irrigation history of this district is not known, but according to what has been told down from generation to generation, the Casa Blanca Ditch [Ancient Sweetwater] [#25] and its construction is very old.[65] *Cultivation of land a hundred years ago were [sic] as it is now. This is also true with Ash Stand, Sweetwater, Many Ants, Bapchil, Wet Camp, Sranuka, Mt. Top Settlement, Cummat, Autum.*[66]

The two villages of Maricopas were made about seventy-five years ago [ca. 1839]. Land cultivation of said settlement commenced about that time, which extended about three miles west of the present railroad bridge of the Arizona & Eastern.[67]

There was plenty of water in the river all the year around. Indians got two crops a year; sowing wheat during the winter, melons, corn, pumpkins and other things in spring, reaping crop in summer. When we planted corn, melons and other things, after we got off our first crop. We got our second crop in winter.

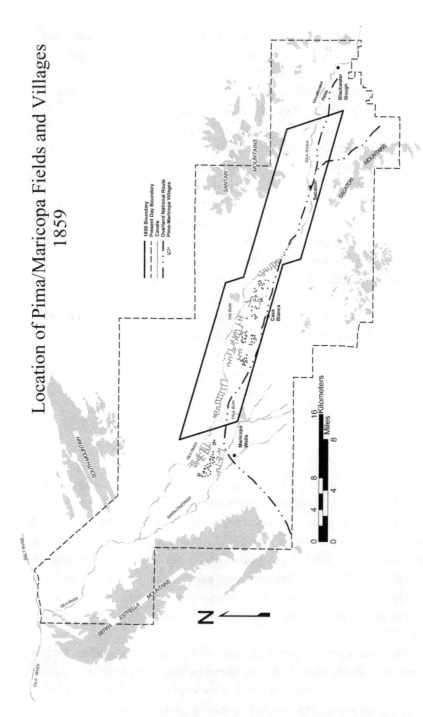

MAP 3.1. Location of Pima and Maricopa Fields and Villages, 1859. (*Source:* Author's map based on 1859 Surveyed Reservation, National Archives and Records Administration)

STATEMENT OF HENRY AUSTIN (CASA BLANCA DISTRICT)[68]

The construction of [the] ditch known as Casa Blanca Ditch [Stotonic/Sweetwater] [#23] is not known.[69] My grandfather told me in my young days that said ditch was already in and was used as an irrigation ditch as far back as he can remember. Same is true with the districts from Sacaton to a little on the other side of the railroad bridge.[70] When I was a young man, a white man by the name of [Ammi] White used to run a store at Casa Blanca.[71] He used to fill up all his store houses with wheat bought from the Indians. People now have no idea how much wheat Indians used to raise in times gone by. I had to wait at the store one time before I could sell my sack of wheat; being so many Indian customers that they had to take their turn before they could sell their wheat.

Water in the river never went down and Indians had plenty of water all the time in their ditches. Somewhere about forty-eight years ago, we began to notice the decrease of the water in the river and our ditches, especially we who have farms and take our water after several other districts take theirs.[72] We felt this shortage more than the people above us.

STATEMENT OF KISTO BROWN
(SNAKETOWN AND BRIDLESTOOD DISTRICTS)[73]

The old Snaketown, or Sratuka Ditch [#21], which you see along the edge of the hill here below the Snaketown Village, is a very old canal; I understand it was built by my ancestors, and it is at least four generations old.[74] Beyond that, I think the people who originally built the ditch lived in these many ruins that you see here in Snaketown. There is, however, a trace of an old or ancient ditch higher up on the mesa that may have been the ditch which brought water to these old ruins.

The present Snaketown ditch [#18] was built in comparatively recent years, as the heading of the older ditch had been washed out by the flood.[75] Also the present ditch, on account of being lower down, does not cover as much land as did the older ditch. Then, too, the water supply has been such that in the later years it has been impossible to irrigate as much land as we did formerly.

The [Old] Bridlestood [#17], or the Palinkirk, which had its headings south and west of the Snaketown canal, is also a very old ditch.[76] It was in existence at the *time of my earliest remembrance, and it was abandoned about twenty-five years ago [1889].*

Of the Indians who lived there, some went to Salt River, some to Gila Crossing, and others went down along the [Maricopa and] Phoenix Railroad and are living there now, cutting wood. Seven or eight years ago, one Paloma, with several other men, repaired this ditch and branching it, made a new ditch [#19] for the purpose of diverting the flood water at a point further up the river.[77]

One of the river channels ran and curves at this point and it seemed favorable to them then. Paloma and others had one year[']s benefit from this ditch, when this channel had taken another course, therefore setting away from this heading. At present, the current is about one-half mile away, and it was this sad occurrence that caused these Indians to depend on the waste water from the Snaketown ditch [#18].

STATEMENT OF BENJAMIN THOMAS (SRANUKA AND SANTA CRUZ)[78]

The old ditch which we call the [Old] Santa Cruz [#11][,] because the Indians who lived there later went over and settled on the Santa Cruz, was built when I was a small boy and the fields under this ditch were abandoned when I was old enough to fight the Apaches.[79] *I think the cause of the abandonment was on account of shortage of water, the diversions of the whites at Florence and by the other Indians who moved up to the Blackwater District. The old Sranaka [Sranuka] District, or at least a large portion of it, was also abandoned about this same time. The Old Sranaka [Sranuka] ditch [#15], however, is much older than the Santa Cruz and was built before my time.*[80]

The Ancient Maricopa [#9], located across the river from the Santa Cruz, is a very old ditch, and it was here that the first Maricopa Indians came from the Colorado River and joined the Pimas.[81] *These Maricopas had been driven away from their former homes by the Yuma Indians, to whom they were related. The Pimas formed an alliance with them and they took out this ditch in the Pima country, and they often joined forces with the Pimas to fight the Yumas, who would come up and attack them from the west. Some of these same Maricopa Indians afterwards moved up and took out the Old Maricopa Ditch [#28] just above the Sweetwater District.*[82] *Most of these old ditches were built about six feet wide on the bottom and twelve or fourteen feet on the top and were figured to carry about a foot and a half or two feet of water.*

The river, in the old days, or when I was a boy, was very much narrower than it is at present and it was no wider at any place than 150 steps, and in some places only 60 steps.[83] *The many floods that have come since I was a boy have widened the river to its present size and width.*

STATEMENT OF GEORGE PABLO
(DETAILED AND GENERAL DITCH HISTORIES)[84]

I was born in a village near a small mountain named by the Pimas Rattle Snake Home (Mt. Top Village). I do not remember how many years I lived in this place, but I can remember very well the time when water in the river was plentiful and the Pimas irrigated their lands and were self supporting people, because there being sufficient water for irrigation, we raised in abundance wheat, corn, melons, pumpkins, native beans and even cotton, which was worked in a way by the Pimas and made into cloth and used as clothing.[85]

Each village had its own ditch and I can recognize at this time eight ditches which carried sufficient amount of water for irrigation, which have been abandoned on account of scarcity of water in the river [fig. 3.1].

When the water in the river got so low during my residence in Mt. Top Village, some of us had to leave our farms there and move further up the river where we could find seepage water and there take up land. I sometimes think of my kin whom I had left in the neighborhood of Casa Blanca and Mt. Top Village my birth-place (now a vanished settlement). It makes me feel sad to think of them because there is not water enough so as to make their lands productive from which they can make their living.

Their only livelihood is in selling mesquite wood they haul either to Mesa, Tempe or elsewhere (a distance of twenty-five or thirty miles). We Indians here under the Cottonwood Ditch [#32] have a little seepage water to irrigate our lands with, but it is not enough to go around and we suffer for want of more water.[86] *And when I think of those relations of mine located in Casa Blanca, Wet Camp, Snaketown, Bapchil, and other settlements below these, I consider them like I do the Papago Indians put on the desert, where they depend only upon heavy rains which causes [sic] high floods, but this run-off water does not last but a short time, usually about three or four days.*[87] *This is just our condition now for a number of years on account of our river being taken from us by the white man.*

FIG. 3.1. Agency project constructed by the U.S. Indian Irrigation Service in 1914. (Courtesy of the National Archives and Records Service)

The Gila River is a river which, in the past, supplie[d] us through our various canals with enough water for the irrigation of our lands, but since that water has been taken by the whites and Mexicans above us, I say we are like the Papagoes out on the desert, because the steady flow has gradually ceased. In the summertime, the flow of rain water lasts about a week or ten days, but in the winter, it lasts a little longer.

I remember the time when a settlement of Pimas, some at this time living yet in the Santan District and other settlements, had good farms just west of the present Government farm (Sacaton School Farm).[88] *Their land was under a large ditch [the Old Santan] [#30] which was made by themselves. This ditch was abandoned, but is yet visible in some places below the Agency. I judge that this particular ditch is about six feet at the widest place, and it was customary for us in those days to have the heading of a ditch much wider than this[;] I judge, [it] was about ten feet at its heading.*

The Pimas in this settlement and under this ditch, when water was enough for us to use for irrigation, we raised lots of wheat, corn, melons, pumpkins and other crops that I have already mentioned to you; these same crops were harvested for winter use, and we never depended on the Government for help, as we had plenty to live on the whole year.

When the Little Gila River water began to get low, these Indians knew that they would suffer, because the Pimas of Cottonwood, Sacaton Flats and Blackwater settlements [were] diverting water from this same Little Gila River, so they had to abandon this ditch and their farms. Some planned to move across the Big Gila River and there take up land and use what floodwater they could get. As there is no steady flow of river water for this present Santan District, wells were drilled by the Government in order to supply them with well water for irrigation of their fields.[89] But not many days ago, I heard that the well water is doing no good to the wheat crops, that the Indians have begun feeding their own stock on said wheat fields, after convincing themselves that there will be no maturity of their planted wheat this year.

Allotments have been made there, but to my opinion, we ought to first be assured of a permanent supply of water and then allotments made afterwards, so that any Indian can willingly take his allotment any where [sic] and know that he can be supplied with water for his land.[90]

We have a little seepage water in the Cottonwood Ditch [#32], and if allotments are to be made now, some of us will have to leave this valuable water supply and be forced to take allotments elsewhere where we will have to depend on flood water, same as the Papagoes on the desert.[91] Sacaton Flats Indians also have a little seepage water for irrigation, and no doubt will not want to leave it and take allotments elsewhere. The Indians at Blackwater are in about the same fix for irrigation water as Casa Blanca and other settlements west of us. No water except in times of floods. The Government has left us in this suffering condition because it has allowed certain white and Mexican people to divert our water above us. What I am telling you now is the truth, as I have seen and known through my own experience from boyhood up to the present time.

I cannot furnish you with any definite information about the Cottonwood Ditch [#32] because I am not one of the original ones who first built this particular ditch.[92] This ditch was constructed some years before I bought this field that I am living on. I do not know exactly how many years has [sic] gone by since I came here, but I remember that it was the same year that the building of the [Southern Pacific] railroad was in progress and was built as far as Casa Grande.[93] I remember that I used to go up there just to see how it was built (S.P.R.R.). If you want the

FIG. 3.2. A Pima granary: the Pima stored thousands of bushels of food in granaries such as this to sell to emigrants. (John R. Bartlett, *Personal Narrative of Explorations and Incidents in Texas, New Mexico, California, Sonora, and Chihuahua* [New York. D. Appleton & Company, 1854], 2:236)

facts about this particular ditch, I would advise you to go to Ho-ke Wilson.[94] *He is about the only living old man who was in the party of Indians who first built this Cottonwood Ditch that you wanted to know about. However, as to myself, I do not know the plans of the builder; but I can say this: that we had enough water some years ago with which we irrigated our crops and we had to build sheds for storage of pumpkins and melons for winter use, for the wheat we made storage baskets of arrow weed and in this way had plenty to live on the whole year, but of late years we do not see such abundant harvests [fig. 3.2].*

There are five in my family and I have about forty-five acres of good land under the Cottonwood Ditch, but since there is not enough water, I cultivate about fifteen acres and thirty acres lies unused. When I left my old home in Mt. Top Village, I went and lived at Sacaton Flats for about two years before I came here. I know of another ditch that was surveyed by the Missionary, Rev. C. H. Cook, near here some years ago, said ditch to have diverted water from the Big Gila River, and water was run through this ditch once, but on account of scarcity of sufficient amount of water, it had to be abandoned.[95] *The Cottonwood Ditch [#32] remained in use because there is a little seepage to divert.*

As to abandonment of Old Woman's Mouth and Cayah Ditch: The Old Woman's Mouth [#41] was abandoned about fifteen years ago, or at least it has died out since that time.[96] *The Cayah [#39] fields were abandoned earlier; I would say about twenty-five or thirty years ago.*[97]

Of the following abandoned ditches of which you have asked me, I will say that the first eight were constructed previous to my remembrance, while the last three were constructed during my childhood. All these ditches were used during my youth.

1. *Ancient Maricopa Ditch [#9] (Below Sacaton Station [Maricopa &] Phoenix RR.)*
2. *Ancient Santa Cruz Ditch [Old Santa Cruz] [#11] (Between Sacaton Station & [Pima] Butte. Indians now in Santa Cruz Settlement near Sierra Estrella Mts.)*
3. *Bridlestood [#16] (North side of the river. Indians now settled through other settlements.)*
4. *Snaketown or [Old] Sratuka [#21] (North side of the river. About nine miles west of Sacaton.)*
5. *Old Sranuka Ditch [#15] (Settlement now at Gila Crossing.)*
6. *Ooist or Bapchil [#22] (Sweetwater District.)*
7. *Old Mt. Top Ditch [#26] (Around Rattlesnake Home.)*
8. *Ancient Sweetwater Ditch [#25] (North of Sweetwater Store.)*

1. *Old Maricopa Ditch [#28] (Northeast of Sweetwater Store.)*
2. *[New] Mt. Top Ditch [#31] (West of Agency.)*
3. *Old Santan Ditch [#30] (Old Sacaton Ditch, north of Agency.)*

The several towns, according to my memory, and naming them in the order in which they were located, east to west, are as follows: Maricopa, furtherest west, next Sweetwater, then Stotonic, Mt. Top, my residence, further west is Ooist (Sticks), Casa Blanca, Wet Camp and Sranuka. East of the [Maricopa and Phoenix] railroad was located the settlement of Skunks, and west of the railroad the Santa Cruz Indians near Pima Butte were located; these Indians were called "The People Under the Hill."

The first ditch referred to was the [Old] Maricopa Ditch [#28], which took out of the Little Gila due north of Old Cook's School House.[98] *At its heading it was twelve feet wide and further down only five feet.*[99] *The Indians in these days made the ditches in this manner. Irrigation began about one mile from the diversion, the* ditch was dug so deep that it was necessary to carry it further in order to get it to the surface for irrigation. The Little Gila River was then deeper than it is now, with not so much brush as now exists. The amount of irrigated area is not known in respect to these fields, as irrigation had been abandoned and the fields been grown over with brush.

The [Old] Maricopa ditch connected with the Sweetwater [or Ancient Sweetwater] ditch [#25] lower down.[100] Some of the irrigation of the fields by the old Sweetwater Ditch is abandoned now. The Stotonic [Old Sweetwater] ditch at the diversion dam, which was destroyed by flood water and which was rebuilt again further up the river and connected lower down with the old ditch. The Old Sweetwater ditch was larger at the mouth, as many Indians lived under this canal, and through this section of the country. The Maricopa and Sweetwater ditches both took out of the Little Gila. The Stotonic ditch is still a little larger than the others, as several settlements are dependent on this ditch. These settlements are as follows: Stotonic, Mt. Top, Casa Blanca, Juit Cooit.

There is not as much land irrigated under this now as in the past, many fields are not cultivated any more. The country was cultivated all through this section between these ditches and the river. From the Stotonic ditch there was another ditch branching off, carrying water to Mt. Top. South of all these ditches are alkali spots, [which] according to my knowledge were never cultivated. The Mt. Top Indians put under cultivation some of this alkali land south of the Maricopa Ditch. The Ooist Ditch [#22] takes out lower down from the Stotonic ditch.[101] The [Old] Sratuka Ditch [#21] on the north side passes the Double Buttes.[102] The Ooist Ditch is about as large as the Sweetwater Ditch or Stotonic Ditch [#23]. Under the Sratuka Ditch, the amount of land is approximate and not definite. The [Old] Sranuka Ditch's [#15] heading was east of the [Maricopa and Phoenix] railroad about six miles.[103] This ditch passes between the Double Buttes, where the settlement was located. The width and depth is approximately the same as other ditches. The cultivated lands began under the Schonic Ditch about two and one-half miles below its diversion.[104]

West of the Sranuka Ditch is the [Old] Santa Cruz Ditch [#11], a rather small ditch, passes close to Small Butte and north of Sranuka Ditch.[105] The diversion for this ditch is about two miles east of the [Maricopa and Phoenix] railroad. The area of cultivated land is about two miles. The fields of the Sranuka and the Skunk connected. A few fields are irrigated from the Sranuka Ditch east of the railroad. The Old (Ancient) Maricopa Ditch [#28] diverted its water on the north side of the Gila River about four miles east of the railroad. The Bridlestood ditch [#16] is about one and a half miles east of the [Ancient] Maricopa Ditch.[106]

The Ancient Maricopa Ditch [#9] is the same in size as the Sweetwater Ditch [#23]. The Pimas and Maricopas have their fields under this ditch. There are only a few Pimas irrigating land east of the railroad now. The Indians did not cultivate this upper section on account of high floodwater in this district. The widest section of this land is about one-half mile across and about one and three-quarter miles in length. The land irrigated by the Santa Cruz Ditch is about one-eighth mile across.

West of the Ancient Maricopa Ditch the Indians used the land flooded by the water whenever it was flooded by storm water, availing themselves of the opportunity to plant pumpkins and melons, etc. The river was, in most places, about two to four hundred feet across, and in some places not even that wide, as the Little Gila was then the main body of the river. I did not think that there was any main river until some time later when the North Blackwater Indians diverted the water into a canal which they built there, the flood water coming down cut through this diversion, destroying this diversion or heading of the slough with deposits of silt. This slough was not very long, probably about two hundred feet. Some of the water, during high floods, washed down the Gila River, cutting the river bottom lower than the Little Gila, and thereby making the Big Gila River as it is now.[107] It never affected the river much, owing to its high banks and great depth. The Little Gila was then deeper than it is now. The amount of flood water coming down the valley now is greater than it was. The Little Gila banks being all solid, but now, as the Big Gila banks are not so solid, they cause the Indians more trouble than formerly.

About in June, the water in the river begins to get low and the next month there is a little water left. The next month flood water will begin. The flood water will begin in about three weeks. In the fall, there will be enough water for irrigation. From this time, there will be a little seepage water, and later on, more seepage water will be available. During the time I was in Casa Blanca, there was also enough water all the year through.

The reason for the moving of the Indians to the different settlements[,] from Casa Blanca to Mt. Top, Santan, Blackwater, and other places, was on account of a shortage of water. The Santan and Blackwater Indians having diverted the water above them and owing it to the river becoming larger and thereby giving the Indians above them more water than they could obtain at their old settlements, they were forced to move to these different settlements in order to live. The Sranuka *people also found out that the water was getting less, and went west and found a seepage slough and are now living at Gila Crossing by diverting seepage water.*[108]

The Santa Cruz Indians also moved near Gila Crossing in order to get this seepage water where they had sufficient.[109] *Some Pimas called the Sratukas also found out that water was getting short and went to Salt River and made a ditch and got their water from Salt River, which is now the Salt River Reservation.*[110] *The western Maricopas went to Salt River, they are at Lehi now. This is a settlement of mixed tribes. The [Old] Santa Cruz Ditch [#11] diverted its water lower down than the [Old] Sranuka Ditch [#15]; the length of the Santa Cruz Indian fields were [sic] about two miles. The Santa Cruz Indian fields are a little wider than the Skunk fields. This is as far as the irrigation extends. From here, there extends much brush and alkali sections [sic].*

The San Carlos Agency was settled when these Indians moved to their settlements. It was about the time the peace treaty was made with the Apaches [May 21, 1872] that the ditch at Blackwater and the settlement there was [sic] made; they still feared the Apaches at this time.[111] *The water in the river began to get low before the Adamsville people began to take out the water, and a few years previously and still more pronounced when the white settlers began coming in.*[112]

As regards the old Sratuka Ditch [#21] and Village: The old Sratuka Village was located on the south side of the river, whereas the principal fields were across the river on the north side under the Sratuka Ditch, or the ditch that is now called Sku-ka-ika, or Snaketown [#18]. When a considerable amount of this ditch and farm lands were washed away, some forty-odd years ago [ca. 1868], and the Indians were beginning to feel the want of water on the Gila, a good many of these Sratuka Indians moved over and located on the Salt River. Those who remained, made new lands under the Snaketown ditch, and a short time after this the Snaketown settlement was established. Some Indians remained and established another Sratuka, or Wet Camp, village on the south side and they got their water from the Bapchil Ditch [#22] [fig. 3.3].

This Bapchil Ditch is often called Ooist by the Indians, and Bapchil mostly by the whites.[113] *It irrigates all the lands in the Bapchil and the old Sratuka district. The present Sratuka Village is located about one mile south of where the former, or Old Sratuka Village, used to be before the floods washed it away about forty-seven years ago.*

The sketch which I have made here on the ground and which you have copied shows the ditches and the land that was in cultivation when I was a youth and before the whites began to take water out of the river above us.

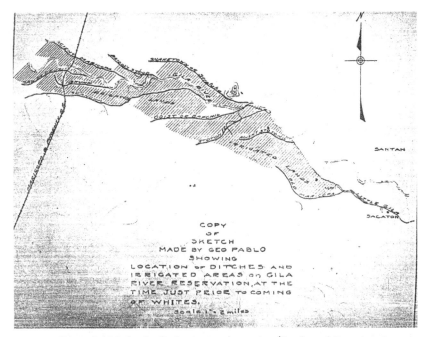

FIG. 3.3. George Pablo's sketch of irrigation canals, ca. 1850. (Southworth Interviews in Arizona State Museum Library Archives)

STATEMENT OF HO-KE WILSON
(SWEETWATER AND OTHER DISTRICTS)[114]

I was born in the settlement of Bapchil about seventy or more years ago, and I can remember that I was about five or six years old when we left this Bapchil home and settled in another place not very far from there (Kow-vot-ka). Here we cleared about five acres of land, but from this Kow-vot-ka home we still owned and culti-vated our farm in Bapchil. We numbered four in the family at that time. We owned about eight acres of land in one place and five acres in another, making a total of thirteen acres in our old home in Bapchil. We have, besides the thirteen acres, about five acres that we had cleared near Kow-vot-ka Village, making eighteen acres in all. We lived just one year in Kow-vot-ka settlement, and we moved to another place called Stone Mortar.[115]

In Stone Mortar Village we lived about two years, when a member of our fam-ily died and we had to abandon our home, as it was customary for us in those days that if someone in the family died, the house would have to be burned and the place abandoned.[116] *The family then moved and located in Mt. Top Village (another vanished settlement). Here we lived about six or seven years. We continued raising wheat, corn and other crops that we had raised in other places.*

Our land was under a ditch large enough to carry sufficient water to irrigate with, about six feet wide at the bottom and top, because we never made our ditches like we now see the white people do, have the bank slope; we made the banks of our ditches in those days nearly straight up and down; this makes the top of a ditch about as wide as the bottom.

A large amount of water entered this canal, and I can still remember when I was old enough to help work in the fields, that sometimes four men and sometimes five men had to be irrigating at the same time from this one particular ditch. There was another ditch right opposite our old Bapchil home, and this is where the Snaketown Indians diverted their water (at foot of Double Buttes).[117]

I had forgotten to mention this before, that I owned another small piece of land under this [Old] Snaketown Ditch [#21].[118] *This ditch is about the same in size as the one already mentioned to you. The field under this ditch belonging to me is about eight acres. I can yet remember very well that there was enough water in various ditches the year round, and we used to raise and harvest lots of wheat, pumpkins, melons, corn and other things. Though there were at that time no modern farming implements, or even work horses, to do our farm work with. We used wooden plows (ox-plows).*[119] *The plows were made by ourselves of mesquite and ox teams to answer for horses. The yoke, a part of the plowing outfit, on the ox teams, were [sic] generally made of willow or cottonwood, such material being lighter in weight than mesquite.*

I have often realized of late that at the present time our young Indians have learned to use modern farming implements, if we had as much water now as we had then, our young people would be prosperous. We also made our own wooden shovels, as a white man's shovel was then unknown, but when the City of Tucson was first settled by the Mexicans, shovels made by the Mexicans were then known, though different from a white man's shovel. Occasionally some of the Pimas would go to Tucson to have a shovel made by the blacksmith in that town. With these two kinds of shovels we were able to clean out our ditches and work in our fields. We sometimes had to use these shovels to do our planting because there was [sic] very few families that owned a yoke of oxen, and the owners were always busy plowing some person's field. Though we did our planting in a crude way, we were always sure of a good crop, as we had sufficient water for irrigating [fig. 3.4].

FIG. 3.4. A Pima plow: made of mesquite or ironwood, the Pima plow easily turned the fertile soil along the Gila River. Steel plows arrived in the 1860s. (Drawing courtesy of Castetter and Bell, *Pima and Papago Indian Agriculture*)

We lived in Mt. Top Village for about six or seven years, as I have stated before. Here my mother died, and about that time, Old Chief Antonio Azul, being a former resident in our neighborhood, brought word that he had found a suitable place to divert another good supply of water, and that he wanted his relations to help him make this ditch and to take up land under it. My father[,] being one of close relations to Old Chief, accepted this invitation, as the family was yet in a mournful condition over the death of my mother not long before. So we left our home at Mt. Top Village and came to our present home here in Cottonwood. To the best of my recollection, this is about forty-five years ago [1869]. So this Cottonwood ditch [#32] is still in use, as there is a little seepage water to irrigate land in this ditch.[120] *This Cottonwood ditch has never been enlarged. It is about five feet wide, but at its heading is about eight feet wide and about one mile from the diversion to where it enters into the Indian fields, and there two main ditches (equal in size) fork out and is [sic] used by various Indians about two miles down to the Agency. We had left our home in Mt. Top, but we did not want to abandon our old farms in the west; so from our new home here in Cottonwood, we worked there continuously during the planting season. My father and I cleared us a piece of land chosen by my father under this new ditch.*

This field is on the north side of the new dam now in construction by the white people ([U.S. Indian] Irrigation Service).[121] *This Cottonwood Ditch [#32] was* made about forty-five years ago [ca. 1869], but Antoni[t]o Azul has better knowledge about this than I. But I remember the time we started clearing on the proposed site, with a number of hired Indians, mostly Papagoes, who were paid in store goods and cash, which had been borrowed by Chief Antonio and his partners from a white man who was then a resident trader near Casa Blanca.[122]

This borrowed merchandise and cash was to be paid back in wheat at harvesting season. We did not raise much wheat the first year[;] still it was ruled that all who had obtained land under this ditch were to pay proportionately of three sacks of wheat at harvesting time so as to meet the payment of this borrowed money and merchandise. The year previous to this payment, we had also raised wheat in our fields in Bapchil and other settlements, so this made it easy for us to meet the payment. Some years afterward, when the water in the river got so scarce in the west, we obtained more land under the Cottonwood Ditch, where seepage water remained for us to divert. We finally abandoned our fields in the west and now are permanently settled here. I have learned through my own experience that this seepage water is not very good water to irrigate with, because I know that in one of my fields, I used to get forty sacks of wheat when we had a steady flow of good river water.

When the white and Mexican people settled in Florence, and further up the river, and had diverted this good river water belonging to us, the crops we raised did not mature or yield as much as it [sic] did formerly, because of the two reasons: uncertainty of good river water and this alkaline seepage water.

At present there are six in our family and we have under this Cottonwood Ditch about thirty-five acres, but about ten acres of this area lies uncultivated on account of scarcity of good water. We have about fifteen acres in alfalfa, as alfalfa seems to stand water containing much alkali. We do not raise much wheat, corn, melons and other crops, as we did when we had lots of water. There is still the Old Santan Canal [#30] below William Stephens ([New] Mt. Top Ditch [#31]), Old Maricopa Ditch [#28] and others west of these. These ditches herein stated and all the other ditches east of these were made during my existence, but the ditches west of the Sweetwater Ditch [#23] were made and used by the Pimas for some time before I was born.

Traces of some of these abandoned ditches are yet visible in some places, and I hope that some day, all these once cultivated land[s] may bring to the coming children abundant harvests again.

STATEMENT OF SLURN VANICO
(ANCIENT SWEETWATER AND OTHER DISTRICTS)[123]

I was born in a settlement near Casa Blanca, what we called Mt. Top Village. There are a number of Indians living now who lived in that village with me. I was about seven years of age when I left with my parents and moved to Blackwater. We left our ditches and farms near Casa Blanca for our relations to use. There was enough water in the Gila River for us to irrigate our lands with at that time. And we knew that we could make a living at this new home in Blackwater just as well as in our old home in Mt. Top Village. We made our own ditches and dams, but as these ditches and dams are not in use now on account of our river water being all taken away from us by the white people and Mexicans, the Government is to blame for the loss of our water.

Lands that had been irrigated from the various abandoned ditches are still unused, but we hope to cultivate them again if the Government would help us get our water back.

We had plenty of water for irrigating some thirty or more years ago, and we never had to depend on the Government for help. I do not remember the number of years ago when the Santan Indians had good farms and were making their own good living from farming under [an] irrigation ditch made by themselves. This ditch is about six feet wide at the bottom and carries enough water for all the Indians irrigating from this ditch. This ditch is about three miles long and can yet be seen in some places (Old Sacaton Ditch No. 13).[124] I will say that the abandonment of this ditch was about forty years ago [ca. 1874].

There are a number of other Indian ditches that I still remember, from which the Indians got their supply of water for irrigating. There is a ditch below William Stephens, but was used only one year and was abandoned for some reason. I think I heard the reason, which was that there was [sic] not enough Indians to keep it in repair. About that time, some Indians who had farms that were irrigated from this ditch had moved to other settlements ([New] Mt. Top Ditch [#31], the Old Maricopa Ditch [#28], Stotonic Ditch [Sweetwater Ditch] [#23] and others).

We had left our home in Mt. Top Village when I was about seven years old; we moved and located in what is now Blackwater settlement. We had obtained about twenty-five acres of land which was under the Blackwater Ditch [#44],[125] on which land we lived about ten years, numbering six in the family at that time when one of our close kin was murdered by the Mexicans at Adamsville, while drunk. This murdered Indian being the grandson of Chief Antonio Azul, Chief Antonio, being our uncle on our mother's side, sent word to us to come and live with him since the sad event happened. So we had to leave our twenty-five acres of land in Blackwater and come here. We were given five acres of farm land under this Cottonwood Ditch [#32] by our Chief and uncle.[126] *This is about forty-five years past.*

Through purchase and otherwise, we obtained more land later on under this Cottonwood Ditch [#32]. One of my brothers now owns the five acres which was given to us by Chief Antonio and is now living separate. We number six in the family now, and we own about thirty-five acres, but about ten acres of this land was washed away by floods in the river. We have about eight acres in alfalfa and raise a little wheat and sometimes a small acreage of corn. We have about fifteen acres under brush at this time for the reason of scarcity of water. When we had enough water some forty years ago, we raised and harvested good crops of wheat, corn, melons and pumpkins, but now we Indians do not raise but very little of such crops. I remember about thirty-five years ago we had to plow with wooden plows (ox-plows) and we used oxen to pull those plows. We made these wooden plows, as also our shovels, from the mesquite wood.[127] *Now we have all modern farming implements and all we need is enough river water to irrigate our lands.*

STATEMENT OF MEGUEL (SANTAN DISTRICT)[128]

I do not know my exact age, but I was old enough to remember the greatest flood we ever had: water rose in the [Gila] river, reaching to the foot of Double Buttes and over to Casa Blanca ruins. I must have been about five years old when this happened, because I remember my parents and I, during this flood, went in search of a higher place from our home in Bapchil, as that was my first home.[129]

The next big flood was when I was a grown man, and that was when the flour mill was flooded and ruined in Casa Blanca settlement (about 1869).[130] *I have been on nearly every raid in the mountains after Apaches, as they were then our enemies. I once went to the Mojave Country to sell horses with Owl Doings, who is now dead.*

I was a full grown man when Big Back, Apache Chief, was killed in the mountains and I was with the party of Indians who went there with American soldiers (about 1871).[131] *I remember well that Louista, the captured Apache Indian who was with the Scouts in subduing Big Back, the Apache Chief.*

*I cannot tell you exactly how much land I cultivated in my old home in Bap-
chil and other settlements in the West, because I do not know what an acre is, but
I can go there and show you various places that I farmed when I was a boy (he
mentioned five different places of his farming lands; the writer then estimated at
four acres in each field, making a total of twenty acres in all).*

*At that time, we did not have any plows or shovels, but we use to make our own
shovels, which were made of the root of the mesquite.*[132] *We planted our wheat, corn,
pumpkins and other crops with those wooden shovels. When the ditches needed
cleaning, those that had no wooden shovels used a basket and sometimes a pottery
disk and even, when they had to, used their hands.*

*Our ditches were about three to four feet wide, but at the diversions, we always
had our ditch heading much wider, which is about six or seven feet. During planting seasons, a number of old men would be seen in a field, all using this crude-made
wooden shovel making holes in the ground, all with one stroke and on a quick pace
and others following them with the seed to be planted, the same person covered the
seed. We planted in this crude manner for some time and many years previous to
my birth.*

*When I was a young man living in the West, ox plows were somehow known
and brought to the Pimas by the Papagoes from the South. Oxen were then bought
from time to time from the Papagoes and a number of them were owned by the
Pimas later. Some close relations would pair these oxen in order to make a work
team and in this way they helped one another in their plowing during planting
seasons. When ox plows were first known to us Pimas, we then commenced to making them ourselves, but the oxen were purchased from Papagoes or Mexicans from
time to time. To make these plows the desired shape, just a few being able to shape
the plow in the right way. It is something like a white man's plow, it has a beam and
a handle, but it is all of wood. The wooden shovels are simple and not so hard to
make; sometimes later a Mexican shovel was known, different from a modern white
man's shovel, and also not hard to make, and any Indian finding a flat iron would
take it to Tucson and have it made into a shovel by a blacksmith. At that time, a
shovel and wooden plow and a[n] ox-team in existence was to us something great.*

*I believe there are three reasons why we left our farms and homes in the West.
1st, That we become so familiar with oxens, wooden plows and this Mexican shovel,
and we knew that we can cultivate more land; 2nd, For the reason of scarcity of
irrigating water; 3rd, Because of peace being made with our then enemies, the
Apaches. My father and his relations were the promoters of the main ditch and of*

course obtained more land than the others, and from them I inherited a number of farms. I can remember when we had the water the year round, we raised lots of wheat, watermelon, pumpkins, corn, cotton, and there was no failure of our crops.

Cotton was raised, and when ripe, was picked and we had a way of separating the seeds, altho it took a number of people and a great deal of time; after the seed had been separated, it was then spun and made into balls and put away, but sometimes we made blankets and shirts.[133] *When the white man first brought calicoes among us, cotton raising was abandoned.*[134] *I know about the Old Maricopa Ditch [#28] that you just asked me about, but I did not help build it, but I remember that the Maricopas who use to live among us were self supporting because they liked to farm as well as we Pimas.*[135]

I have often thought of late when we had no farming implements, and now when we have good farming tools but no water. When I had left my farms in the West, I came and settled where the old man preacher (Rev. C. H. Cook) use to teach in a school. The ruins of the house is [sic] still there. I do not remember how many years I did live at this place, but anyway, we made the ditch, the remains of which can be seen. Water was still plentiful then and our crops matured, so I cannot tell you how wide this ditch is, but it is about that wide (indicating about five feet). Old Sacaton Ditch extended to where the Maricopas lived; ditch about two and a half miles long.[136]

We made another ditch on the other side (South side) making the Little Gila River, now [New] Mt. Top Ditch [#31], but only one crop of wheat was harvested and that was all; it has never been used since.[137] *One reason for its abandonment is because about that time, Indians in that neighborhood had moved to other settlements so there were not enough left to keep it in repair. This is nearly forty years ago, so I think that this Santan Ditch [#27] is about forty years old, because I remember that we started making this Santan Ditch some years before the battle was fought between the Pimas of Blackwater settlements and Pimas of the settlement around Mr. Cook's school house.*[138] *My brother (Jose Enos) assist[ed] them in this battle but we refused. I went to Adamsville, near Florence, and lived three years there after this trouble among the Pimas. When I came back from Adamsville, I settled here in Santan to build some of the ditch we had begun some time before the battle had been fought. This ditch had been extended and a number of Indians had cultivated small pieces of land. We did not finish making this Santan Ditch [#27] in one year or two years. Every year or so we made it a little longer, as the Pimas from other settlements began to come and take up land. We did not at first make it as wide as it is now, it was only about so wide (indicating about five feet); it was widened lately and remained as you now see it.*[139]

I have about twenty acres of land left under this ditch and I do no work on this land because I am too old, but this man that lives with me, son-in-law, uses this land, some years only half and some years not as much because irrigating water is uncertain. To my recollection, the first five or six years in this Santan Canal [#27] the water was in it continuously, but afterwards, it began to decrease, and of late about this time of the year the river dries up. Lots of Indians here in Santan owns [sic] mowers and other machinery, but they have not enough water to get rich on. I don't know much about the Cottonwood Ditch [#32], Sacaton Flats [#36], Blackwater [#44] and other ditches east of the Sacaton Agency, but I know they make their own good living by farming, especially at the time before the white people diverted our water above us. All of our ditches are large enough to carry enough water for our land, but we have to depend on the flood water for irrigation. I remember I use to visit my relatives at Blackwater years ago and I use to help work in their ditch, though I owned no land there. To my recollection, Blackwater settlement is over fifty years old. We Pimas are "Poor Pimas" now, but in the older times, while poor in horses and plows, we were rich in harvests.

STATEMENT OF WILLIAM JOHNSON (CASA BLANCA)[140]

I am about sixty-five years old. I was born in Casa Blanca settlement. There my father, mother and myself lived together. At that time we had a farm of about twenty-five acres, near the Casa Blanca ruins. We always tried to keep our fences, ditches and farms in good condition. Indians in those days were in close touch with each other. They knew their relation towards each other and cared for one another, but now the white man's laws has [sic] broken up this tribal relationship. Some say it is because there is no water, so there is no use working on our ditches, but I say some are hanging too much on the white man and have little or no respect for their own people. I wish every young Indian boy or girl was like us before the white man came among us. Our fathers have taught us to have respect for our father and mother first and our kinsmen second. So it is today, that some of our young men have dropped and have forgotten their kinsmen and are looking upon the white man as tho he and the Indians were close kin. This is causing trouble, and already some Old Indians have been thrown in jail without good reason.

We had one or two reliable Superintendents some years ago, and perhaps would have gotten our lost water back by working together and with the Superintendent. I cannot say for sure that some Indians have actually died of starvation, but I suspect, for the reason that some of those that have passed away were unable to produce crops, as there is not enough water for irrigation, neither have they any cattle from which they can obtain provisions or money to support themselves.

I stated that I had twenty-five acres of land in Casa Blanca, and when I was probably about fifteen years old, I left that place and migrated to Blackwater settlement. While living in Casa Blanca, I had always helped my father about the farm work, and I clearly remembered at this time what abundant harvests of wheat, corn, beans, pumpkins and watermelons we use to work at. I do not mean that our individual farms are as large as a white man's forty acres of today, but every crop we raised, matured to its completeness.

About the age of fifteen, I left this home in Casa Blanca and located in Blackwater. We obtained about twenty-five acres more in this settlement; said land was already under ditch as Blackwater had been a settlement some years before our arrival. For several years we still plant crops in our old farm in Casa Blanca. From our Blackwater home we go there to do the planting. When the normal flow of the river began to decrease, we finally abandoned this western farm in Casa Blanca, as we knew that this Blackwater settlement is above all the other settlements. We had a good ditch in this Blackwater Village, like those in the vicinity of Casa Blanca. Our ditches are none too large or none too small; they are just large enough to carry water and to be easily kept in repair, as we have only the wooden shovels to work with some fifty years past. Two of the main ditches in the vicinity of Casa Blanca from which I use to irrigate my field are still in use at present by the Indians now living there, but they depend entirely on flood water. These ditches have either a four or six foot bottom.

I lived in this Blackwater settlement about seven years and I remember the Papagoes from the South use to come there and trade with various Indians, the Papagoes would bring their cattle to the Pimas for wheat and other subsistence in the fall.[141] *Blackwater settlement was to the Papagoes a well known trading place and there was no hesitation on the part of the Papagoes in bringing in their cattle. After residing in Blackwater seven years, Chief Antonio, an uncle on my mother's side, sent word by one Manuel Cook to come to Cottonwood and help work on a ditch that was then in construction, and that he was holding for me a piece of land,* that if I did not come the same day that I was notified, I would not be entitled to the land. So I obeyed this order and came the same day and the next day I help on this ditch, tho' I had not yet seen my land.

We made the ditch about one mile from where I started to help when my uncle came to me and said, "This is enough for you, you have obeyed my word, you go back to your home, but come back some other time and I will then show you the piece of land I wish to give you." So within a year, I came and I was shown the field I was to own. To my recollection, this is about forty-two years ago [1872]. I afterwards obtained more land under this Cottonwood Ditch [#32], besides this field given to me by my uncle. I finally abandoned my field in Blackwater because it was too much work going back and forth during planting season.

We have a little seepage water to divert for our lands here in Cottonwood, but this seepage water is about as bad as well water. I have about fifty-five acres of land besides about five acres which high flood in the river had washed away. About eight acres of this is cultivated by myself, which leaves forty acres uncultivated. The lands I cultivate are partly in wheat, alfalfa and a little barley. I also own about fifteen acres of land in Santan settlement[;] six acres is owned by one of my sons and he has alfalfa sown in this six acre piece and nine acres are unused.

Santan settlement is the youngest of all other settlements east and west of the Sacaton Agency. It is somewhere about thirty-five or forty years old. The majority of the older Indians now living in Santan use to live and had farms that was [sic] irrigated from a good ditch made by them (Old Sacaton Ditch). The reason why they abandoned these farms is on account of the battle which had been fought. I was in that battle and was on the Blackwater side.[142] Another reason is that too much land had been taken up by various Indians above them, that is, Cottonwood, Sacaton Flats and Blackwater settlements, all diverting water above this settlement out of the Little Gila River. So they had to move across the Big Gila and use what flood water they could get. The supply has been favorable for the first ten years, but now it is about the same as other settlements.

STATEMENT OF COS-CHIN (SANTAN)[143]

The general history in this particular district, to the best of my knowledge and memory, is that the ditch known as Santan Ditch [#27] was constructed and *completed thirty-four years ago [ca. 1880].*[144] *Irrigation and farming were practiced among the Pimas for many centuries. The time when the Mexicans and Papagoes had trouble it was a time of two years. This happened about seventy-five years ago [ca. 1839].*[145] *The Papagoes fled to the Pimas for protection and subsistence. They lived with the Pimas for several years. No white man ever inhabited any of the Pima land then.*

The Pimas owned all of the Gila River Valley. They lived by agricultural pur-suits. They were not a war-like people nor led nomadic lives. Time afterwards white people immigrated through Pima land going West.[146] *They generally stopped with the Pimas who were always willing to share their food and shelter. The present farming district and more land was then in cultivation. Some land had since been neglected on account of shortage of water.*

The farm tools used then were very crude. Often made of wood. The plows were made from mesquite wood and worked by oxen.[147] *Shovels were made from cotton-wood. They made picks from the hard part of ironwood. Ashwood was another wood used for making tools. With these tools they made their ditches and worked their fields. Time came when the Mexicans or Spaniards introduced a new spade made of iron shaped something like the shoulder bone of the horse and the Pimas named it "Shoulder shovel."*

The Pimas planted wheat in the winter and in the summer they planted corn, sorghum, melons, pumpkins, [tepary] beans and other things. Cotton was another main crop; from it they made their own clothes. Tobacco was also culti-vated. What is known as Island land was then in cultivation. About fifty-four or fifty-five [ca. 1860] years ago. About the same time [Ammi] White was robbed of his store.[148] *It was known that previous to this time this same district was under cultivation many years before, and the reason that the land was neglected was this: The villages all went after mescal and during their stay the men went on a deer hunt and before they returned to their camp, Apaches had robbed them of their wives and children.*[149] *The men returned to their farms, burned their kis, which was the custom when anyone of the family dies.*[150] *They also destroyed the dam from which their fields were irrigated. This land was deserted until the time [of] which I have spoken. Then it was again deserted on account of shortage of water, which was taken away from us by white settlers above us. The Santan Ditch [#27] I remember was started and finished while we were farming on the Island.*[151] *After it was fin-ished, we moved over to the present Santan District on account of shortage of water on the Island. This was about thirty-three or thirty-four years ago [ca. 1880].*

STATEMENT OF TOR WHITE (SANTAN AND SWEETWATER)[152]

My recollection of the Santan Ditch [#27], when completed and put in use, under which I work and farm, is about 34 years ago [ca. 1880].[153] I lived and farmed at Sweetwater before I came to Santan. The ditch at [Ancient] Sweetwater [#25] was a much older ditch.[154] I cannot say how old, but it was in use before I was old enough to farm. At the same time, there was plenty of water and the Pimas planted a good many things all the year round. Ditches were in constant use. But time came when our water got short and farms were neglected.

During the early days when Apaches raided the country, no white man ever inhabited any of our land and water was plentiful. Land was divided to families no matter how small a family a man had.[155] It was the idea of a Pima father to encourage his children in farming. When they got older, they were given land to work on; so, in that way, nearly everybody had a piece of land.

The reason why we came to Santan District was because our water supply got short on the Island and Sweetwater District. Mr. Cook surveyed the land for the Santan Ditch [#27].[156] The mouth of the ditch was about nine feet bottom running to about five feet at the end. The ditch extended to about 5 1/2 miles in length. More people came under this ditch to farm and the ditch was enlarged and extended to its present size and length.[157] We had a good supply of seepage water for a while, when it got short we depended wholly on flood water. So that farming here got to be just as uncertain as in other districts. As to fertilizing our farms, we do not have to use any fertilizer, soil is rich except in some districts where there is alkali, then flood water is needed to fertilize it.

STATEMENT OF JOSE ENIS (SANTAN DISTRICT)[158]

The general history of irrigation in this particular district, to the best of my knowledge and memory, is that the ditch known as Santan Ditch [#27] was constructed and completed thirty-four years ago [ca. 1880]. I lived at Sweetwater many years before I came to the Island to farm. It was about the same time White was robbed of his store, which is about fifty-three or fifty-four years ago [ca. 1860].[159]

I farmed on the Island for about twenty years. Water began to get short, yet people wanted more land and water, so we decided to come to this present Santan District. We worked on the ditch about ten or eleven years before we finished it.

We have lived and farmed here ever since. The Santan Ditch is about thirty-three or thirty-four years old.[160] *The time the ditch was started, it had a width of about ten feet bottom and ten feet high. This ditch extended about five miles. After more people came to Santan, the ditch was increased to its present size and length.*[161] *We had a good supply of seepage water for a while and when flood water comes, it does not last as long as there are other dams built above us.*

The farming here got uncertain just as it had in other districts. The Pima Indians, who were a self-supporting tribe, are now forced by these new dams above us to do the best we can for subsistence. It must be understood that the Pimas never suffered so before the white man came. They raised all kinds of produce to keep themselves. Their farming tools were then very crude, but they always managed to do well with them.

STATEMENT OF JUAN JOSE (SANTAN DISTRICT)[162]

The general history of irrigation in this district, to the best of my memory, is that the ditch known as Santan Ditch [#27] was constructed and completed about thirty-three or thirty-four years ago [ca. 1880].

My remembrance of the finishing of the Santan Ditch is about thirty-three or thirty-four years ago, and it took about ten or eleven years to finish it. It has a width of about two shovel lengths and a depth of about ten feet at the head. It was extended some distance, gradually diminishing until finally it ended with a width of about one shovel length. From time to time, as more people came, we worked on our ditch, making it wider and longer, until it was as you see it today. My early days were spent at Sweetwater. Then I moved to what is now called Island land, about the time White was robbed of his store, some fifty-three years ago [ca. 1861].[163]

On the Island, I farmed with other Pimas for about twenty years, then we moved to Santan where we have lived ever since. Our purpose was to get and work more land for our water had diminished on the Island. We had a good supply of seepage water for a while. It soon dried up, as there were other dams constructed above us, depriving us of all the water we had used in former years. The Pimas were greatly affected by this shortage of water, for they were almost pauperized. Some of the older Indians, who were once self-supporting, are now drawing rations, while some of the Pimas are living on what little they can make by selling wood [table 3.1].[164]

TABLE 3.1. Grain Production and Cords of Mesquite Cut, 1887–1904

Year	Winter Grain (bushels)	Corn (bushels)	Wood Cut (cords)*	Wood Cut (acres)#
1887	105,000	5,000	—	—
1888	110,000	2,700	—	—
1889	144,000	3,600	—	—
1890	114,000	3,000	—	—
1891	50,000	—	200	256
1892	110,000	5,500	300	384
1893	76,000	3,000	350	448
1894	62,000	0	1,000	1,280
1895	70,950	500	1,500	1,920
1896	51,250	0	4,000	5,120
1897	51,250	0	1,500	1,920
1898	117,819	0	1,500	1,920
1899	34,488	1,072	5,000	6,400
1900	12,980	180	19,000	24,320
1901	25,417	36	11,000	14,080
1902	16,955	18	14,896	19,066
1903	42,051	18	10,600	13,568
1904	12,000	500	5,300	6,784

Source: Annual Reports of the Pima Agency, 1887–1905, in Annual Reports of the Commissioner of Indian Affairs, 1887–1905.
* Based on an average of 128 cubic feet of mesquite per cord.
# Based on 100 cubic feet of three-inch or greater diameter wood per acre.

STATEMENT OF HARVIER (SANTAN DISTRICT)[165]

The ditch known as Santan Ditch [#27] was constructed and completed about thirty-four years ago [ca. 1880]. I was a young man when the Pimas started to work on the Island Ditch, which was finished in about four years.[166] About the time a white man was robbed of his store, this man's name was White, by soldiers unknown to the Pimas.[167] Water was plentiful and there was no water question. Indians raised nearly all kinds of products and were always a self-supporting people until up to the time when white people settled and built their dams above us [between 1864 and 1890] [fig. 3.5].

It was while I was farming on the Island, we commenced to work on the present Santan Ditch [#27].[168] It took us about ten or eleven years to finish it, for we did not work on it constantly. That is about thirty-three or thirty-four years ago

FIG. 3.5. Ration day in Sacaton, ca. 1900. (Courtesy of the Arizona Historical Society, 7457)

[ca. 1880]. The ditch was not a very wide one, it started with a width of about ten feet bottom, ten feet deep and about five miles long. Towards the end, it was nar-rower, about five feet wide and three feet deep. The water supply on the Island got short and, as there was a good supply of seepage water in the new ditch, we moved over to the present Santan District. But the seepage water soon got short and we now depend on flood water, but even that is deprived from us by the other dams built above us. We now suffer every year, something which we never endured before the white man came. The Pimas depend on what little they raise and what they can get by selling wood, which is often very little.

STATEMENT OF JUNA OSIF (SWEETWATER DISTRICT)[169]

To the best of my knowledge and memory, this district was under cultivation before I was born, because I was old enough to remember I saw all the land now covered with mesquite near the hill known as Rattlesnake Home was cultivated fields. Casa Blanca and Sweetwater had one main irrigating ditch known as Sweetwater Ditch [#23] at that time.

Said ditch was used to irrigate all lands now under cultivation and what is now abandoned and covered with brush. We had plenty of water in the ditches all the time and raised two crops a year. Wheat being sown in winter time, melons, pumpkins, corn, beans or teparies, were planted in spring, getting first crop in summer. Then as soon as we reaped our crop, we planted melons, corn or other seed for fall crop. We were happy and contented. Cotton was also raised by the Indians. They weaved it into blankets and crude clothing.[170]

The Sweetwater Ditch [#23] was about three yards wide and much deeper than it is now.[171] In my younger days, the Indians used a wooden plow made from mesquite trees, having a pole or tongue of willow tree.[172] These were pulled by oxen. Somewhere about thirty years ago, the water in the river and ditches began to decrease as the waste in the river decreased year after year, [and] the Indians were accordingly forced to abandon our fields. Poverty began to stare us in the face. Being always a self-supporting people, we did not know how to take it. Some Indians are now in the begging business like some whites. Indians would not now be beggars had their water been retained for them. All the settlements from Sacaton to the railroad crossing between Maricopa and Phoenix was [sic] a solid, cultivated land.[173]

STATEMENT OF JUAN MANUEL, CHIR-PURTKE (SRANUKA DITCH)[174]

The Ditch known as [Old] Sranuka Ditch [#13] was built long before I was born. When I was old enough to know and see, I remember seeing that this ditch was used as an irrigating ditch.[175] I cannot tell anything about it as to when or how it was dug. But it was several generations ago and was built with wooden shovels, same as any other old ditch. These implements were made from ironwood or any hard wood good for digging. For shoveling dirt, paddles were made of cottonwood trees. The Indians helped each other in planting and harvesting their crops.

In my time oxen were used for plowing. This method of cultivation was introduced by the Spanish and was in use until thirty-five or forty years ago, when the U.S. Government gave us the plows and harness.[176] As the Indians were being supplied with better equipment of farming implements, they continued to increase their cultivated land and were prosperous and contended [sic].

White people began to take water from the river about forty years ago [ca. 1874]. The first diversion being so small we hardly noticed it, but they gradually took more out each year till we noticed our loss by not being able to irrigate all our fields. We were forced to abandon them little by little, until some twenty years ago when we were left high and dry. Some districts where seepage water can be obtained for irrigation, the Indians use it, well knowing that seepage water is not so desirable for irrigating purposes as is the river water. Seepage water is only resorted to when the others fail. In the other districts where there is no seepage water, the Indians are forced to be constantly on the road with a load of wood to the market in order to keep their families alive.[177] Floodwaters just run long enough to make a scant crop.

The old ditches, as I remember them, were not as wide as they are now, but were deeper than they are now. When shovels were furnished by the U.S. Government, the Indians then began to widen their ditches. The original cultivated land extended from Sacaton to about two miles west of the present railroad bridge at Sacaton Siding [along the Maricopa and Phoenix Railroad], both sides of the river being cultivated. The nature of crops commonly raised by the Pimas in olden times were wheat, corn, lima beans (bintes)[,] t[e]p[a]ris, melons, pumpkins, cotton and tobacco. The ditches on the average were three miles long.

STATEMENT OF CHIEF THOMAS (SRANUKA DISTRICT)[178]

About the time Big Back, the Apache Chief, and his band were killed by the U. S. soldiers and the Pima Scouts near the Four Peaks in the Superstition Range of mountains, that the Pimas from time to time began to move away (to Gila Crossing) from this village of Sranuka, and that the western part of the cultivated fields, which is a part of the Sranuka District, were completely abandoned as late as the construction of the railroad from Maricopa to Phoenix, Arizona [in 1887]. This subduing of the Apaches is about forty years ago. I do not know when the [Old] Sranuka Ditch [#13] was first constructed; it was made previous to my birth.[179] I also know of three different locations of where we Sranuka people previously diverted the water for irrigation. I think that about the same amount of acreage that we now see in the old abandoned fields of Santa Cruz District have [sic] been washed away.

STATEMENT OF JUAN LAGONS (HOLLEN DITCH)[180]

The ditch known as Hollen Ditch [#7] was built thirty-seven years ago [ca. 1877].[181] The Indians worked on said ditch one year before it was finished. As soon as the ditch was completed, the Indians put their claims under cultivation, planting wheat as their first crop. While waiting for their wheat to ripen, they kept on clearing more land, and by the following spring, when corn planting time come [sic], they had more land under cultivation. Three years after this particular ditch was first put into use as an irrigating ditch, all the land under it was cultivated as you see it now.

From the very beginning, crops did not yield as good as our old fields two miles west of Sacaton Siding did.[182] We use seepage water for irrigation nearly altogether. Plants which are sensitive to alkaline are not doing any good, and even those which are suppose[d] to stand it do not yield as good as when river flood water is used for irrigation.

As I call to memory, the old fields near Sacaton Siding, when flood water was plentiful, I cannot refrain from saying that civilization did us more harm than good; we were self supporting then, had plenty to eat all the year round. When civilization or enlightened people came, they robbed us of our water[;] we were then left without any resources at all. Our fields were scorching dry, we had to do something or we would all starve to death. So our fathers sought for the seepage water, knowing that it was not as good as river water. Floodwater is the only thing that keeps our fields alive, otherwise they would have been useless long ago. Wheat, corn, melons, pumpkins, beans (or teparis), lima beans, peas, blackeyed peas, cotton and tobacco were raised in early days. Now we have added several other new products.

When water was first taken out by the white people above the reservation, we felt it and suffered first, as we were the last to take out our water from the river. There was water enough left for other Indians to irrigate their fields above us, but we were left high and dry.

STATEMENT OF JAMES HOLLEN (HOLLEN DITCH)[183]

The ditch known as Hollen Ditch [#7] was constructed thirty-seven years ago [ca. 1877]. Was in construction for one year before it was finished. It was about three or four feet wide and about three miles long.[184] Said ditch was completed and used as an irrigation ditch one year after construction work had started. About one-third of the present cultivated land was put under cultivation, and four years afterwards, all the land under said ditch was cultivated.

The nature of crops raised on this particular district are [sic] wheat, corn, melons, peas, pumpkins, lima beans, blackeyed peas, cow-peas, pink beans, barley, succum, tobacco, cotton and other things. The Indians got two crops a year when the river water was running all the year round. Now they cannot do it, as there is not a continuous flow of water in the river. We who cultivate land in this district do get two crops a year, as we use seepage water on our land. Although the water supply is small, we manage to distribute it equally among us, thereby getting a crop of some kind each year.

Seepage water is not desirable water to be used on account of the alkali it contains. It leaves a hard crust on top of the soil, and plants that are sensitive to it do not do well at all. As more land was put under cultivation, the Indians soon saw that the old ditch was too small for the amount of land under cultivation; they at once enlarged it to its present size of five feet wide. This was done about five years after the first construction of the ditch [in 1882].

Our cultivated land is limited on account of the scarcity of water. Before white people took away our river water, we used to cultivate more land than we do now. Quite a number of ditches are now lying idle and covered with brush. Our fathers were forced to leave their old fields in the District of Sacaton Siding (Sra-nuka) where they built their homes and cultivated land. We felt the decrease of water first as we were the last to take out our water from the river. Therefore, we left the old homes and fields and moved to this district. The seepage water we are now using is not sufficient to bring us crops to keep us alive all the year through, so we have to sell wood to tide us over to harvest time. Some Indians who have no wagons to haul their wood to market are the ones to suffer most, because they have to wait for their neighbors to get through with their own wagon so that they can borrow it to sell their wood. In the meantime, these families have to do the best they can.

STATEMENT OF JOSEPH HEAD
(CASA BLANCA AND OTHER DISTRICTS)[185]

The ditch known as Hoover Ditch [#5] was constructed forty-one years ago [ca. 1873].[186] It was in the springtime when work on said ditch commenced. The following spring, the construction of said ditch was all completed and water turned into it to irrigate what lands the Indians had cleared and had it ready to be irrigated. About one-half of their claims under this ditch was put under cultivation, planting corn, melons, pumpkins, t[e]p[a]ris, and other vegetables; this was their first crop.

The Hoover Ditch, when first dug, was about four feet wide at the bottom and five feet wide at the top; the water was knee deep and deeper at some places. It was also used to float poles and logs before Indians had wagons. These poles and logs were used in building houses. Implements used in building this ditch were white man's tools, but before the white man's tools were seen and used by the Indians they used wooden tools made of ironwood and mesquite trees, also of Cottonwood trees. Baskets were also made to carry dirt to the banks or where there was a fill.

About four years after said ditch was completed, all the land under it that could be irrigated was put under cultivation. Three years after Hoover Ditch was constructed, the John Thomas Ditch [#4] (now called Lancisco by some) was being worked.[187] It took two years to finish this ditch. When completed, about one-third of the present cultivated land was put under cultivation. Three years after, all the bottom land was cultivated and a branch ditch was connected to irrigate a highland and is now known as Lancisco Ditch.[188] Nearly all the bottom land that was first irrigated by the John Thomas Ditch was washed away by the flood of 1903 [1905].

Three years after the above mentioned ditch was constructed, Joseph Head's Ditch [#6] was in progress.[189] It took Joseph Head and his party two years to finish this ditch. Land under this ditch was covered with dried, dead brush, so those claiming it only set fire to it and it was all cleared. As soon as the construction of the said ditch was finished, all land under it was put under cultivation. James Hollen's Ditch [#7] was constructed thirty-seven years ago [1877]; it was in construction one year before it was finished.

The Cooperation [Cooperative] Ditch [#3] was constructed fourteen years ago [1900].[190] It was in construction for six months. About one-third of the present land under it was cultivated. One year afterwards, all the land was cultivated as it is now. There was plenty of water in the river the whole year through, before the white people diverted it. Indians had all they wanted in their ditches all the time. Had all kinds of crops, both grain, vegetables and plants. They were contented and prosperous. But when the white people took our water, we were left without any resources. We had to fall back on the seepage water, but it is not enough to keep us and families alive, so in order to keep alive we had to cut and sell wood in Phoenix and other towns.[191]

Our crops do not yield as good and as abundantly as when irrigated with river or floodwater. Many acres of the old cultivated land on both sides of the river from Sacaton to this place (Gila Crossing) were abandoned on account of the diversion above. We protested to the U.S. Government to protect our water rights from time to time but nothing has been done to this day. The width of the river in my young days was about twenty-five to fifty steps. Indian fields on both sides of the river[,] which have been washed away by the floods, were nearly one-quarter of a mile wide.

White people have no idea how the Pima Indian has suffered by the diversions of their [sic] water by the whites above the reservation. It has caused us to abandon our old farms and homes which we loved so dearly, in order to seek for seepage water.[192] Others went to live in the mesquite forest to get their bread by selling wood. Others stayed on their farms depending altogether on floodwater.

As to the Stotonic, the present Stotonic [#23] is the later and lower heading of which you call the Ancient Stotonic [#25].[193] The heading of this canal has been changed several times. About thirty-five years ago, however, the greatest change was made, although its heading has been changed slightly once or twice since then.

STATEMENT OF JOHN RHODES (GILA CROSSING DISTRICT)[194]

The ditch known as Hoover Ditch [#5] was built forty-one years ago [ca. 1873].[195] This ditch was in construction for one year before it was finished. I was not old enough to do the work, but I used to carry water for the men who did the work. According to the historical stick kept by Joseph Head, the date of construction of this was forty-one years ago. The date of construction of John Thomas Ditch [#4], on the south side of the river, is thirty-eight years ago [ca. 1876].[196] This ditch had a five foot bottom when first constructed. They worked on said ditch for two years before they finished it. About one-third of the land under it was cultivated the first year, and three years after all the land under this ditch was put under cultivation, also a branch ditch was dug to irrigate a highland. Said ditch is now known as Lancisco Ditch, I think.[197] The irrigated farm lands under this particular ditch have been reduced a great deal by flood waters washing off nearly all the bottom lands or the old cultivated land under said ditch.

James Hollen Ditch [#7] came in one year [1877] after the John Thomas Ditch, which is thirty-seven years ago.[198] It was one year being constructed and was about four feet wide. About one-half of the land under it was cultivated the first year.

Joseph Head's Ditch [#6] came in next, about twenty-eight years ago [ca. 1886]; it was two years in construction.[199] When finished, all of the land under it was put under cultivation, as it was level and hardily [sic] and brush. It did not require much work in clearing. The size of this ditch must be about three feet wide at the bottom.

All of the above mentioned districts or ditches received their water from the river when first constructed. They continued so until about twenty-five years ago, when all our river water was taken by white men above our reservation.[200] We have suffered much loss[;] our cultivated land was reduced and what fields we do cultivate do not bring us as much as they did when irrigated by river water.

In order to get the seepage water, which rises below Hoover Ditch dam, a company was formed by the most progressive Pima Indians. This company was named Cooperative Company. They dug a ditch known as the Cooperative [#3], about fourteen years ago.[201] The ditch was eight feet wide when first constructed. Water about knee deep in said ditch. Seepage water is very poor water to irrigate with. It leaves a hard crust on the ground after irrigation. If not cultivated, plants will not do well. Plants which are sensitive to alkaline will not do well for this district, which uses seepage water for irrigation. Even alfalfa, which is said to resist the alkali, is showing the effects.

STATEMENT OF OLIVER SANDERSON (GILA CROSSING DISTRICT)[202]

The following named ditches were already constructed and used when I came here thirty-four years ago [ca. 1880]: Hoover Ditch [#5], John Thomas Ditch [#4], James Hollen Ditch [#7]. All land which is cultivated now was cultivated at that time, except a few high places which were leveled and irrigated after my arrival. River water was used then as irrigating water, although it had already started to decrease, but not enough to be noticeable here in this district because there was a big lake above the head of these ditches and it flowed into the river, making it quite a stream.[203]

The districts like Casa Blanca and others had already noticed it and had suffered already to some extent. As more land was cultivated by white people above our reservation and more water diverted from the river, the less land the Indian is able to cultivate and [the] more land he is forced to abandon. And, finally, when the Florence Canal was constructed [1886–89], it took all the water available, leaving the Indians with a dry farm. Where the Indians do not have seepage water to rely upon, they are compelled to cut wood and are on the road continually to either Phoenix, Tempe or Mesa City.[204] Wood is cheap and does not pay much for labor and time involved, but the "Poor Indian" cannot help this. He is forced to do so by his white brother.

Four

FRIENDS OF THE PIMA SPEAK OUT

When Southworth was interviewing the Pima elders, he also solicited information from three individuals that he believed might add to the understanding of Pima agriculture. He wrote letters regarding the nature and extent of Pima agriculture to Dr. Charles H. Cook, longtime missionary to the Pima; Dr. Charles H. Ellis, former Presbyterian missionary; and the Reverend David M. Wynkoop, also a Presbyterian missionary. While the three letters do not provide any revelatory information, each offers a unique perspective and adds to the overall understanding of Pima conditions at the turn of the twentieth century.

Of the three, Charles Cook had the most intimate knowledge of Pima agriculture and water loss. He arrived among the Pima in December 1870 and remained for forty-four years, retiring in 1914. He not only met the spiritual needs of the Pima during a difficult time of transition but also advocated for restoration of their water. In September 1910 Reverend Dirk Lay arrived to succeed Cook, who remained with Lay nearly four years before retiring to Nodaway, Iowa. When Lay arrived in Sacaton, Cook demanded that he "promise that you will not leave my people until their irrigation water has been restored to them."[1] Cook died in Nodaway on May 4, 1917, having established Presbyterian churches in each village on the reservation.

Ellis and Wynkoop played lesser roles in Pima affairs. Ellis served as a Presbyterian missionary (and assistant to Cook) at the turn of the century and was stationed in Sacaton. He periodically visited the churches in Gila Crossing and Blackwater. He is not to be confused with C. E. Ellis, who spent nearly fifteen years on the reservation as an employee of the Pima Agency. Wynkoop was sent to the reservation by the Presbyterian Board of Home Missions in October 1896 to assist the Reverend Cook. Wynkoop served at Gila Crossing until 1903. In the tradition of Cook, Wynkoop was devoted to the spiritual well-being of the Pima but also took an active role in water matters, recognizing that he had to consider both their spiritual and economic well-being.

LETTER FROM CHARLES H. COOK (GENERAL OVERVIEW)

Nodaway, Iowa, June 1st, 1914
Mr. C. H. Southworth
Sacaton, Arizona

Dear Sir:

Received your kind letter and will endeavor to answer it in a measure at least. I first came to Pima Agency or Sacaton in Dec. 1870, and was shortly after employed as teacher for the Pima Indians by the Agent, Capt. [Frederick] Grossman, the Military officer in charge. Since that time up to a year ago my home has been with the Pimas. Capt. Grossman was a noble man and the first to introduce a few modern farm implements [fig. 4.1].[2]

At that time the Pimas and Apaches were at war with each other and with the whites. The Pimas taking sides with the whites[;] they gave protection to the overland travel and to the early white settlers. The Pimas were farmers. They would learn to raise corn, wheat, barley, beans, melons and cotton from childhood. They Pimas [sic] would raise some cattle and work-oxen, but very few horses.

The Pimas then lived in some 10 to 12 villages in the Gila valley. They had an head [sic] chief and each village one or more sub chiefs and generally one or more ditch-captains. Each village had their own ditch. In digging their ditches, or fencepost holes without any steel or tool implement, as strait as an arrow, and quicker than we could have any idea of, would appear as something new to us palefaces. Yet in those early days the Pimas would have an abundance of food and manufacture, though some little scant, their own clothing. They had all the water needed for irrigation. The Pimas occupied the lower Gila valley. The Papagoes and Jofquaatom had for a long time been residents of Salt River valley.[3] As late as 1880 the Quachartys [Kwahadk] occupied the Vekol valley, about 35 miles south-west of Casa

FIG. 4.1. The Pima Agency, ca. 1890. (Courtesy of the Arizona Historical Society, 109077)

Grande, Ariz.[4] Most of the soil is good, but some of it as well as some of the well water contains too much alkali for the rains to wash it away.

The Quacharty Indians had their reservoir befor[e] the whites had come near them. But your Missionary sadly missed it. An Indian wanted to show him where near his home silver & the cactus would grow. Had he trusted the Indian & gone with him and located the $600,000.00 silver mine, he could have supplied the Pimas and Quachartys with the needed water so that they could have lived comfortable, as in the days gone by. The Quacharty Indians had a rich mine, but they loved their valley and hills.

They would fence in some 10 acres with the cactus and mud & long grass, some 6 or more foot high. Then when the rains came they would fill their reservoir and irrigate their farms, & sow & reap. Our Tucson people early felt that they needed the Papagoes as neighbors, as protection against the Apaches. Also as hunters & guides. I came to a Papago village once, and what was my surprise when I saw a tame dear [sic]. In the early days the Papagoes would bring much gold from placer diggin[g]s to the white settlements, and assist the whites in locating mines.

The Pimas for many years have made the Gila River (as far as we know) their principal home. Before the days of the R.R. in New Mexico and Cal[ifornia] the grain from which the flour came was raised by the Indians. A half a doz. or more trading places were kept busy in trading stores, selling wheat for dry goods and groceries.

Each village was responsible for its own ditch and at times dam in the river. With plenty of silt in most places the fields were very fertile and large crops were raised.

At one large village north of the river and for a distance of near ten miles, there were fine ancient fields without a ditch, and near the head of it there was a fine strata [*sic*] of rock in the river bed.[5] The Indians were anxious to build a ditch there, commencing about a mile east of the Agency. Some 4 villages took part in the work. We found a little difficulty in getting the ditch started. However this we did overcome. It showeth the ability of our ditch-capt. After digging through quite a hill, toward the river, instead of toward the high hill, we secured a good level and fine flow of water. This ditch has done good service for 4 villages for some 20 years.

I am told by some Indians that some whites have dug a much larger ditch parallel to the Indian ditch, but the water will not come. The Indian ditch keeps running close to the river, and the ditch of the whites close to the hill back of it, and has not the necessary fall. The government supplied the whites with the Roosevelt reservoir. Why not the Pimas, the Pimas were as willing as the whites to pay for the water?[6]

There may be a possibility of securing good water from the mountains north of the Pima Reservation, which if the Pimas do not get, the whites are likely to appropriate it. The south side of the Gila does not show as if it ever would furnish much water for irrigation.

I am not well posted as to the San Carlos Reservoir project. I do not remember much about the San Pedro. I have traveled over much of the Apache country. The Pimas live now and have lived for a long time at peace with the Apaches. The Apaches have some beautiful patches of country suitable for grazing, cattle raising and gardening. My health has not been very good for the past year, otherwise would have come to Sacaton in the spring.

I believe much can be done toward supplying the Pimas with water, but it will be no easy matter.

> Very respectfully yours,
> Chas. H. Cook

P.S. Up to within 15 years the Pimas were able to make a comfortable living, farming and irrigating the soil.

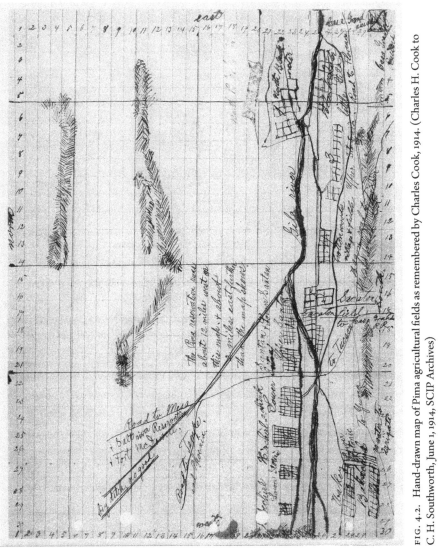

FIG. 4.2. Hand-drawn map of Pima agricultural fields as remembered by Charles Cook, 1914. (Charles H. Cook to C. H. Southworth, June 1, 1914, SCIP Archives)

P.S. My health has not been very good during the past year, for that reason I have not visited the Pimas last spring nor my Apache friends. I am 76 years and over, old, and so it is likely that ere long I shall have to give up a work which I have enjoyed over 40 years. Of late years we have found much alkali in the river and also more or less in the well water. Please do the best you can for the Pimas.

With best regards, yours respectfully,

Chas. H. Cook

LETTER OF C. H. ELLIS (GENERAL OVERVIEW)

The Mission Salt River, Arizona, May 25th, 1914
Mr. C. H. Southworth
U.S. Indian Service
Sacaton, Ariz.

Dear Sir:

I thank you for an opportunity to give you what information I can as to the water question as your line of work is, in my opinion, just what is needed and I so urged years ago.

I am sorry that I cannot give you more information but as I have only lived among the Pimas, or more correctly speaking have had a personal knowledge of them[,] for only fifteen years I can not give you as much information as I would wish.

If I remember correctly I was at Sacaton in April 1900 and learned from obversation [*sic*] and from the Indians that they were at that time in great need as there was no water in the Gila to speak of. While I was there, Rev. Chas. H. Cook returned from Washington D. C. where he had appeared before a committe[e] of congress to try to get aid for the Indians in that vicinity. They were living on the little money they got for wood that they sold wherever they could. I also visited Blackwater and was struck with the fact that tho they were so poor they came to church with clean clothing showing that they were willing to take on civilization.

I also made a trip to Gila Crossing at that time and found that they were depending on seepage water for their supply which was *not* furnishing any silt or fertilizer for their land.

About that time they had just taken out a ditch known as the [C]ooperative [#3] to enable them to get new land as there was much that had become less fertile than formerly.

Changes in cultivated areas.

I noticed at the time I speak of that near Sacaton there were fields that were vacated and dry but how long that had been the case I am unable to say except that the acreage was very much decreased and they seemed to be depending on the little seepage water there was.

Width of river floods etc.

In the fifteen years there has been a good deal of land washed away by [the] flood but I have no way of knowing the acreage.

In 1905 I think it was, there was a very destructive flood and at Gila Crossing I estimated that at the junction of the Gila and Santa Cruz the water was a mile wide. Much damage was done to the farms and ditches.[7]

My observation leads me to believe that the Pimas on the Gila are growing poorer and poorer because of the lack of water and being compelled to use seepage water since the diversion took place higher up the stream.

Th[e]re have been years when they had some fairly good crops but it was during the exceptionally wet years.

I only wish that I could give you from my own observation more as to the early history and will be ple[a]sed to give any other facts should you think that a knowledge covering that length of time would avail any thing. Permit me in closing to say that I believe that if some thing cannot be done to restore them their water the outlook for them is dismal indeed.

     Respectfully,
     C. H. Ellis

LETTER FROM DAVID M. WYNKOOP (GENERAL OVERVIEW)

Cornville[,] Arizona[,] June 19[,] 1914
Mr. C. H. Southworth
Sacaton, Arizona

Dear Sir:
     Your letter relating to the water rights for the Indians on the Gila Reservation received. Not being in the Government service during my stay at Gila Crossing, I have no written reports to refer to and must trust to my memory in regard to

the ditches and conditions of the reservation. If you would care to do so I might arrange to make a trip to Sacaton and Gila Crossing and with you go over the former ditches and country and I might give you some information that would be valuable. I located at Gila Crossing Oct[.] 17[,] 1896, and left there some time in 1903 during this time my time was devoted to the wellfare [*sic*] of the Indians and I spent most of my time planning to advance their interests. During the years I was located at Gila Crossing there was no way to go up the Gila River other than horse or wagon and I never ascended the River farther than Florence, Ariz. I know nothing about the advance of the settlements of the whites at San Carlos, Thatcher, Pima, Safford and other places along the Gila, but prior to 1896 and a short time afterwards there seemed to be no great shortage of water in the Gila River. Then came a time of gradual failure. Their acreage was decreased year after year until they raised but little up the Gila River above the Rail Road. My field of labor extended from the Rail Road to the junction of the Salt and Gila Rivers. On this district we were much more prosperous than on the Gila above the Rail Road extending to the Eastern line of the Reservation for towards the mountains the rocks brought the underflow of the river to the surface and the Indians put in dams and took the water to their fields and the Indians at Gila Crossing would have lived very well had they not assisted those of their kinfolks on the Eastern end of the Reservation above the Rail Road. When I first came to Gila Crossing, most of the land North of the Gila was watered from a main ditch (know[n] as the Joept Manuel or afterwards John Hoover ditch [#5])[.] It was taken from two sources, one branch tapped *Mass Acumult* and the other branch was taken out of the river just south of the lower end of *Mass Acumult*[.] This ditch was about seven feet wide on the bottom and carried a good head of water. There were two other ditches taken out of the Gila North of the river, but some smaller than the John Hoover ditch. One large ditch was taken out South of the river and the land of the *Yat-tupt-Autum* was watered from it[.] [A]bout two miles below the *Yat-tupt-Autum* ditch was another large ditch taken out on the South side and know[n] as the *Volk-est-a-bia* or John Thomas ditch [#4], and watered the land of the *Com-madt-worcho-Autum* and about three miles below this ditch a nother [*sic*] was taken out on the South Side and know[n] as the *Boy-o-man* or Joseph Head ditch [#6].[8] Except the John Hoover ditch two others were taken out on the North side of the river. I presume in 1896 enough water was taken from the Gila River to irrigate between five and six thousand acres of land. In 1896 the Indians had about discarded the service of oxen and the wooden plows. They used horses and small plows they bought from the Government or other places. Their main crop was wheat[,] which they sowed in the late fall and winter and harvested the last of May or first of June[,] after which the[y] planted corn, melons, beans, pumpkins. We must confess that they did not do as well as they might have done with the land and water they had but they produced all they needed while they could obtain enough water.

They understood that they could wash the alkali from their land and that the river water when silty was a fertilizer. The Pimas were governed by clans with a Chief over each village, but the lands were divided to the families and I would guess that a good average would be ten acres to each family. Just below the Rail Road a whole village has been abandoned on account of a shortage of water. I understand *Her-wa-chuit* was chief and he came down to Gila Crossing.[9] Since I have been away[,] I understand that *Mass Acumult* (a lagoon) has been destroyed and that many of the Indians farms have been washed away. I have been away for eleven years and do not know what has taken place on the reservation since I left. I believe I could take you to each old ditch for I studied the conditions while I was on the reservation. In the year about 1901, the Indians organized a new company and under the sanction of the Agent[,] Mr. Elwood Hadley[,] started to take out a new ditch for the development of new land[s], and have [given] it the name of the Co-operative ditch Company [#3][.] I believe this was and is still a success[.] Now I believe it is known as the ditch Comp[any], and while then the owners in the ditch were young men, I think they are the leading men in the tribe now[.]

Please excuse my delay in writing this letter, but it arrived in a very busy time for a farmer to stop making hay and write letters.

If Mr. Herbert Martin is still at Sacaton[,] you may find him a great help in assisting you to understand this letter for we have been to these places together[.][10] If I can assist you any farther in this matter, feel free to call on me.

Respectfully Yours,

David M. Wynkoop

Five

TWO PIMA CALENDAR STICKS

Charles Southworth obtained the translation of two calendar sticks. One belonged to 66-year-old Juan Thomas, whom Southworth interviewed in 1914. The second calendar stick belonged to Mejoe Jackson, another Pima elder. The events recorded on the calendar by the stick holder are etched into a canelike mesquite branch. In almost all instances, these etchings are intelligible only to the holder of the calendar stick.

Many of the events recorded by Thomas and Jackson are matters of historic record and are described in the early historical writings of Arizona Territory. Following this historical timeline, Southworth dated the calendric events "to the different [recorded historic] events." As he observed, "It should be borne in mind that the [Pima] year begins in the summer at the time of the Saguaro harvest, and correspondingly, their year interval contains a portion of two of our calendar years."[1] Southworth reproduced the sticks as he received their translations in 1914.

CALENDAR OF JUAN THOMAS OF BLACKWATER

1850–51
Black vomiting, a certain sickness which prevailed through all the settlements, killing the Indians by hundreds.

1851–52

Mesquite Root, an Indian name for a Papago Village, near Quijotoa, which Apaches attacked, killing all the men, elderly women, and taking captive all the young.

Near Gray-back Mountain, Apaches ambushed Pimas and Maricopas, killing six warriors.

1853–54

Pimas went on a campaign in the mountains against the Apaches. They found a settlement and killed every person in the village. One of these Apache had a pet eagle.

1854–55

Pimas and Papagoes join forces and pursue Apaches, who stole some horses; they killed the horse thieves and recovered the horses.

1855–56

Pimas attacked a settlement of Apaches near where the San Carlos Dam site is now, killing many; the Apaches were grinding mesquite beans when attacked. Among the dead was a blind man.

1856–57

Pimas attacked Apache village, killing many. There was a corn field near by the village. Pimas roasted corn after the battle was over.

1857–58

Iriaqaw Indians were killed by Apaches while fishing near Gila Crossing.[2] Four days later Joseph Roberts was shot by an Apache. Roberts thought the man was a Pima and he was talking to him when he was shot.

An army of Yuma Indians came from the Colorado River to fight Pimas and Maricopas. In battle which took place, the Yumas were slaughtered.

1858–59

The star fell, or meteor. Apache kill a Pima in battle.

Apache[s] kill Pima; he was a chief of Casa Blanca village.

The first white man came to Casa Blanca village, and open[ed] a store.

1859–60
Second white man came to Casa Blanca; he went with Pimas on war campaign and killed two Apaches, father and son. It was in spring.

1860–61
The Pimas helped themselves to several sacks of wheat belonging to a trader.

Two Pima war leaders were wounded in a fierce battle between Pimas and Apaches. One died four days after and the other died one year later.

1861–62
A white man by the name of White was captured by troops coming from the east, supposed to be Texas volunteers.

Apache[s] kill Pima near Gila Crossing (Estrella).

Soldiers with Pimas chased Apaches.

1862–63
Two medicine men were killed by their own people for causing sickness and death. They were father and son.

A white woman was taken away from Apaches after fierce battle. It was in the fall when this took place.

1863–64
In fall Pima kill Apache near Silver King, Globe.

In winter Apache kill Pima about two miles south of Four Miles Post.

In spring Pima kill Apache and stood the body up on a hill near Sacaton Siding.

Old Santan fields were put under cultivation, corn, melons and pumpkins yield bountiful crop.

1864–65
Early in the fall Pima kill Apache, cut his ears off and tied them to a long pole. Stood the pole in the midst of the villages between Sacaton and Sweetwater.

Many Whiskers [Cyrus Lennan, postmaster at Maricopa Wells], a white man, deceived Apaches by telling them he was their friend. He issued flour to them and after the Apaches put their arms away, Many Whiskers signaled to the Pimas fire on them. Battle issued in which Many Whiskers was killed with a spear by the Apaches.

1865–66
Many Apaches were killed in a battle with Pimas at a place called Wild Gords Piles. This happened in the fall and the Blackwater Indians had just reaped their first crop of corn, melons and pumpkins.

1866–67
In fall an Apache was killed who had a long foot.

1867–68
In fall Pima killed several Apaches. One Pima was wounded.

1868–69
Having an Apache woman for their guide the Pimas and Papagoes joined forces and lead [*sic*] a war campaign into the country which is now known as the San Carlos Indian reservation.

1869–70
Rained two days and nights continuously, washing down rocks and leaving white strips on the mountains.

Pimas kill Apaches while they were drunk and having a good time, and took several horses away with them.

1870–71
An Apache was killed while getting Giant Cactus fruit. About the same time Louis [Lewis] Nelson's father was killed by the Apaches at Peacho [Picacho] Mountains. One month later another Pima was killed.

1871–72
A Pima was bitten by a rattlesnake.

An Apache was killed known as Canteen.

[A] Pima was shot with a gun.

1872–73

Apaches were slaughtered on top of a mountain known to the Indians as Black Butte, and Doctor Montezuma was captured. Two brothers were killed.

1873–74

In summer Old Man Blackwater lead [*sic*] a successful campaign killing many Apaches.

An Apache was killed known as Big Back. One Pima was killed in this battle. The U.S. Army was with the Pimas at this battle.

Telegraph line went through the Pima settlement. About the same time an Apache was killed by the Pimas, being the last one killed and peace was made.

1874–75

Two Indian runners ran races with balls.[3]

1875–76

Man and woman ran race and woman won.

1876–77

A mare gave birth to twin colts.

1877–78

A Pima died while away in the mountains after mescal.

In spring a man from Blackwater was killed by Santan Indians. Eclipse of the sun occurred.

1878–79

In spring Casa Blanca Indians tried to kill Juan Thomas' brother and father. In summer the S.P.R.R. was extended to Casa Grande.

1879–80

A white man was shot and killed by two Blackwater young men near Casa Blanca.

1880–81

In spring Mr. Donkey, one of the boys who killed a white man the year before, was hung at Florence.

1881–82

In the beginning of spring snow fell. In summer two Indians were killed by the Agency police.

1882–83

Whooping cough swept through the Pima settlement, killing many children.

1883–84

Freight train ran over a Pima and killed him, cut him in two.

1884–85

The First Government wagon issued to Pima Indian.

1885–86

Two prominent men at Blackwater died, Owl and Heart.

1886–87

The Pimas were called upon to run Geronimo down.

1887–88

Blackwater and Sacaton Flats runners ran a race with balls. Earthquake occurred.

1888–89

Government building burned at Sacaton. Blackwater Presb. Church was built.

1889–90

Three prominent men at Blackwater died, Juan Thomas' father and others.

1889–90[4]

Pimas were called to guard the paymaster from being robbed at Ft. McDowell.

1890–91
In spring high flood but did not wash away fields.

1891–92
Two brothers died. Makil Anton and Juan Makil.

1892–93
Cow hooked Catherine Sampson.

1893–94
Chief Yellow, of Blackwater, died.

1894–95
The smallest pony ran [the] race. Peter James owned one of them.

1895–96
A man died in jail at Sacaton.

Nelson's horse raced at Sacaton Flats.

John Thomas shot himself at Phoenix Indian School.

1896–97
Presbyterian Church built at Gila Crossing. The River practically dry. The Blackwater Indians were forced to leave homes to sell wood.

1897–98
Agent Hadley issued beef to Indians.

1898–99
Another year in which beef was issued.

1899–1900
A rattlesnake bite [*sic*] a woman and she died.

Pima Indians went to work on a railroad in Nevada. Sam Anton was ran over [*sic*] and killed by train while he was drunk.

1900–1901
President McKinley assassinated. Pimas worked on railroad somewhere in California (Salton Sea).

1901–2
A & E extended from Tempe to Florence.[5]

1902–3
Floods washed away Indian fields.

1903–4
Two women struck by lightening [*sic*].

1904–5
A Presbyterian church was built at Sweetwater north side of river.

1905–6
Two young men died, one fell from a wagon and struck his head on hub.

1906–7
Sioux Indian, La Blanc and known to Indians as Feather Hat, came on the reservation.

1907–8
Two Indians died in an old well.

1908–9
J. B. Alexander attacked Louis [Lewis] Nelson.

1909–10
Inspector E. B. Linnen investigates J. B. Alexander's administration.[6]

1910–11
John Nelson and Nellie Roberts died.

1911–12

An Indian said to be killed by lightening [*sic*].

1912–13

Five prominent people died. Little Gila opened up in Spring.

CALENDAR OF MEJOE JACKSON

1842–43

Mexicans fought the Papagoes. Papagoes fled to the Pimas for protection, and lived with them for several years where the town of Sacaton is now situated. Pimas pursued and killed two Apaches about six miles southwest of Sacaton. One Pima was killed, *Pe-wa-cum*'s father.

1843–44

Apaches ambushed two Pimas, one was killed and the other escaped. This took place about 15 miles west of Tucson.

1844–45

An Apache captive was traded for a horse in Tucson, the horse was brought to Sweetwater but later ran away. Two elderly men and a boy started after the horse, and while on their way were ambushed, the two men were killed and the boy was thought to have been taken captive.

1846–47

In the early spring an Apache General known as *Ah-gee-cau-cum* (Small Leg) was captured across the river opposite Casa Blanca. The Apache was allowed to be killed by the relatives of the lost boy who was thought to have been taken captive the year previous. This same spring two Maricopa women were killed near a little hill southeast from Santan Village; known as Maricopa women slaughter.

1846–47

An Apache Indian was killed by the Pima and Maricopas, at Kelvin, and was scalped by a Maricopa Indian known as Thirsty Hawk. The Pimas went on a campaign, one Pima was wounded, near Superstition Mts. This Indian was known as Ragged G. String.

1847–48
Maricopas went to fight the Yumas at Yuma and were all slaughtered. Measles prevailed throughout the settlement, the old and young becoming affected.

1847–48
Snow, to the depth of a foot and a half, fell.

1848–49
Maricopas and a few Pimas went after mescal. They were slaughtered on the other side of Pecacho [Picacho] Mts., by the Apaches.

1849–50
Maricopas and Pimas went on a war campaign, and two Coquans were killed. After five days a Pima woman was killed by the Apaches while gathering cholla fruit. A daughter of this woman escaped and fled to the village notifying the people. In the summer a certain sickness prevailed among the Indians called by them "Black Vomiting" (probably black malaria).

1850–51
Pimas went on a war campaign and returning they were forced to jump a precipice, one Indian was killed. During the winter of the same year, an Apache, while trying to steal from the Pimas, was killed at Shon-ke-whib. In the spring a Papago Indian village, known as Mesquite Root[,] was attacked by the Apaches and everyone [was] either killed or taken captive. A few days after the Pima Indians went on a war campaign in order to avenge the attack. An Apache woman was captured and her husband wounded, the woman was brought to a Pima village and murdered, her body was then stood up at the foot of Double Butte.

1851–52
Two Papago women who were captured at Mesquite Root returned to their people. Four Apaches were chased from Casa Blanca hills towards Table Top

Mountain. They were overtaken about half way and killed. Some Pimas were wounded but none of them died. After this happened a war party of Apache Indians came to Tal Grey Mountains and sent four of the tribe to the Pima village for the purpose of getting the Pimas to follow to where the main party was in ambush[;] this plan was successful, six Pimas were killed.

1852–53
Pimas went on a war campaign and killed several Apaches on top of Silver King Mts. At the same time Pima and Papagoes joined forces against the Apaches at Catalina or Turkey Neck Mts., and took a number of horses which the Apaches had stolen from Old Mexico. Nearly all the Apaches were killed.

1852–53
On the south side of the river at Ray, Pimas met Apaches driving a number of horses and mules, the Apaches were killed and the horses and mules were taken by the Pimas. Near the McDowell Mt. a Pima was shot and left for dead, but he was only unconscious, and on recovering returned home several days after the others.

1853–54
Apache[s] were killed by the Pimas, they were grinding and making cake of mesquite beans, this took place ten miles north of Ray. A blind Apache was killed north of McDowell.

1854–55
An Apache who was supposed to be unbalanced in mind was wandering in Lower Santan District, and was noticed by a Pima woman who notified the men and they killed him.

1855–56
Four Apaches came down to the village at West [Wet] Camp and stole oxens. The Pimas followed them and overtaking them near Tempe Buttes, they left the oxen and climbed up the Butte. The Pimas surrounded them, killing three, one escaped. Pimas killed several Apaches where the Roosevelt dam in [sic] now situated. After the battle was over they roasted corn belonging to the Apaches.

1855–56

The Pimas start on a war campaign and camped about ten miles above Florence. During the night, their horses were frightened. The next night they returned home. Soon after, some Maricopa Indians went fishing at the foot of the Estrella Mts., while fishing they were attacked by the Apaches. One man killed, one was wounded and died soon after. Maricopas and Pimas joined forces and followed the Apaches. They caught and killed them at their camp. Early in the fall Joseph Roberts was shot by an Apache while talking to him, thinking he was a Pima. The Apache fled leaving the horse which Joseph Roberts and his party took. A short time after this happened Yuma Indians came down to Maricopa home and made war on the Maricopas. The Maricopas called for aid, the Pimas responded and assisting the Maricopas they killed nearly all the Yuma warriors, leaving a few, who escaped to the Estrella Mts.

1856–57

The digging of the Island Ditch. A star was seen with a long tail. The Maricopas believed that a star of that appearance showed a sign that a prominent man was to die. In the fall Pimas went on a war campaign[;] *Va-cache's* father was killed. In the winter an Apache who had come to steal was killed, at Maricopa village. In the spring an Apache was killed by a white man at a trading post.

1857–58

The Pima Indians were given clothes by a white man who had one arm. Abright [*sic*] light was seen in the sky. A medicine man was accused of the death of a patient and was killed by the dead man's relatives. In the winter a party of emigrants passed through Pima lands with a herd of tame buffalo.

1858–59

About thirty miles north of Florence Apaches were hunting wood rats when the Pimas and one white man attacked them, killing an Apache man and boy.

1859–60

Pimas went on a war campaign, when they got to Hat Mts. they sent back some of their party. Leaving some that were on horses they continued until they ran across tracks of Apaches. They started after them, until they ran across another party who were returning from a stealing expedition. The Pimas killed them all and then returned home. A few days after this, some

Pimas had a quarrel over some long standing trouble and a fight ensued, both parties lost several members.

1861–62
The Cottonwoods were budding when a white man, named White, was robbed of his store and taken prisoner by a company of soldiers. A few months after a regiment of soldiers and cavalry came to Casa Blanca and stationed there for several months. They bought hay from the Indians, which the Indians cut from their wheat fields. In the early summer the Island Ditch was completed and the Pimas planted melons, pumpkins and corn.

1862–63
After the Island land was put under cultivation a Pima while looking for his horse was killed by an Apache, four miles east from Sacaton.

1863–64
In the spring an Apache who did some stealing at *Ah-ke-chin* village, west of Maricopa Station, was killed by the Pimas. His body was dragged several miles to where Sacaton Siding is now located. The body was put on poles and stood up.

1864–65
A Pima who had a ranch near Pecacho [Picacho] had his horses stolen by Apaches. He came to notify the Pimas. They started after the thieves and caught them on the desert, killing all four Apaches and cutting their ears off.

1865–66
East from Silver King Mts. some Apaches were killed by Pimas. Among the Pimas who killed Apaches were Juan Thompson, *Ch-cho*, (Earth) and *Co-sho-pa-cho*. This happened at a place called Gourd Piles. One Apache tried to hide in the water but was soon discovered.

1866–67
In the summer the Pimas were made Gov't Scouts and on their first campaign killed some Apaches. Among those killed was one known as Long Feet[;] one woman was captured, brought to the Pima and there killed at Double Butte. North Blackwater [#43] ditch was in use.

1867–68

In the fall the Pimas went on a war campaign, killing one old Apache and a boy, this happened on the Globe Mts. while they were getting some plant seed.

1868–69

A Papago woman, one of the captives of Mesquite Root, returned to the Pimas [and] planned a war expedition against the Apaches, taking the woman as their guide[.] Their expedition was not successful and they returned home disappointed.

1869–1870

Santan Ditch was started in its construction. It rained many days and nights, washing down rock and soil from the mountain side, leaving marks on the mountains which could be seen for many miles. The River overflowed its banks, washing down the store at Casa Blanca.

1870–71

Deers came to the Pima fields and were grazing on the Pima corn when they were killed. In summer Pimas went on a war campaign to Superstition Mt. One Pima was killed, and one Apache taken captive[;] his name was "Red Eye."

1871–72

In the fall Apache war parties were raiding the country. They were making their night stop at Red Rock; during the day the Pimas fell on their tracks and followed them to their camp at Red Rock. During the night they attacked the Apaches, killing nearly all. The few left escaped with much difficulty. At the same time some other Pimas were on a war campaign to the Globe Mts. They killed an Apache woman. The man who killed her was known as *Ni-se-pe*. In the winter Pimas were returning from a war expedition and were waylaid by Apaches at a little red hill about five miles from McDowell, one Pima was killed. The same winter while on a hunting trip some Pimas and Papagoes were met by raiding Apaches. The Pimas and Papagoes had scattered to look for game. One of the Pima party who was on a horse had wandered to a hill, tying his horse he went to look for game. The Apaches were on the hill at the same time, laying [*sic*] in wait for this party. The man returned from another direction to where he had tied his horse. Not finding his horse he saw the Apache who took it, he then attempted to escape. Being fleet of foot he outran his pursuers for a long distance, before one of the Apaches mounted the horse and gave chase. He was caught and a fierce fight followed by the time the rest of the Apaches caught up with him. He shot and killed one Apache before he received the wound that disabled him, though fighting till the last bullet was fired he fell to the Apaches[;] this dead hero was "Kisto" the father of Lewis D. Nelson.

Half a year after all these happenings *My-how-kee* called a war council to avenge and make date for a war campaign. Their expedition to the Superstitious Mts. was successful. They met the enemy and killed two Apaches, who fought them with guns[;] one Pima was wounded name[d] Ni-se-pe.

1873–74

Mesquite beans were ripe. Two Pima brothers, living at Blackwater[,] were accused of killing another Pima. They were tried by the friends of the dead man and was [*sic*] killed. The two brothers were old timers at Blackwater and had lived and farmed there[;] an old family quarrel was the cause, as the man was murdered by a Mexican. In the fall the Pimas went on a war campaign to Globe Mts., they came to an Apache camp where they fought the Apaches at night[;] the Pimas killed many Apaches, and took many captives, among them was a boy, now Dr. Montezuma.[7]

In the winter Pimas went on a war campaign to Silver King Mts. They fought with the Apaches and were again victorious, taking many captives[,] among them a well known Apache known as "Mountain Grandchild," captured by *O-le-bin*. At the same time, U.S. Soldiers with some Pimas and some Apache captives went to the Roosevelt Mts., to fight Apaches who were still hostile after the Gov't had settled them on the reservation. They killed their leader and many of his followers. The leader, a Pima, was called Big Back.

1874–75

The first telegraph line was constructed through the reservation. At the same time some Pima chiefs went to Washington on land matters. Apaches were taken to San Carlos Reservation from Hot Springs in wagons.

1875–76

Pima went after mescal to Globe Mts. A man and a woman disputed about a race, so the people decided a race between the man and woman. Bets were made. The man won the race.

1876–77

A year after this race and during mescal time at the same place (Globe Mts.), a mare foaled twin colts.

1877–78

A year after this the Pimas again went after mescal to the Globe Mts. A man by the name of Tall Miguel took sick. They started home with him but he died on the way.

1878–79

Two Pimas [who] were accused of being medicine men with power to kill were shot and killed two miles west of Sacaton. They were the sons of Juan Thomas.

The party who killed the two brothers were not satisfied so planned to kill some more relatives of the dead men. They went south of Casa Grande, where the Pimas were having a general meeting. There they killed three more persons. The relatives then formed a party to make revenge. Making their headquarters at Blackwater. A date was made when they were to meet each other for battle. Day came and they fought and killed three of the party who killed the two brothers.

Six

EPILOGUE

Pima Water Rights, 1914–2007

When the U.S. Supreme Court ruled that Indian water rights were reserved rights, the United States for the first time accorded legal recognition of tribal nations' rights to water resources. This remained true even though officials of the U.S. Indian Service believed the Pima had lost their rights to the low flow of the Gila River due to upstream diversions and beneficial applications of the water under Arizona prior appropriation laws. Nonetheless, interior secretary Richard A. Ballinger asked that the Justice Department look into the matter of Pima water rights in 1911, with the attorney general then requesting data regarding the Indians' use of the water before initiating any proceedings. The U.S. attorney for Arizona Territory, J. E. Morrison, acknowledged that the Pima had sufficient water only in times of flood and that the chief cause of their stress was Upper Gila Valley diversions. These Upper Valley users had acquired their water in accordance with local prior appropriation laws and were beneficially using the same, however, so no injunction was issued.[1]

Pima chief Antonito Azul attempted to persuade Congress to mitigate the loss of Pima water. "Can the United States Congress and the people of this country," he wrote, "whose money has been squandered by the rogues who have robbed us, come to our aid?"[2] While the Indian Service made an effort to collect data, John Truesdell, assigned by the Justice Department to represent Pima claims and convinced that the Pima had prior and legitimate rights to the waters of the Gila River, opposed a survey of "all the lands affected" by irrigation along the river.[3] Charles Olberg, aware of the inherent conflict between reserved and prior appropriation rights, did not believe that it was morally right to take water from upstream users after they had put it to beneficial use with the blessing and approval of the United States government in order to restore it to the Pima.[4] Representative Carl Hayden (D-AZ), meanwhile, persuaded Congress not to authorize litigation of Pima claims.[5]

Between 1905 and 1921 Congress appropriated funds for a series of irrigation projects designed to protect the limited water that remained in the Gila River for the benefit of the Pima. With the 1916 Florence–Casa Grande Project (FCGP), Congress authorized two diversion dams, one above Florence twenty-five miles east of the reservation and one on the reservation. An inadequate conveyance system and an insufficient supply of water, however, limited the effectiveness of these efforts. Only with passage of the San Carlos Act in 1924, which authorized the construction of Coolidge Dam (with San Carlos Reservoir to store water) and the San Carlos Irrigation Project (the distribution system to convey water to both Indian and non-Indian land), did it appear that the Pima would receive the water they needed. The dam and conveyance system was to provide water first "for the irrigation of lands allotted to Pima Indians on the Gila River Reservation" and second to non-Indian farmers in the Florence–Casa Grande and Upper Gila Valley areas, but only if such water did not "diminish the supply necessary for said Indian lands."[6] In 1928 the Florence–Casa Grande Project was merged into the San Carlos Irrigation Project.[7]

In 1923 a lack of water in the Gila River led to the complete loss of the Pima wheat crop, prompting commissioner of Indian affairs Charles Burke to request legal action on behalf of the Pima against Upper Valley users. Truesdell recommended that the Justice Department file a general adjudication of the Gila River in federal court to determine priorities. On October 4, 1925, nearly forty years after the Pima had originally asked the government to intervene on their behalf, the Justice Department initiated legal proceedings against upstream users in *United States v. Gila Valley Irrigation District*.[8]

When Congress authorized construction of Coolidge Dam in 1924, the Pima were to receive their water before all other users. In representing the Pima in court, Truesdell worked to secure water for ten irrigable acres for each of the Pima and Maricopa (totaling 50,546 acres on-reservation, including 650 acres for government purposes) rather than asserting Pima claims to the entire natural flow of the river based on the proposition that the Indians would have continued to expand their agricultural endeavors were it not for upstream users.[9] On December 5, 1927, suit was filed in the U.S. District Court in Tucson. While the court called many expert witnesses over the next eight years, none of them were Pima, effectively silencing their concerns. By 1934 government attorneys had agreed in principle to divide the water that would be stored behind Coolidge Dam equally, despite the protests of the Pima that the intent of the San Carlos Act was to provide them with all the water they might need before any other user was served.[10]

By June 1935 the federal district court in Tucson was prepared to issue its ruling, calling for an equal division of both stored and pumped water. The Pima, having priority rights to the natural flow of the Gila, objected and did not consent to the decision, attempting to intervene on their own behalf. The court rejected this effort when it accepted the Gila Decree. Federal attorneys representing the Pima feared that the court would not sustain reserved rights and instead agreed to accept 210,000 acre feet of water for the Pima under time-immemorial rights. Upper Gila Valley and Florence–Casa Grande farmers retained their rights to water.

The ink on the decree was barely dry when the first challenge appeared in 1939. Upper Gila Valley users argued that all water flowing into San Carlos Reservoir was temporarily stored and was therefore technically stored water, subject to allocation. The court rejected this argument and ruled that water flowing into the reservoir with an equal amount flowing out was not stored water but natural flow. With the Gila Decree not yet five years old, upstream users were already seeking to gain access to Pima priority rights to the natural flow of the Gila as determined in the decree.[11] Over the next forty years government attorneys continued to litigate Pima rights; the Indians even filed suit in 1951 under the provisions of the Indian Claims Commission Act. Despite construction of Coolidge Dam, the Gila Decree and insufficient water limited the Pima to just one-quarter of their irrigable land.[12] Consequently, despite water rights to 50,546 acres, the Pima farmed just one-quarter of their eligible lands.[13]

Inadequate water caused the Pima to consider alternative water supplies. In 1948 Pima governor David A. Johnson told Arizona senator Ernest W. McFarland that the Pima were interested in Colorado River water in lieu of Gila River water. "If it will do us good, we want it," Johnson explained, but "if it will take us into court later on, we don't want it." McFarland had opened hearings on a proposal to bring Colorado River water to central Arizona to be used in part for Indian tribes without adequate water. Johnson, all too familiar with empty commitments and insufficient water, stressed the Pima's desire to secure water to meet their needs.[14] Because Colorado River water was some of the last remaining unappropriated water available in Arizona, there was little chance of the Central Arizona Project (CAP) being approved by Congress until the matter of Indian water rights was settled. In 1957, for instance, U.S. attorney general David Warner informed Simon H. Rifkind, special master for the Colorado River in the *Arizona v. California* case, that Indian tribes along the river were entitled to water as well. Rifkind recognized that Colorado River water might be used to satisfy Indian water claims in central Arizona, including the claims of the Gila River Indian Community. There was "enough [Colorado River] water," Rifkind argued, "to satisfy the future expanding agriculture and related water needs of each Indian reservation" in central Arizona. This opened the door to bringing Colorado River water to central Arizona Indian tribes to be used as a substitute source (in the case of the Pima) for an overappropriated Gila River.[15]

When the Central Arizona Project was authorized by Congress in 1968, the political maneuvering in regard to allocation of the water began. By 1971 five central Arizona Indian tribes—the Gila River Indian Community, Salt River Pima-Maricopa Indian Community, Fort McDowell Yavapai Nation, Ak-Chin Indian Community, and Tohono O'odham Nation—requested 1,219,200 acre-feet of CAP water based on the application of the Practicably Irrigable Acreage (PIA) standard to each of the reservations. The PIA was a court-sanctioned principle that Indian tribes were entitled to all the water necessary to irrigate reservation lands that were susceptible to irrigated agriculture. Non-Indian users requested an additional 4,175,137 acre-feet, for a total request of 5,394,305 acre-feet, nearly four times the expected annual delivery capacity and two times Arizona's total entitlement of 2.8 million acre-feet.[16] The following year the Pima encouraged the secretary of the interior to approve their rights to irrigate all of their San Carlos Irrigation Project (SCIP), Gila Crossing, and Haggard Decree lands as well as an additional 25,000 acres of irrigable land.[17] At the same time, the Gila River Indian Community feared that "non-Indian interests [were] actively conniving to steal [its] water rights."[18] In 1975 interior secretary Rogers C. B. Morton published in the *Federal Register* a proposed allocation of 176,000 acre-feet of CAP water for the Gila River Indian Community.[19]

Pima governor Alexander Lewis, Sr., objected to this allocation in a letter to Morton, arguing that the proposed amount would limit the tribe to "presently-developed lands" when more than 250,000 acres of "reasonably irrigable lands" could be served with 1,350,000 acre-feet of water. Nonetheless, Lewis, desirous of a "friendly settlement," argued that the tribe would accept "not less than 278,000 acre-feet per annum." Z. Simpson Cox, the lead attorney for the Pima, threatened to initiate litigation "and legal and political protests" if the tribe did not receive its fair share of water.[20]

In 1975 the five central Arizona tribes formally joined together to invoke Indian reserved rights to irrigate all PIA lands and demand that the rights of each of the tribes be determined before any CAP water was allocated. In October the Senate opened hearings on central Arizona Indian water rights, during which Loyde A. Allison, a Pima farmer and spokesman for the Five Central Tribes of Arizona, asked the Senate not to confirm any CAP allocations "until there has been a full and final settlement of the water rights of each of the five tribes."[21] The following March Senator Edward Kennedy (D-MA) introduced the Central Arizona Indian Water Resources Act of 1976, a bill that directed the secretary of the interior to "acquire, by purchase or eminent domain," 170,000 acres of non-Indian land with surface water rights and transfer such rights to the five central Arizona tribes for the purpose of removing "the cloud over water rights in central Arizona."[22]

The bill was bitterly opposed by Arizona interests and ultimately put to rest when the Bureau of Reclamation reported that it would not solve Indian water rights because it dealt only with surface rights.[23] In October interior secretary Thomas Kleppe published a revised decision of CAP water allocations in the *Federal Register*, providing the Pima with 173,100 acre-feet of water.[24] The Pima then filed suit against the federal government, seeking 1,188,000 acre-feet of CAP water, "all the water" behind Coolidge Dam, and "not less than ten percent of the Salt River Project."[25] In April 1979 the Arizona legislature enacted a bill transferring all water rights determinations to the Superior Court of Arizona. Despite the appeals of the Pima and other tribes, the U.S. Supreme Court upheld the transfer with the *San Carlos* decision of 1983.[26]

As the federal courts moved toward state jurisdiction and quantification of water rights, President Jimmy Carter initiated a plan for water policy reform that encouraged negotiated settlements. In February 1978 interior solicitor Leo M. Krulitz informed interior secretary Cecil Andrus that it made more sense to negotiate settlements with each of the central Arizona tribes on a "tribe-by-tribe" basis and that the best way to do so was to use litigation as an inducement. By April 1979 the Interior Department was caucusing to "plan and execute departmental actions which are calculated to encourage water rights settlement negotiations, or other action which by themselves will make water available in Arizona for use by the Indian tribes."[27] By June Andrus grew impatient that the Gila River Indian Community was not being "treated equitably" in its water rights discussions and stated that he would "consider reopening the October 1976 allocation regarding Indian use of CAP water" if the claims of the Indians could not be worked out.[28] Arizona officials publicly complained that CAP allocations were being held "hostage" to Indian water claims, with Arizona's congressional delegates fearing that the main stem CAP system would be completed before "actual delivery of water" could be made.[29]

State legislators in June 1980 enacted into law the Groundwater Management Act, which created four Active Management Areas (AMAs) in the populated regions of the state and established the Arizona Department of Water Resources (ADWR).[30] The ADWR then began advocating that Indian tribes, including the Pima, be required to accept treated effluent water in exchange for some of their CAP allocations. In the case of the Pima, the ADWR wanted the tribe to accept up to 50,000 acre-feet of Chandler effluent water and another 25,000 acre-feet of effluent from the City of Phoenix. The Bureau of Indian Affairs opposed the proposed exchanges, arguing that a combination of treated effluent and saline groundwater "could have disastrous long-term effects" on Pima agricultural lands.[31] Andrus indicated that he would act "upon suggestions" made by Arizona officials, freeing up additional CAP municipal and industrial (M & I) water for non-Indian use. The Gila River Indian Community opposed such an exchange, asking for an additional 103,476 acre-feet of CAP water in addition to the 173,100 acre feet already allocated in 1976.[32]

In October the Gila River tribal council officially acted to oppose any mandatory exchange of CAP water for treated effluent. In December Andrus announced a revised CAP water allocation plan. Gila River retained its 173,100 acre-feet of water, but non-Indian M & I users now "share[d] a first priority," meaning that the Indians' priority could be reduced by 10 percent in time of shortage, which would place their water on equal terms with non-Indian M & I users.[33] The ADWR then filed suit against Andrus to bar the Indians' "share[d] first priority" and the lack of effluent exchange.[34] Nonetheless, by mid-December eleven Arizona tribes, but not Gila River, had signed water contracts. Pima governor Alexander Lewis, Sr., suggested that the tribe did not sign a contract because it feared a new presidential administration might void the contract and did not wish to have two irrigation delivery systems: one for treated effluent and one for CAP water.[35]

In December 1981 the Bureau of Reclamation issued a draft CAP environmental impact statement, including a provision that changed the formula for Pima priority water, which increased its reduction in times of shortages to 25 percent and left the door open for mandatory effluent exchanges. The rationale for these changes was the belief that the Gila River Indian Community sat upon "one of the best developable ground water sources in the State" and that the tribe also had "access to a developed surface supply of irrigation water through the San Carlos Project."[36] Just 75 percent of Pima CAP water would be first priority, while 90 percent of other Indian and non-Indian M & I water would have such priority. The Pima saw this proposition as "unfair" and discriminatory.[37] On March 24, 1983, interior secretary James Watt published the allocations in the *Federal Register,* making them official.[38]

The Pima, aware that successful litigation might provide "paper" entitlements without financial assistance to put the water to a "wet" beneficial use, were encouraged by federal officials to sign a contract. Consequently, after the allocation of CAP water was official, the tribe began negotiating a water delivery contract. In March 1985 Pima governor Donald Antone reiterated the tribe's need for "a stable supply of water sufficient to sustain the expansion of the reservation's economy." This concept that gained added value when the tribe released its 1985 "Master Plan Report for Land and Water Use," which outlined a goal of irrigating 146,330 acres of land and developing seven riparian wetlands within the reservation. These goals would require an annual water budget of 771,581 acre-feet of water.[39]

After years of fruitless talks, the tribe and the Salt River Project, the largest utility and water supplier in the Salt River Valley, agreed to begin discussing a "comprehensive water rights settlement proposal." In October 1990 the tribe appointed a water negotiating team to press forward toward a negotiated settlement with all parties that might be involved in a comprehensive settlement. By 1991 a framework that included a proposed annual water budget of 653,500 acre-feet of water and funding to rehabilitate or construct the water delivery system was in place.[40] In June of that same year the Bureau of Reclamation informed Pima governor Thomas White that the mandatory effluent exchange provision would be dropped, clearly an effort to entice the tribe to sign a water delivery contract.[41] On October 22, 1992, the Gila River Indian Community signed its delivery contract for 173,100 acre-feet of CAP water.[42]

A water delivery contract was not a full and complete water settlement; tribal claims against upstream users, mining corporations, neighboring irrigation districts, and cities remained. The Interior Department, however, sought to discharge its trust responsibility and see a final settlement of all tribal water claims and consequently supported the Pima in the Gila River General Stream Adjudication, which the State of Arizona initiated in 1976 with the goal of clarifying and quantifying all water rights within the Gila River basin. The adjudication hearings were transferred to the Maricopa County Superior Court in 1979 and were combined as *In re the General Adjudication of All Rights to Use Water in the Gila River System and Source* and classified W-1 (Salt River), W-2 (Verde River), W-3 (Upper Gila River), and W-4 (San Pedro River) consolidated.

As settlement talks progressed, the question remained: from whence would settlement water (above the CAP delivery contract) come? While many elderly Pima longed for Gila River water, that was not politically practical or feasible. Consequently, short of buying out existing water users (an unpopular proposition, as evidenced by the 1976 Kennedy bill), the only source of settlement water was the reallocation of 240,000 acre-feet of uncontracted CAP non-Indian agricultural water. This proposition was agreed to in principle by the Central Arizona Water Conservation District (CAWCD) Board of Directors in 1995.[43] The Pima also remained concerned with how the water would be delivered to the reservation so that it could be put to beneficial use.

On October 13, 1995, the water delivery question was answered when the Gila River Indian Community and the Bureau of Reclamation agreed to an annual funding agreement for the tribe to build the federal portion of the on-reservation CAP irrigation delivery system under the provisions of the 1994 Indian Self-Governance Act. Reclamation committed $386 million, to be adjusted for cost increases, to construct the on-reservation portion of the CAP delivery system. This led to the creation of the Pima-Maricopa Irrigation Project as a tribal program using federal funds to construct the backbone delivery system and laterals to irrigate tribal land with CAP contracted water. Within a year the Pima-Maricopa Irrigation Project "Draft Programmatic

Environmental Impact Statement" was made public, outlining four alterna-
tives for constructing a water delivery system across the reservation.[44]

Senator Jon Kyl (R-AZ) offered to assist the CAWCD in bringing about
a legislative solution to the Gila River water settlement beginning in the
spring of 1998. A framework for settlement was discussed, although interior
secretary Bruce Babbitt expressed concern that if an agreement could not be
worked out before the end of the Clinton administration "it could be a very,
very long time" before one might be concluded.[45] Rita Pearson, director of the
ADWR, feared that litigation could "take decades in the courts" and present
risks to both tribal and state interests. Since a court could rule that the Pima
had priority rights to the waters of local watersheds (Salt, Gila, and Verde),
metropolitan cities and the Salt River Project favored reallocating CAP water
to settle the Indians' claims. Important allies were added to the list of settlement supporters.[46] On July 30, 1999, Babbitt published a notice in the *Federal Register* modifying previous CAP allocations to "assist in the resolution
of outstanding Indian water rights claims."[47] Settlement of Gila River Indian
Community claims, however, was now being tethered to the CAWCD's
repayment of the construction costs of the CAP mainstem system, an issue
that was the subject of its own lawsuit between the CAWCD Board and the
federal government. In November the Arizona Supreme Court affirmed a
Maricopa County Superior Court ruling acknowledging that reserved rights
applied to groundwater but that "a reserved right to groundwater may only
be found where other waters are inadequate to accomplish the purpose of a
reservation."[48]

Kyl, meanwhile, moved toward the front of water negotiation and in
July introduced an amendment to a Defense Department appropriation bill
that prevented Babbitt from reallocating any CAP water. Congress approved
the bill on July 20, placing Kyl as the central figure in bringing about a final
negotiated and legislatively approved water settlement.[49] Kyl then introduced
S. 3231, the Arizona Water Settlements Act of 2000. Although the bill died at
the end of the legislative session, it raised the hope that a final settlement was
imminent.[50]

Litigation continued concurrently, and in March 2002 the Arizona Superior
Court ruled in *In re the General Adjudication of All Rights to Use Water in the Gila
River System and Source* (W-1-203) that the 1935 Gila Decree covered upstream
agricultural wells but that the Gila River Indian Community could not claim
more water out of the Gila River than was granted it by the Gila Decree of 1935.

In addition, the court opined that the tribe could not claim any additional water from the Salt River other than the water that already had been allocated by the Haggard Decree.[51] On February 4, 2003, the Gila River Indian Community agreed to a water settlement proposal. Three weeks later Senator Kyl and Senator John McCain (R-AZ) introduced S. 437 (the Arizona Water Settlements Act [AWSA] of 2003) in the Senate, with Representatives J. D. Hayworth (R-AZ), Jim Kolbe (R-AZ), Trent Franks (R-AZ), Raul Grijalva (D-AZ), and Ed Pastor (D-AZ) introducing H.R. 885 in the House.[52] The Senate approved the bill on October 10, 2004, with the House following suit on November 17. On December 10, 2004, with a simple stroke of the pen and without political fanfare, President George W. Bush signed into law the Arizona Water Settlements Act of 2004, which, in addition to the Gila River Indian Community Water Settlement Act (Title II), also included adjustments to the CAWCD repayment contract for constructing the CAP (Title I), amendments to the Southern Arizona Water Settlement Act of 1984 (Title III), and provisions for an adjustment to the San Carlos Apache water settlement (Title IV).

The Gila River Indian Community Water Settlement brought to a historic conclusion one of the most egregious and long-standing Indian water disputes in the United States. This negotiated agreement approved by Congress provided water that the courts had refused to confirm for decades. It also allocated $147,000,000 (in 2000 dollars and indexed for cost increases) to rehabilitate the San Carlos Irrigation Project and $53,000,000 (in 2000 dollars and indexed for inflation) to buy down the cost of CAP water for tribal farmers, something the courts could never have provided.[53] On December 10, 2007, secretary of the interior Dirk Kempthorne signed the "Statement of Findings: Gila River Indian Community Water Settlement Act of 2004," which was then published in the *Federal Register,* making the settlement fully enforceable.[54] An enforceable settlement act restored a total annual tribal water budget of 653,500 acre-feet and established a level of certainty in water planning for all of central Arizona.[55]

CONCLUSION

A unique history precedes every legislative act. Outside of this historic context, events are interpreted in a vacuum. The Arizona Water Settlements Act of 2004 is no different. Title II of the AWSA—the Gila River Indian Community Water Settlement Act—is directly connected to the Pima voices of the past. While the elders that Southworth interviewed in 1914 have all passed on, they represent a stepping stone in the long history of Pima water use, water deprivation, water rights, and, ultimately, water restoration.

I have heard Pima elders explain how they fought their entire lives to bring water back to their people, even though they knew they would never see the day when the water actually returned. Most knew that they would never enjoy the benefits of water settlement, but all of them looked forward to the day when their children, grandchildren, and great-grandchildren would once again enjoy the benefits of an abundant supply of water.

The 1914 interviews hint at the day when the Pima would regain use of the waters of central Arizona. I believe that some of the Pima elders conceptualized the day when the Gila River Indian Community would again become the breadbasket of Arizona and the Pima would again become the River People in all facets of this meaning, including becoming water masters once again. While the restoration of water will greatly influence the Pima agricultural economy, the Gila River Indian Community is also poised to become a major water player in central Arizona water politics. The Gila River Indian Community today is the largest single contractor of CAP water, with 328,800 acre-feet. The Community also lies in the middle of the three-county CAP service area (Maricopa, Pinal, and Pima counties) and holds some of the last remaining agricultural lands to be developed (or redeveloped) in Arizona.

The future of the Gila River Indian Community will always be linked to the past, not only because the Akimel O'otham are the River People but also because generation upon generation of Pima leaders have listened to the voices of their elders and built a clear moral and legal basis for water settlement. This vision, which predates the 1914 interviews, is nonetheless poignantly illustrated and epitomized in the interviews, for these Pima voices provide the context and interpretative framework for the Arizona Water Settlements Act of 2004. While the Pima were "forced to abandon [their] fields" a century ago, the interviews hint at the day when the Indians' water would one day flow again across the reservation and irrigate the land. "Some day," Pima elder Ho-ke Wilson told Southworth in 1914, "all these once cultivated land[s] [will] bring to the coming children abundant harvests again."

NOTES

INTRODUCTION. "INDIANS STARVING TO DEATH"

1. "Indians Starving to Death: Six Thousands Perishing on the Gila Reservation Because of Lack of Water," *Chicago Tribune*, June 18, 1900.
2. "The First Irrigators, Gross Injustice to the Friendly Pima Indians of Arizona," *New York Tribune*, reprinted in the *Florence Tribune*, March 17, 1900.
3. Frank Russell, *The Pima Indians*, pp. 64–66.
4. C. H. Southworth, "Statements by Pima Indians Regarding Irrigation on the Gila River Indian Reservation," Arizona State Museum Library Archives (hereafter cited as "Statement" with the name of the informant), Statement of Joseph Head, p. 82.
5. Statement of John Rhodes, p. 84.
6. Statement of Jose Enis, p. 65.
7. Statement of James Hollen, p. 79.
8. Statement of Frank Hayes, p. 8.
9. Statement of Ho-ke Wilson, p. 46.
10. Statement of George Pablo, p. 29.
11. Statement of Juan Lagons, p. 77.
12. C. H. Southworth, "The History of Irrigation along the Gila River."
13. C. H. Southworth to Mr. Odd S. Halseth, dated March 9, 1931, San Carlos Irrigation and Drainage District, Florence, Arizona, Arizona State Museum Library Archives. Halseth became Phoenix's first city archaeologist in 1929. He was born in Moss, Norway, in 1893. After serving in World War I, he worked at the San Diego Museum and as curator of archaeology at the Museum of New Mexico in Santa Fe. Halseth arrived in Phoenix in 1927 to initiate excavations at Pueblo Grande, serving as its first director and remaining there until he retired in 1960. "Odd S. Halseth, Archaeologist, Dies," *Arizona Republic*, July 16, 1966.
14. Robert A. Hackenberg to William H. Kelly, dated August 30, 1962, Tucson, Arizona, Arizona State Museum Library Archives.
15. Ibid.
16. Russell, *The Pima Indians*.
17. Hackenberg to Kelly, August 30, 1962.
18. Statement of James Hollen, p. 78.
19. David Rich Lewis, *Neither Wolf Nor Dog: American Indians, Environment, and Agrarian Change*, pp. 170–74.
20. Donald Pisani, *Water and American Government: The Reclamation Bureau, National Water Policy, and the West, 1902–1935*, p. 154.

21. Leonard A. Carlson, *Indians, Bureaucrats, and Land,* discusses the economic impacts of the advent of land severalty on tribal nations. Carlson theorizes that allotment policies hastened the demise of Indian agriculture rather than promoted it.
22. Statement of Meguel, p. 55.
23. Statement of Juna Osif, pp. 71–72.
24. Statement of Oliver Sanderson, p. 85.

CHAPTER 1. "HIGH AND DRY"

1. "Huhugam" is the O'otham word for "those who came before." Archaeologists and other social scientists tend to use the term "Hohokam" to refer to those Native Americans who farmed the valleys of south-central Arizona for millennia. I prefer to use the O'otham spelling to refer to the prehistoric culture group.
2. Herbert E. Bolton, ed., *Father Eusebio Kino's Historical Memoir,* pp. 195–97; Herbert E. Bolton, *Anza's California Expeditions,* 2:389.
3. Edward Castetter and Willis H. Bell, *Pima and Papago Indian Agriculture,* pp. 80–82; Bolton, *Father Eusebio Kino's Historical Memoir,* p. 195.
4. Bolton, *Anza's California Expeditions,* 1:263; Herbert E. Bolton, *Rim of Christendom,* p. 248.
5. Juan Mateo Manje, *Unknown Arizona and Sonora, 1693–1721, from the Francisco Fernández del Castillo Version of Luz De Tierra Incognita,* p. 121.
6. The Papago practice of harvesting crops on share apparently predates contact: José Augustín de Campos found the Tohono O'odham who visited the Río San Ignacio in 1693 performing such labor. Peter Masten Dunne, ed., *Jacobo Sedelmayr, 1744–1751: Missionary, Frontiersman, Explorer in Arizona and Sonora, Four Original Manuscripts,* p. 23. La Encarnación del Sutaquison (Sudaccson) is between the modern communities of Sweetwater and Casa Blanca. Wheat likely was grown before 1744, although the earlier written record does not document its cultivation among the Pima. Eusebio Guiteras, ed. and trans., *Rudo Ensayo,* p. 15.
7. Dunne, *Jacobo Sedelmayr,* pp. 29, 31; Manje, *Unknown Arizona and Sonora,* pp. 88, 89, 122; Bolton, *Anza's California Expeditions,* 2:304 (citing Díaz).
8. Bolton, *Anza's California Expeditions,* 2:124, 126, 304. One fanega, a unit of dry measure used in Latin American countries, equals 1.58 U.S. bushels, so de Anza estimated that about 95 to 126 bushels of wheat had been broadcast over the field during its initial planting.
9. Bolton, *Anza's California Expeditions,* 4:34, 45; Elliot Coues, ed., *On the Trail of a Spanish Pioneer: The Diary and Itinerary of Francisco Garcés in His Travels through Sonora, Arizona, and California, 1775–1776,* pp. 107–8; Bolton, *Anza's California Expeditions,* 3:19. The river would have been low due to its seasonal fluctuations. Winter rains and spring snow runoff in the upper Gila watershed would increase the flow across the middle Gila. Late spring and early summer are the driest months.
10. Robert A. Hackenberg, "Pima and Papago Ecological Adaptations," pp. 169–70; Bolton, *Anza's California Expeditions,* 1:263 and 4:44; William H. Emory, *Notes of a Military Reconnaissance from Fort Leavenworth, in Missouri, to San Diego, in California, Including Parts of the Arkansas, del Norte, and Gila Rivers Made in 1846–1847. House Executive Document 41,* p. 85 (quotations); Russell, *The Pima Indians,* p. 87.

11. Bolton, *Anza's California Expeditions*, 2:390 (quotations) and 4:43; Paul H. Ezell, *The Hispanic Acculturation of the Gila River Pimas*, pp. 39, 104; Emory, *Notes of a Military Reconnaissance*, House Executive Document 41, p. 83.

12. Statement of George Pablo, p. 29.

13. Statement of Frank Hayes, p. 8.

14. Russell, *The Pima Indians*, p. 87.

15. Richard White, *Roots of Dependency: Subsistence, Environment, and Social Change among the Choctaws, Pawnees, and Navajos*, p. xv.

16. Patricia Limerick, *The Legacy of Conquest: The Unbroken Past of the American West*; William H. Goetzmann, *Exploration and Empire: A History of the Exploration of the American West from 1805 to 1900 Which Reveals the Impact of the Great Adventure on the Whole American Culture*, pp. xii–xiii.

17. Christopher McGrory Klyza, *Who Controls Public Lands?: Mining, Forestry, and Grazing Policies, 1870–1990*; Robert F. Berkhofer, *The White Man's Indian: Images of the American Indians from Columbus to the Present*, pp. 154–56.

18. Lewis Henry Morgan, *Ancient Society or Research in the Lines of Human Progress from Savagery through Barbarism to Civilization*, p. 17. According to Morgan, only Africans and Australian Aborigines were lower on the evolutionary scale.

19. Frederick E. Hoxie, *A Final Promise: The Campaign to Assimilate the Indians, 1880–1920*, pp. 83–115.

20. White, *Roots of Dependency*, pp. xiv–xv, argues that the collapse of Native American economies was an intentional by-product of federal policy designed to foster dependency by conditioning Indian economies to rely on the American market.

21. R. Douglas Hurt, *Indian Agriculture in America: Prehistory to the Present*; Francis Paul Prucha, *The Great White Father: The United States Government and the American Indians*, pp. 50–51.

22. Treaty with the Creek Nation, dated August 7, 1790, in *Statutes at Large of the United States of America, 1789–1873* (hereafter *Statutes at Large*), 7:35.

23. Treaty with the Great and Little Bands of Osage, dated June 2, 1825, in *Statutes at Large*, 7:24.

24. David Rich Lewis, *Neither Wolf Nor Dog*, p. 7.

25. Emmerich de Vattel, *The Law of Nations or Principles of the Law of Nature: Applied to the Conduct and Affairs of Nations, Book I*, chapter 7, pp. 34–35.

26. Quoted in Lewis, *Neither Wolf Nor Dog*, p. 8.

27. Thomas Jefferson, "Notes on the State of Virginia" and "Letters," pp. 290, 818.

28. "An Act to regulate trade and intercourse with the Indian tribes and to preserve peace on the frontier," in *Statutes at Large*, 2:139.

29. "An Act making provision for the civilization of the Indian tribes adjoining the frontier settlements," in *Statutes at Large*, 3:516.

30. Henry Rowe Schoolcraft, *The American Indians, Their History, Condition and Prospects, from Original Notes and Manuscripts*, p. 367.

31. Marc Reisner, *Cadillac Desert: The American West and Its Disappearing Water*, p. 43.

32. Earl Zarbin, "Desert Land Schemes: William J. Murphy and the Arizona Canal Company"; John Wesley Powell, *Report on the Lands of the Arid West, with a More Detailed Account of the Lands of Utah*. Chapter 2 of this work specifically deals with Powell's proposals to

reform federal land laws by marrying water with the land. The loopholes in federal land laws, Powell argued, encouraged monopolization of the water.

33. Wallace Stegner, *Beyond the Hundredth Meridian*, p. 211; Reisner, *Cadillac Desert*, pp. 45–47 (quotation).

34. Samuel P. Hays, *Conservation and the Gospel of Efficiency: The Progressive Conservation Movement, 1890–1920*, pp. 6–8.

35. *United States v. Rio Grande Dam and Irrigation Company*, 174 U.S. 690 (1899); Robert G. Dunbar, *Forging New Rights in Western Water*, pp. 61–81 (quotation).

36. "An act to provide for the sale of desert lands in Certain Territories," March 3, 1877, in *Statutes at Large*, 19:377.

37. Pisani, *Water and American Government*, p. 35.

38. Daniel McCool, *Command of the Waters: Iron Triangles, Western Water Development, and Indian Water*, pp. 14–15; Karen L. Smith, "The Campaign for Water in Central Arizona: 1890–1903."

39. McCool, *Command of the Waters*, pp. 66–110; Pisani, *Water and American Government*, pp. 275–76 (quotation); Donald Worster, *Rivers of Empire: Water and Aridity and the Growth of the American West*, pp. 171–72.

40. Gerald D. Nash, *The Federal Landscape: An Economic History of the Twentieth-Century West*, pp. 21–39; Pisani, *Water and American Government*, pp. xi–xvii.

41. Congress based its authority on the United States Constitution, art. 1, sec. 8, cl. 3, which states that Congress has the authority "To regulate commerce . . . with the Indian tribes."

42. Francis Paul Prucha, *American Indian Treaties: The History of a Political Anomaly*, pp. 9–12.

43. *Lone Wolf v. Hitchcock*, 187 U.S. 553 (1903).

44. *United States v. Winans*, 198 U.S. 371 (1904); *Winters v. United States*, 207 U.S. 564 (1908).

45. Janet McDonnell, *The Dispossession of the American Indians, 1887–1934*, p. 121; D. Otis, *The Dawes Act and the Allotment of Indian Lands*, p. 17.

46. Powell was not a proponent of the neatly surveyed grids in the American West, arguing that the West should be reorganized by watersheds. This would enable scientific planning of irrigation works and enjoin legal disputes that were otherwise inevitable. Such progressive thinking could only be done under the authority of the federal government and was ultimately rejected in the National Reclamation Act, which provided none of the safeguards advocated by Powell. Charles F. Wilkinson, *Crossing the Next Meridian: Land, Water, and the Future of the West*, p. 239.

47. Statement of Cos-Chin, p. 61.

48. Dwight Clarke, ed., *The Original Journals of Henry Smith Turner with Stephen Watts Kearny to New Mexico and California, 1846–1847*, pp. 107–8.

49. William H. Emory, *Notes of a Military Reconnaissance from Fort Leavenworth, in Missouri, to San Diego, in California, Including Parts of the Arkansas, del Norte, and Gila Rivers Made in 1846–1847. Senate Executive Document* 7, p. 82 (quotations); "Report of A. R. Johnston, aide-de-camp to S. W. Kearny," in ibid., p. 598 (Carson quotation).

50. Emory, *Notes of a Military Reconnaissance. Senate Executive Document* 7, p. 85.

51. Ibid., p. 84.

52. *Report from the Secretary of War, Communicating a Copy of the Official Journal of Lieutenant Colonel Philip St. George Cooke, from Santa Fe to San Diego, etc.*, p. 49; Frank Alfred Golder, *The March of the Mormon Battalion Taken from the Journal of Henry Standage*, p. 198; Philip St. George Cooke, *Report of Lieutenant Colonel P. St. George Cooke of His*

March from Santa Fe, New Mexico, to San Diego, Upper California, pp. 254–55 (Cooke and Tyler quotations).

53. George P. Hammond and Edward D. Howes, eds., *Overland to California on the Southwestern Trail, 1849: The Diary of Robert Eccleston,* p. 204; Marjorie Tisdale Wolcott, ed., *Pioneer Notes from the Diaries of Judge Benjamin Hayes, 1849–1875,* p. 45; Jake B. Goodman III, ed., *Personal Recollections of Harvey Wood,* p. 12; "Diary of Judge Benjamin Hayes' Journey Overland from Socorro to Warner's Ranch, from October 31, 1849, to January 14, 1850."

54. Anna M. Perry, ed., *Travels in Mexico and California: Comprising a Journal of a Tour from Brazos Santiago, through Central Mexico, by Way of Monterey, Chihuahua, the Country of the Apaches, and the River Gila, to the Mining Districts of California,* p. 72; Anna Raschall Hannan, ed., *The Adventures of Charles Edward Pancoast on the American Frontier: A Quaker Forty-Niner,* pp. 244–45; Henry F. Dobyns, ed., *Hepah, California! The Journal of Cave Johnson Couts from Monterey, Nuevo León, Mexico, to Los Angeles, California, during the Years 1848–49,* pp. 66–67; Lansing B. Bloom, ed., "From Lewisburg to California in 1849: Notes from the Diary of William H. Chamberlin," p. 173.

55. John D. Walker to James L. Collins, dated December 2, 1859, Tucson, New Mexico Territory, and John D. Walker to James L. Collins, dated June 8, 1860, Tucson, New Mexico, RG 75, T21, National Archives and Records Administration; John P. Wilson, "Peoples of the Middle Gila: A Documentary History of the Pimas and Maricopas, 1500s–1945," chapter 9, p. 10.

56. J. Ross Browne, *Adventures in the Apache Country,* p. 107.

57. Statement of Henry Austin, p. 24.

58. Ammi White to Charles Poston, dated June 30, 1864, Agency of Pima and Maricopa Indians, Pimo Villages, RG 75, M234, National Archives and Records Administration, Roll 3.

59. John Nicholson, ed., *The Arizona of Joseph Pratt Allyn,* p. 109.

60. M. O. Davidson to D. N. Cooley, dated January 12, 1866, Enriquilla, RG 75, M234, Roll 3.

61. C. H. Lord to D. N. Cooley, dated June 4, 1866, Tucson, Arizona Territory, in *Annual Report of the Commissioner of Indian Affairs* (hereafter *ARCIA*), 1866, p. 112.

62. Levi Ruggles to George Dent, dated March 4, 1867, Pima Villages, RG 75, M234, Roll 3.

63. Charles D. Poston to William P. Dole, dated April 15, 1863, in Charles D. Poston Letterbook, RG 75, M734, National Archives and Records Administration, Roll 8.

64. Roger Nichols, "A Miniature Venice: Florence, Arizona, 1866–1910," pp. 339–40.

65. *ARCIA, 1869,* pp. 219–20.

66. George W. Dent to Nathaniel Taylor, dated April 15, 1869, La Paz, Arizona Territory, RG 75, M734, Roll 3; John Stout to Ely Parker, dated October 25, 1871, RG 75, M234, Roll 2.

67. Roger Jones to Randolph B. Marcy, dated July 21, 1869, Washington D.C., in *Records of the Inspector General,* p. 662.

68. J. D. Cox, Secretary of the Interior, to John Rawlins, Secretary of War, dated June 9, 1869, Department of Interior, Washington, D.C., RG 393, National Archives and Records Administration, Roll 6.

69. Frederick Grossman to George W. Andrews, dated November 9, 1869, Sacaton, Arizona Territory, RG 75, M734, Roll 3; Frederick Grossman to George W. Andrews, February 15, 1870, RG 75, M734, Roll 4; *Weekly Arizona Miner,* September 26, 1868 (quotation).

70. Frederick Grossman to George W. Andrews, dated November 11, 1869, Sacaton, Arizona Territory, RG 75, M734, Roll 3.

71. David H. DeJong, "See the New Country: The Removal Controversy and Pima-Maricopa Water Rights, 1869–1879."

72. John Stout to Ezra Hayt, dated December 21, 1877, Pima Agency, RG 75, M234, Roll 19.

73. John Stout, Agent, to Commissioner of Indian Affairs Ezra Hayt, dated August 15, 1878, Pima Agency, in *ARCIA, 1878,* p. 3; A. B. Ludlam to Ezra Hayt, Commissioner of Indian Affairs, dated September 5, 1880, Pima Agency, in *ARCIA, 1880,* p. 4 (quotation).

74. Statements of Juan Manuel (Chir-purtke), p. 73; Juan Lagons, p. 76.

75. P. McCormick, United States Indian Inspector, to Cornelius Bliss, Secretary of the Interior, dated April 4, 1897, Sacaton, Arizona Territory, p. 3, RG 48, M1070, National Archives and Records Administration, Roll 36; Statement of William Wallace, p. 6 (quotations); "Report of Elmer A. Howard to Commissioner J. D. C. Atkins," in *ARCIA, 1887,* p. 4.

76. "Gila River Priority of Irrigated Acres, Water Distribution Chart #3," San Carlos Irrigation Project (hereafter SCIP) Archives.

77. *ARCIA, 1890,* p. 5; William Junkin, United States Indian Inspector, to John Noble, Secretary of the Interior, dated September 30, 1890, Pima Agency, RG 48, M1070, Roll 36, p. 3.

78. *ARCIA, 1896,* p. 115. The Pima soon earned a reputation as workers par excellence. Over the next few years they were employed in Arizona and Nevada. When working in the Ray copper mine railroads in 1900, they were described as "far superior to the Mexicans." In 1900 they earned nearly ten thousand dollars working on the railroad. *ARCIA, 1900,* p. 196.

79. Russell, *The Pima Indians,* pp. 64–66, notes that at least five persons died of starvation in 1898–99 alone. The following year a woman from Blackwater died after being bitten by a snake. "This woman had gone far out on the desert to search for mesquite beans, as she was without food; indeed the whole community was starving because of the failure of the crops owing to the lack of water in the river for their ditches." John Ravesloot, "The Anglo American Acculturation of the Gila River Pima, Arizona: The Mortuary Evidence," p. 16.

80. Cornelius Crouse, U.S. Indian Agent, Sacaton, Arizona Territory, to Commissioner of Indian Affairs Daniel Browning, dated May 10, 1893, RG 75, Letters Received, Office of Indian Affairs, National Archives and Records Administration; "Report of C. C. Duncan, United States Indian Inspector, to the Honorable Secretary of the Interior Michael H. Smith, dated Pima Agency, November 23, 1894," RG 48, M1070, Roll 36, p. 1 (quotation).

81. Statement of Joseph Head, p. 82.

82. *ARCIA, 1895,* p. 121; J. R. Young to Secretary of the Interior Michael H. Smith, dated December 4, 1894, RG 75, Letters Received, Indian Division, Office of Indian Affairs.

83. This includes filed acreage, not irrigated. "Report of C. C. Duncan," RG 48, M1070, Roll 36.

84. "Gila River Priority of Irrigated Acres, Chart #2," SCIP Archives.

85. *ARCIA, 1898,* p. 126; *ARCIA, 1900,* p. 196; Frank C. Armstrong, United States Indian Inspector, to Lucius Q. C. Lamar, Secretary of the Interior, dated February 26, 1887, Pima Agency, RG 48, M1070, Roll 35, p. 57.

86. Copy of Minutes of the Florence Canal Company Board of Directors, November First, AD 1887, in Duncan to Smith, dated November 23, 1894, Pima Agency, RG 48, M1070, Roll 36.

87. Fred Nicklason, "Report for the Gila River Pima and Maricopa Tribes," pp. 657–59.

88. Statement of James Hollen, p. 79.

89. Frank C. Armstrong, Special Agent, to the Secretary of the Interior, dated November 23, 1901, in "Conditions of Reservation Indians, Letter from the Secretary of the Interior, dated February 21, 1902," p. 56.

90. *The United States of America as Guardian of Chief Charley Juan Saul and Cyrus Sam, Maricopa Indians, and 400 Other Maricopa Indians Similarly Situated, v. Haggard et al.,* June 11, 1903.

91. Robert A. Sauder, *The Yuma Reclamation Project: Irrigation, Indian Allotment, and Settlement along the Lower Colorado River*. Sauder refers to this showdown as the final irrigation frontier.

92. *Thirteenth Census of the United States Taken in the Year 1910, Volume VI, Agriculture*, pp. 70–76. The counties were Maricopa, Pinal, and Graham.

93. Eric V. Meeks, "The Tohono O'odham, Wage Labor, and Resistant Adaptation, 1900–1930."

94. *Fourteenth Census of the United States Taken in the Year 1920, Volume VII, Irrigation and Drainage*, p. 110.

95. Ibid., pp. 111–12.

96. Testimony of Wendell Reed, in House of Representatives, *Indians of the United States*, pp. 1014–15.

97. "Gila River Priority Analysis, Water Distribution Chart #3."

CHAPTER 2. "FORCED TO ABANDON OUR FIELDS"

1. Pinal County Historical Society, File Folder "Irrigation in the Florence District," p. 3.

2. Author interview with Robert H. Southworth, Scottsdale, Arizona, November 13, 2007.

3. Roy V. Peel, Director of the Bureau of the Census, to Clay H. Southworth, dated April 25, 1952, Department of Commerce, Bureau of the Census, Washington, D.C., Southworth Family Files. The June 1, 1900, census records from Genoa precinct (Douglas County, Nevada) referred to Clay as Charles. Clay had three brothers named Hartford, Stoddard, and George.

4. Olberg designed Ashurst-Hayden (or Florence) Diversion Dam (dedicated in 1921), Sacaton Dam (dedicated in 1925), and Coolidge Dam (dedicated in 1930), all of which are on the Gila River and were constructed for the benefit of the Pima.

5. Clay H. Southworth Employment Biography, Southworth Family Files.

6. "Appropriation Is Double for Fort Hall Project," Southworth Family Files.

7. H. W. Dietz of the Indian Service did not recommend the release of Southworth. The Water User's Association voted on September 28, 1918; C. H. Southworth to Major C. R. Olberg, dated April 14, 1924, Sacaton Diversion Dam, Southworth Family Files.

8. H. W. Dietz to the Commissioner of Indian Affairs, dated March 4, 1920, Salt Lake City, Southworth Family Files.

9. David H. DeJong, "An Equal Chance?: The Pima Indians and the Florence–Casa Grande Project, 1916–1924."

10. Clay H. Southworth Employment Biography, Southworth Family File.

11. C. H. Southworth to Commissioner of Indian Affairs through Major C. R. Olberg, dated December 10, 1928, San Carlos, Arizona, Southworth Family Files. Southworth assumed the management of the San Carlos Irrigation and Drainage District on January 1, 1929.

12. Herbert W. Clotts to C. H. Southworth, dated December 8, 1936, Los Angeles, California, Southworth Family Files.

13. "I'd have died if I had stayed back there [Washington, D.C.] any longer," Southworth stated. "West's Pioneer Reclamation Expert Retires," *Arizona Republic* (no date), Southworth Family Files.

14. H. Rex Lee, Acting Commissioner of Indian Affairs, to Clay H. Southworth, dated July 26, 1951, Washington, D.C., Southworth Family Files. Southworth received numerous

congratulatory letters on his retirement, including letters from Senator Ernest McFarland (D-AZ), a lifelong friend.

15. Dillon S. Myers to Ralph M. Gelvin, dated September 12, 1952, Washington, D.C., Southworth Family Files.

16. Gene M. Gressley, Director of the Western History Research Center, to Mrs. Clay H. Southworth, dated July 21, 1966, Laramie, Wyoming; and Gene M. Gressley, Director of the Western History Research Center, to Mrs. Clay H. Southworth, dated May 26, 1966, Laramie, Wyoming, Southworth Family Files.

17. Fred C. Clark, Jr., to Mrs. Clay Southworth, dated February 11, 1963, Brigham City, Utah, Southworth Family Files.

18. Southworth, "The History of Irrigation along the Gila River," p. 143. The main areas for seepage flows were found in Blackwater, Sweetwater, and Gila Crossing, where bedrock beneath the river channel forced the subflow to the surface.

19. E. B. Merritt, Assistant Commissioner of Indian Affairs, to the Honorable Charles Curtis, United States Senate, dated March 24, 1916, Washington D.C., SCIP Archives.

20. *Winters v. United States.* 207 U.S. 564 (1908). The Winters case defined Indian water rights as implicitly reserved by the federal government on behalf of the Indians. The Winters right is referred to as a "reserved right" in perpetuity and is dependent on the extant needs of the tribe, whether or not such water is actually put to beneficial use at the time, as state prior appropriation laws demand.

21. *Hearings before the Committee on Expenditures in the Interior Department of the House of Representatives on House Resolution No. 103 to Investigate the Expenditures in the Interior Department, June 5, 1911,* pp. 135, 193. The secretary could allot up to 80 acres of agricultural land, up to 160 acres of grazing land, and up to 40 acres of irrigable land. Commissioner Robert Valentine believed that this gave him the authority to allot anywhere from 0 to 40 acres of irrigable land at his own discretion. "We are the judge," he told the House subcommittee in 1911. "A Petition Addressed to the Indian Rights Association by the Chiefs of the Pima Tribe of Indians," dated July 31, 1911, in "Conserving the Rights of the Pima Indians of Arizona, Letters and Petitions with Reference to Conserving the Rights of the Pima Indians of Arizona to the Lands of Their Reservation and the Necessary Water Supply for Irrigation," pp. 11, 17.

22. *Hearings before the Committee on Expenditures,* p. 671.

23. The largest Pima farms were Jose Mendoza (100 acres), Jack Stone (96 acres), Lewis Porter (60 acres), Frank Armstrong (55 acres), Pancho Lopez (54 acres), Joseph Smith (52 acres), John Jones (50 acres), Jose Kalka (50 acres), and Ed Wood (50 acres). Many others farmed between 30 and 50 acres, growing wheat, barley, alfalfa, corn, cotton, beans, squash, and a variety of garden crops.

24. Reverend Sheldon Jackson and Reverend George L. Spining, "Our Red Reconcentrados—Some Facts concerning the Pima and Papago Indians of Arizona," p. 1515.

25. *ARCIA, 1904,* p. 16.

26. "J. R. Meskimons, Superintendent of Irrigation, to The Honorable Commissioner of Indian Affairs, dated Phoenix, Arizona, August 15, 1904," RG 75, Records of the Bureau of Indian Affairs, Records of the Irrigation Division, Gila River Project, National Archives and Records Administration.

27. *Annual Report of the United States Geological Survey, Part 4,* p. 357.

28. *The United States of America as Guardian of Chief Charley Juan Saul and Cyrus Sam, Maricopa Indians, and 400 Other Maricopa Indians Similarly Situated, v. Haggard et al.*

29. *ARCIA, 1903*, pp. 131–33; Willis T. Lee, *The Underground Waters of Gila Valley, Arizona*, pp. 63–64.

30. *ARCIA, 1904*, p. 16.

31. Lee, *The Underground Waters of Gila Valley, Arizona*, pp. 65–66.

32. Narcisse Porter, John Seota, and others wrote to Stephens and members of the House Indian Affairs Committee, asking for support in addressing their water claims. "A Petition Addressed to the Indian Rights Association by the Chiefs of the Pima Tribe of Indians," dated July 31, 1911, in "Conserving the Rights of the Pima Indians of Arizona," p. 10. On December 29, 1911, the Pima published their "Appeal for Justice."

33. *The Pima Indians and the San Carlos Irrigation Project: Information Presented to the Committee on Indian Affairs, House of Representatives in Connection with S. 966, an Act for the Continuance of Construction Work on the San Carlos Federal Irrigation Project in Arizona and for Other Purposes*, pp. 58–59.

34. Charles E. Ellis, Special Agent, to Robert G. Valentine, Commissioner of Indian Affairs, dated April 10, 1912, RG 75, Letters Received, Indian Division, National Archives and Records Administration; "Annual Statistical Report, Narrative Section, Pima Agency," Sacaton, Arizona, dated May 28, 1912, RG 75, M011, Roll 104, pp. 2, 33.

35. "Olberg to Valentine," in "Annual Report of the United States Indian Irrigation Service, District 4," fiscal year 1913, p. 44.

36. Wendell Reed to Cato Sells, dated March 26, 1913, Washington D.C., RG 75, Irrigation Division, National Archives and Records Administration.

37. C. R. Olberg to Cato Sells, through Wendell Reed, dated February 19, 1914, Sacaton, Arizona; John S. Layne to C. R. Olberg, dated May 20, 1914, Solomonville, Arizona; C. R. Olberg to Wendell Reed, dated February 20, 1914, Sacaton, Arizona: all in C. R. Olberg Letterbox, SCIP Archives; Charles H. Southworth to N. W. Irsfeld, dated June 22, 1915, C. H. Southworth Letterbox, SCIP Archives.

38. Ashurst told the *Arizona Blade Tribune* that many congressional delegates were opposed to any appropriation for "white settlers in Arizona"; but because of the interest of the Indian Service, Indian Rights Association, and other "kind red societies," the Florence–Casa Grande Valley would ultimately "obtain the money necessary" for the FCGP. "Diversion Dam Sure Says Ashurst," *Arizona Blade Tribune*, dated May 8, 1915.

39. *Diversion Dam on the Gila River at a Site above Florence, Arizona, Excerpts to Be Used by the Committee on Indian Affairs*, pp. 14–16.

40. Quoted in Jack L. August, Jr., "Carl Hayden's Indian Card: Environmental Politics and the San Carlos Reclamation Project," p. 402. Hayden also faced opposition from Upper Valley water users (in the Safford, Duncan, and Virden valleys), who were fearful they would be "compelled to abandon their homes" to benefit the Florence–Casa Grande and reservation farmers. "Upper Gila Valley Alarmed over San Carlos Project," *Arizona Blade Tribune*, April 4, 1914.

41. "An Appeal of the Pimas," *Casa Grande Bulletin Print*, n.d. [ca. 1920] (University of Arizona Microfilm 621 I 1267).

42. "Farmers and Indians Are Unit [*sic*] on San Carlos Matter," *Arizona Blade Tribune*, March 28, 1914.

43. N. W. Irsfeld to C. H. Southworth, Pima, Arizona, dated February 11, 1915, Sacaton, Arizona, C. H. Southworth Letterbox, SCIP Archives; "Annual Report of the United States Indian Irrigation Service District 4," fiscal year 1915, pp. 42, 45, 46; Franklin K. Lane, Secretary of the Interior, to the Honorable Senator Henry Ashurst, dated January 28, 1915, Department of the Interior, Washington D.C., in *Diversion Dam on the Gila River at a Site above Florence, Arizona, Excerpts*, p. 5 (quotation); "Extracts from the Hearings before the Senate Committee on Indian Affairs, Thursday, January 28, 1915," in ibid, pp. 6, 8.

44. "Reed to Sells," in "Annual Report of the United States Indian Irrigation Service, District 4," fiscal year 1915.

45. Wendell Reed to C. R. Olberg, dated February 10, 1914, Washington D.C., C. R. Olberg Letterbox, SCIP Archives.

46. C. R. Olberg to Wendell Reed, dated February 20, 1914, Sacaton, Arizona, C. R. Olberg Letterbox, SCIP Archives.

47. U.S. Senate, *Indian Appropriation Bill: Hearings before the Committee on Indian Affairs, United States Senate, on H. R. 20150*, p. 503.

48. August, "Carl Hayden's Indian Card," p. 402.

49. The Florence newspaper noted that in many instances off-reservation landowners were "reluctant to give accurate data" to the Indian Service, which was collecting the information. The newspaper urged its readers to cooperate fully, because the truth would eventually come out. "Water Rights Data Coming Slowly," *Arizona Blade Tribune*, June 27, 1914; F. M. Schanck to C. R. Olberg, dated April 28, 1914, Los Angeles, California; Merritt to the Director of the Geological Survey, dated March 7, 1914, Washington, D.C., both in C. R. Olberg Letterbox, SCIP Archives.

50. C. R. Olberg to Wendell Reed, dated February 9, 1914, Sacaton, Arizona, in C. R. Olberg Letterbox, SCIP Archives. The Justice Department, believing it was progressing in its protection of Pima water rights, did not intervene on behalf of the Pima. Attorney general James Clark McReynolds erroneously believed that the *Lobb v. Avenente* case would take Pima water rights into consideration. *Annual Report of the Attorney General 1914*, pp. 38–39. The *Arizona Blade Tribune* stated on May 30, 1914: "While it is known that the Indian Department has been looking into the matter of water rights in the valley on behalf of the Indians there is nothing to indicate the department will ask to have the case transferred to the federal court."

51. August, "Carl Hayden's Indian Card," p. 420, note 10. The complaint filed in *George Lobb v. Peter Avenente et al.* included more than 250 defendants. The court adjudicated water rights to 11,039 acres in the Florence–Casa Grande area with priority rights between 1868 and 1915. Supplemental decrees recognized water rights appurtenant to additional lands.

52. "Report on the San Carlos Irrigation Project: The History of Irrigation along the Gila River," pp. 9–10.

53. Statements of George Pablo, p. 29; James Hollen, p. 79.

54. Cooperative village was an anomaly, with 49 percent of its fields abandoned. Established during a time of minimal seepage flow in 1900, Cooperative's high abandonment rate might be due to being last in line to receive water off the Gila River.

55. Statements of Antonito Azul, p. 18; George Pablo, p. 33.

56. Statement of Juan Lagons, pp. 76–77.

57. Statements of Juan Thomas, pp. 1–2; Havelena, p. 3; and John Makil, p. 23.

58. Testimony of Wendell Reed, in House of Representatives, *Indians of the United States*, p. 1002.
59. Ibid., pp. 1014–15.
60. Statements of Havelena, p. 3; William Wallace, p. 6; Samuel Scoffer, p. 9; Henry Austin, p. 24; George Pablo, pp. 29–31, 38; Slurn Vanico, p. 47; Meguel, p. 52; Harvier, p. 69; and Joseph Head, p. 82.

CHAPTER 3. THE SOUTHWORTH INTERVIEWS

1. C. H. Southworth to Mr. Odd S. Halseth, dated March 9, 1931, San Carlos Irrigation and Drainage District, Florence, Arizona, Arizona State Museum Library Archives.
2. Ibid.
3. Ibid.
4. File Folder "Irrigation in the Florence District," Pinal County Historical Society, pp. 3–4.
5. Statement of Oliver Sanderson, p. 85.
6. Southworth to Halseth, March 9, 1931.
7. Southworth published the calendar stick of Juan Thomas in C. H. Southworth, "A Pima Calendar Stick," *Arizona Historical Review* 4:2 (July 1931).
8. Southworth to Halseth, March 9, 1931.
9. Southworth received calendar sticks from Joseph Head and Juan Jackson.
10. Juan Thomas was sixty-six years old at the time of the interview. He was born in the Casa Blanca District. When he was twenty-eight he came to the Blackwater District, where he lived and farmed in 1914. At that time he had fourteen acres of land under cultivation. Thomas did not speak English. He was the possessor of one of the calendars recorded in chapter 5.
11. Southworth, "The History of Irrigation along the Gila River," p. 129 (hereafter Southworth, "History"). The Cholla Mountain ditch was also known as the North Blackwater ditch and was 7.56 miles in length. It was located on the north side of the Gila River, with its heading 3 miles above the reservation. The ditch carried 16 cubic feet per second (cfs) of water and irrigated 941 acres; an additional 309 acres of previously irrigated land had been abandoned due to insufficient water.
12. The Island Ditch Blackwater carried 35 cfs and irrigated 1,029 acres in 1914, with an additional 30 previously irrigated acres. The ditch was 9.73 miles in length and headed on the Gila River. Southworth, "History," p. 130.
13. The Florence Canal was located upstream from the Gila River Indian Reservation and was 50 miles in length. Southworth, "History," pp. 147–52. It was chartered in 1886 and constructed between 1886 and 1889. The canal took most of the remaining surface water flow of the Gila River. When combined with Upper Valley diversions in the Safford and Duncan-Virden valleys in the 1870s, it left little water in the river for Pima farmers.
14. Havelena was eighty years old at the time of the interview. When he was twenty-six, he left his place of birth in Casa Blanca and moved to Whitea (off-reservation), near Adamsville, where he cultivated land for three years. He enlisted in the United States Army at Maricopa Wells in 1865 and served five years. He then moved to the Blackwater District, where he lived for fifty-one years. In 1914 Havelena had about seventy acres under cultivation. He did not speak English. His statement was given to Lewis Nelson in May 1914.

15. See note 11 above.
16. On September 2, 1865, the United States Army mustered ninety-seven Maricopa men (six more joined later) and ninety-four Pima men into Companies B and C, respectively. The men served one year as volunteers in the army, securing the fledgling settlements in central Arizona. A number of the men continued to serve as scouts into the 1870s. Lonnie E. Underwood, *The First Arizona Volunteer Infantry, 1865–1866.*
17. See note 12 above.
18. See note 13 above.
19. The Cayah ditch carried 15 cfs and was constructed in 1869. Old Woman's Mouth was constructed in 1881 and carried 20 cfs. Old Indian Ditch was constructed in 1884 but was never put in use.
20. William Wallace was eighty-one years old in 1914. He resided in Casa Blanca before moving to the Blackwater District, where he lived for fifty-two years. At the time of the survey, he had about twenty acres in cultivation, which his granddaughter and her husband irrigated and cultivated. He did not speak English. His statement was given to Lewis Nelson in May 1914.
21. See note 12 above.
22. See note 13 above.
23. Frank Hayes was seventy-one years old at the time of the interview. He was born in Casa Blanca District and at the age of twenty moved to the Blackwater District, where he lived and farmed in 1914. He had about twelve acres under cultivation. He did not speak English. His statement was given to Lewis Nelson in May 1914.
24. See note 12 above.
25. See note 11 above
26. Samuel Scoffer was fifty-eight years old at the time of the interview. He spent eleven years in Casa Blanca before moving to the Blackwater District, where he had about eighteen acres under cultivation. He did not speak English. His statement was given to Lewis Nelson in May 1914.
27. This peace "treaty" was made with the Apaches on May 21, 1872. *ARCIA, 1872,* pp. 154–55, 317–18.
28. The Cayah ditch was on the north side of the Gila River; it was 2.11 miles in length. It once irrigated 235 acres of land before it was abandoned in 1880 due to insufficient water. Southworth, "History," p. 121.
29. The Old Woman's Mouth canal once irrigated 173 acres; it was 1.8 miles in length. It was abandoned in 1905 due to lack of water. Southworth, "History," p. 121.
30. The Pima constructed the Old Indian Ditch (sometimes called the Upper Blackwater ditch) through land that was later homesteaded under the Desert Land Act. It was also cut through very poor ground and consequently was never put into use. The ditch was 6.7 miles in length. Southworth, "History," p. 121, note 1.
31. Jose Pablo was about sixty-five years old at the time of the interview and lived at Sacaton Flats. His statement was given to Rudolph Johnson in October 1914.
32. Cornelius W. Crouse was Pima Indian agent from July 1890 to August 1893. During dry times the Yaqui ditch took water from Blackwater slough. The Yaqui ditch irrigated 44 acres in 1914, although an additional 289 acres had been irrigated earlier. The Yaqui ditch carried 22 cfs of water and headed on the Little Gila River. It was 2.67 miles in length and was constructed in 1891. When the Little Gila River dried up, the ditch received its water exclusively from Blackwater slough. Southworth, "History," pp. 122, 132.

33. Blackwater Lake (or slough) was fed by underground springs, which served to irrigate land downstream. The lake went dry due to groundwater pumping. The name "Blackwater" came from the dark waters of the lake, which according to Pima tradition was home to strange and awesome animals. J. William Lloyd, *Aw-aw-tam Indian Nights: Being the Myths and Legends of the Pimas of Arizona*, p. 241.

34. J. Roe Young served as Pima Indian agent from August 1893 until July 1897.

35. Elwood Hadley was the Pima Indian agent from 1899 to 1902. J. R. Meskimons was the irrigation engineer who conducted the first comprehensive evaluation of agriculture (past and present) in 1904. He was replaced in 1905 by William Code, who conspired with Salt River Valley speculators, including Dr. Alexander John Chandler, to deprive the Pima of their water. Code resigned in disgrace in 1911. David H. DeJong, "A Scheme to Rob Them of Their Land?: Water, Allotment and the Economic Integration of the Pima Reservation, 1902–1921."

36. Juan Enas was fifty-seven years old at the time of the interview. He was born and raised in the Casa Blanca District. His parents moved to the Blackwater District when he was a child. He still lived there in 1914, with about thirty acres of land under cultivation. He did not speak English. His statement was given to Lewis Nelson in May 1914.

37. John D. Walker was part Indian (Peoria) and served in the California Column during the Civil War. He should not be confused with Indian agent John Walker, who was agent for the Gadsden Purchase Indians from 1857 to 1861, based in Tucson. John D. Walker served as the agency farmer until the 1870s.

38. See note 16 above.

39. The Price and Powell ditch was originally called the Montezuma Canal and was upstream from the Pima Reservation. It was reconstructed in 1909. In 1914 some 317 acres of non-Indian land was under this ditch. Southworth, "History," p. 154.

40. Albert Steinfeld of Tucson acquired the ranch just above the reservation. Southworth, "History," p. 155.

41. The Largo land was abandoned in 1889. In 1910 two brothers (the Padillas) leased the Steinfeld land and constructed the Padilla ditch. Two Pima farmers had 78 acres of land in cultivation in 1914 and also irrigated 44 acres on the reservation. Southworth, "History," p. 155.

42. John Hayes was sixty-four years old at the time of the interview. He was born in the Sweetwater District and moved to Sacaton Flats at the age of twenty-seven. In 1914 Hayes had about eighteen acres of land under cultivation. He did not speak English. His statement was given to Lewis Nelson in May 1914.

43. The Sacaton Flats ditch was also known as the Upper Stotonic ditch. It carried 40 cfs of water and headed on the north side of the Little Gila River. At one time the ditch irrigated 1,283 acres of land; due to water deprivation, it irrigated just 899 acres in 1914. The ditch was 3.72 miles in length. Southworth, "History," 132–33.

44. Has Makil was fifty-five years old at the time of the interview. At the age of twenty he left Sweetwater and moved to Sacaton Flats, where he lived in 1914. The flood of 1905 washed away most of his field except for three acres, which he still cultivated. He did not speak English. His statement was given to Lewis Nelson in May 1914.

45. See note 43 above.

46. See note 32 above.

47. Antonitte (Antonito) Azul, the son of former Pima chief Antonio Azul (who served from 1855 to 1911), was sixty-seven years old at the time of the interview and lived in Sacaton. He

was the last head chief and took an active role in Pima political affairs. He spoke English. His statement was given to Lewis Nelson in May 1914.

48. William Bichard (and his brother Nicolas) bought Ammi White's trading post, mill, and storehouses in Sweetwater in the spring of 1867 and then extended his operations in 1869 to include a second trading post in the village of Adamsville, just off-reservation. The Sweetwater (Casa Blanca) flour mill and storehouse were destroyed in the 1868 flood. Bichard rebuilt them in 1869.

49. The Cottonwood irrigated 819 acres in 1914, with an additional 153 previously irrigated acres. The ditch was 2.98 miles in length and had a capacity of 20 cfs of water. Southworth, "History," p. 133.

50. Russell, *The Pima Indians*, pp. 56–57, describes this fight from February 1879 as translated from Major Johnson's calendar stick. A majority of the men from Blackwater conspired to kill "men of a certain faction" from Casa Blanca. The factions met at the Indian school near Santan. The Blackwater delegation killed three men outside the schoolhouse "and could have killed more with their superior weapons" but chose not to pursue the fight further.

51. Amadeo M. Rea, *At the Desert's Green Edge: An Ethnobotany of the Gila River Pima*, pp. 250–51, states that the Pima harvested mescal (or agave) in the Sierra Estrella Mountains. Castetter and Bell, *Pima and Papago Indian Agriculture*, p. 64, state that mescal was used primarily in times of famine. It was also gathered from the mountains near Superior and in the Superstition Mountains. Edward Castetter, Willis H. Bell and A. R. Grove, *The Early Utilization and the Distribution of Agave in the American Southwest*.

52. David H. DeJong, "The Granary of Arizona: Civil War, Settlers and Pima-Maricopa Agriculture: 1860–1869," pp. 229–34.

53. The New Mount Top ditch took its water from the Little Gila River. At one time it irrigated about 182 acres. It carried 10 cfs of water and was 2.29 miles in length. The Pima abandoned the fields under this ditch in 1869. Southworth, "History," 123–24.

54. The Old Maricopa ditch was separate and distinct from the Ancient Maricopa ditch, which was located farther west. The Pima abandoned the Old Maricopa ditch around 1870; the ditch once irrigated about 239 acres of Maricopa farmland from the Little Gila River. It carried 15 cfs of water and was 2.67 miles in length. Southworth, "History," 124.

55. This may be the incident that Juan Thomas described in his calendar stick entry from 1870–71, in which the father of Lewis Nelson was killed. See Calendar of Juan Thomas of Blackwater, 1870–71, in chapter 5.

56. John Manual was fifty-seven years old at the time of the interview. He lived at Santan, where he had about ninety acres under cultivation. Before coming to Santan, he lived at Mount Top Village, although he did not remember how many years he lived there. Manual spoke a little English. His statement was given to Lewis Nelson in May 1914.

57. The earliest attempts to construct this ditch date to 1869. Little work was completed until 1877, when Charles H. Cook surveyed the canal and laid out the fields. It was completed in 1883. In 1914 this ditch (along with the Santan Flood Canal) carried at least 75 cfs of water and irrigated 3,319 acres of land, with an additional 201 previously irrigated acres. The canal was 14.88 miles in length. Southworth, "History," pp. 133–38.

58. The Lower Santan ditch carried 15 cfs of water. After its head was washed away, the ditch was consolidated with the Santan Indian Canal. Southworth, "History," p. 134.

59. Apachoes was seventy years old at the time of the interview and lived in the Sweetwater District all his life. He served as ditch captain and owned a few acres of land. He did not

speak English. His statement was obtained by Charles Southworth and Rudolph Johnson in June 1914.

60. The Ancient Sweetwater (Stotonic) ditch headed on the Little Gila River and carried 28 cfs of water. It is among the oldest ditches in the Gila River Indian Community, believed to extend back to the Spanish era. At one time it irrigated 590 acres and was 6.39 miles in length. In 1914 the Stotonic or Sweetwater ditch (#23) was 6.39 miles in length and irrigated 1,559 acres, with an additional 810 previously irrigated acres. The Stotonic or Sweetwater ditch carried 29 cfs of water and is still in use today as the Casa Blanca Canal. Southworth, "History," pp. 124–25.

61. See note 54 above.

62. Charles H. Cook arrived among the Pima as a schoolteacher in December 1870. He served as a Presbyterian missionary until 1914. He died in Iowa on May 4, 1917, having spent most of his years among the Pima advocating for the return of their water. See Minnie Cook, *Apostle to the Pima Indians: The Story of Charles H. Cook, the First Missionary to the Pimas*, pp. 211–19.

63. See note 57 above.

64. John Makil was sixty years old at the time of the interview. He was born and raised in the Casa Blanca District and farmed about twelve acres in 1914. He did not speak English. His statement was obtained by Lewis Nelson in April 1914.

65. See note 60 above.

66. These are all historic villages in the central portion of the reservation. Sweetwater, Many Ants (Stotonic), Bapchil, and Wet Camp remain today. Mount Top, Sranuka, and Ash Stand (Matai Kek) no longer exist. Cummat Autum refers to the "people from Komatke" or those who live at the base of the Sierra Estrella Mountains. I am indebted to Henrietta Lopez, an Akimel O'otham from the Gila River Indian Community, for these translations.

67. The Southern Pacific Railroad arrived in Maricopa in April 1879 and reached Casa Grande by summer. The Arizona Territorial Legislature authorized the Maricopa and Phoenix Railroad in 1885, and the line across the reservation began in November 1886. The railroad reached Tempe by June 1887 and reached Phoenix on July 4, 1887. In November 1895 the Maricopa and Phoenix Railroad consolidated with the Phoenix, Tempe and Mesa Railway. David F. Myrick, *Railroads of Arizona*, pp. 495–512.

68. Henry Austin was eighty-one years old at the time of the interview. He lived in Casa Blanca and had about ten acres under cultivation. He did not speak English. His statement was given to Lewis Nelson in May 1914.

69. The Stotonic (or Sweetwater) ditch is nearly identical with the Ancient Stotonic except that its head was moved from the Little Gila River to the Gila River. See note 60 above. The Stotonic ditch was known as the Casa Blanca Canal in 1914 and is still known as the Casa Blanca today.

70. This was the old Maricopa and Phoenix Railroad crossing on the Gila River between Maricopa and Tempe.

71. Ammi White arrived as a trader to the Pima in the spring of 1860 and operated the trading post in Casa Blanca along with his partner, Ebenezer Hoyes. White purchased Pima wheat during the Civil War and sold it to the Union; he was captured by the Confederates in April 1862. White later cornered the wheat market on the reservation. He sold out to William Bichard in 1867.

72. These diversions resulted from the founding of Florence by Pima agent Levi Ruggles in 1866 and Adamsville by Ammi White in 1864. Both towns were just upstream from the reservation.

73. Kisto Brown was sixty years old at the time of the interview. In 1914 he lived in Snaketown Village, but he formerly lived in the Bridlestood District. He had been the ditch captain for the Snaketown Canal since the early 1900s. He did not speak English. His statement was given to Charles Southworth and Rudolph Johnson in June 1914.

74. The Old Snaketown canal was on the north side of the Gila River. The original Sratuka village was on the south side of the river, meaning that Pima farmers crossed the river to work in their fields. Having the villages on the south side of the river provided protection against Apache raids. In 1872 most of the villagers moved to the Salt River Valley. Under the Old Snaketown canal were 1,273 acres of previously irrigated land. It had a maximum capacity of 30 cfs of water and was 1.36 miles in length. Southworth, "History," pp. 126–27.

75. The Snaketown ditch, part of an old irrigation system, headed on the Gila River and was 5.64 miles in length. It was on the south side of the Gila River and still irrigated 354 acres in 1914. Southworth, "History," p. 138.

76. The heading of the Old Bridlestood ditch was on the north side of the Gila River. It once irrigated 1,143 acres. The ditch had a capacity of 20 cfs of water and was 1.24 miles long. It was abandoned due to water loss and a shift in its heading on the Gila due to flooding. Southworth, "History," pp. 127–28.

77. Paloma constructed this ditch in 1906 but abandoned it after one season when the head works were left dry by a shift in the channel of the Gila River. It was 1.74 miles long. Southworth, "History," p. 128.

78. Benjamin Thomas was about seventy years old at the time of the interview. He had lived in Casa Blanca all his life and owned and cultivated about twenty acres of land in 1914. He did not speak English. His statement was obtained by Charles Southworth and Rudolph Johnson. No date is given.

79. Just downstream from Sacate most of the ditches served by and the land irrigated under the Santa Cruz ditch washed away during times of flooding. Consequently it was not possible to determine previous acres irrigated under this ditch. Nonetheless, Southworth thought that perhaps 500 acres were irrigated with a 10 cfs ditch. The canal was 3.47 miles in length. Southworth, "History," pp. 128–29.

80. Most of the land under this ditch washed away in flooding of the Gila River. The Pima moved to Gila Crossing in the late 1870s, and the ditch was abandoned by the 1880s due to water loss. An estimated 736 previously irrigated acres lay under this ditch. In later years it was modified and called the Alkali Camp ditch. The ditch was 8 miles in length. Southworth, "History," p. 126.

81. The Ancient Maricopa headed on the north side of the Gila River and was 3.29 miles in length. Most of the land irrigated was washed away in 1914. About 750 acres previously irrigated lay under this ditch. It carried 10 cfs of water. Southworth, "History," p. 129.

82. See note 54 above.

83. Henry F. Dobyns, "Who Killed the Gila?"; Wendy Bigler, "Exploring and Analyzing Historical Native American Irrigated Agriculture Using Geographical Information Systems."

84. George Pablo was sixty-five years old at the time of the interview. He was a prominent member of the Pima tribe. Prior to 1910 he held the position of judge of the Court of Indian Offenses. He lived and farmed in the Cottonwood District and formerly lived in the Old Mount Top District. He did not speak English. His statement was obtained by Charles Southworth and Rudolph Johnson in June 1914.

85. Russell, The Pima Indians, pp. 148–51, discusses Pima textiles, including weaving with cotton.

86. See note 49 above.

87. The Papago or Tohono O'odham were more nomadic than their relatives the Pima. The Tohono O'odham moved their villages from summer cropping sites to winter mountain gathering sites.

88. Pima Boarding School opened in September 1881, and the school farm was in use by 1883. The farm suffered from a lack of water until groundwater pumps were installed in 1901.

89. See DeJong, "A Scheme to Rob Them of Their Land?"

90. In 1904 the United States Indian Service proposed to allot in severalty three acres with water to each Pima and Maricopa. This was part of the government's effort to dissolve tribalism by dividing tribal property in severalty. When allotment occurred at Gila River, 4,869 Pima and Maricopa received two allotments: an "A" allotment with water and a "B" allotment for grazing. Most allotments were random, and many were too impregnated with alkali to be of much agricultural use. Many Pima complained about the allotment process. See note 35 above.

91. Some Pima traded allotments or "bought" the improvements made by others. Lloyd Allison, *The White Man's Friend*.

92. See note 49 above.

93. The Southern Pacific Railroad reached Casa Grande in the summer of 1879. Myrick, *Railroads of Arizona*.

94. See Statement of Ho-ke Wilson (Sweetwater and other Districts) below.

95. This was likely the Lower Santan Canal (see note 58 above), which was abandoned after its head washed away. It was later used as an extension to the Santan Canal. See note 57 above.

96. See note 29 above.

97. See note 28 above.

98. Charles Cook arrived as a schoolteacher/missionary among the Pima in December 1870 and retired in 1914. The school was a mile west of the modern Sacaton Public School. It was on the south side of the Little Gila River.

99. See note 54 above.

100. See note 60 above.

101. The Ooist ditch was also known as the Bapchil ditch. This ditch irrigated 1,937 acres in 1914, with an additional 936 previously irrigated acres. The Ooist had a 14-foot bottom and narrowed downstream to carry 10 cfs of water. It was 5.7 miles long. Southworth, "History," p. 138.

102. See note 74 above.

103. See note 80 above.

104. No information is available on this ditch. It appears to refer to a ditch that branches off from the Snaketown or Sratuka ditch.

105. See note 79 above.

106. The Old Bridlestood (#17) was abandoned about 1889 and was 1.24 miles long. The ditch was rehabilitated (as the Bridlestood Ditch [#16]) and put into use again but was abandoned in the early 1900s due to channel changes in the Gila River. The new ditch was 2.11 miles long. Southworth, "History," pp. 127–28.

107. This was the flood of 1904–5. See Dobyns, "Who Killed the Gila?"; and Bigler, "Exploring and Analyzing Historical Native American Irrigated Agriculture Using Geographical Information Systems."

108. The Sranuka people moved to Gila Crossing in 1877.

109. The Santa Cruz villagers moved around 1875.

110. The Sratukas moved the Salt River in 1872 (Southworth, "History," p. 127). The move was due to scarcity of water, loss of land due to flooding, and a request from Mormon settlers in Lehi that the Pima move into the Salt River Valley to help protect the Mormon settlements from Apache raids. The Salt River Indian Reservation was established by presidential executive order in 1879.

111. See *ARCIA, 1872*, pp. 154–55, 317–18.

112. Ammi White founded Adamsville in 1864. By 1868 it had more than 400 residents. Roger Nichols, "A Miniature Venice: Florence, Arizona, 1866–1910."

113. See note 101 above.

114. Ho-Ke Wilson was about seventy years old at the time of the interview. He lived in the Cottonwood District and had about twenty-five acres in cultivation. He did not speak English. His statement was given to Rudolph Johnson in May 1914.

115. Stone Mortar (Ho Thia Kek) and Kow-vot-ka (meaning different or separate people) villages no longer exist.

116. Russell, *The Pima Indians*, pp. 193–95, discusses mortuary practices among the Pima.

117. Double Buttes is commonly known as Gila Butte. This canal is the Old Snaketown or Sratuka canal.

118. See note 75 above.

119. The wooden plow dominated Pima agriculture between the arrival of Americans in 1848 and about 1860, when steel plows became more readily available. The wooden plow was made from mesquite or ironwood, with a tongue made of cottonwood. A beveled end was covered with an iron or steel shovel and dug 8 to 10 inches into the soil. The Pima were known to ride to Tucson to purchase or repair such shovels for their plows. Russell, *The Pima Indians*, p. 98.

120. See note 49 above.

121. This reference is to the Wing Dam constructed at the mouth of the Little Gila River in 1914. The structure washed away with the 1915 flooding on the Gila River.

122. This trader was William Bichard, who owned the trading post in Sweetwater, near Casa Blanca. See note 48 above.

123. Slurn Vanico was about sixty years old at the time of the interview. He was born in Mount Top Village and moved to Blackwater when he was seven years old. His statement was obtained by Rudolph Johnson in May 1914.

124. This may refer to the Old Santan or Old Stotonic ditch. There is no record of an Old Sacaton Ditch #13.

125. See note 12 above.

126. See note 49 above.

127. See note 119 above.

128. Meguel was one of the oldest Pima interviewed by Southworth, at an estimated age of eighty-six. He was born in the Bapchil settlement and later moved to the Santan District, where he cultivated twenty acres of land with his son-in-law. His statement was given to Rudolph Johnson in June 1914.

129. This was the 1833 flood recorded by Russell, *The Pima Indians*, p. 38. Many Pima saw the flood as punishment for their transgressions. A meteor shower preceded the flood, which the Pima saw as an augury of disaster.

130. This flood occurred in September 1868. The flood destroyed three Pima villages, William and Nicolas Bichard's Sweetwater (Casa Blanca) wheat mill and storehouse, and George Hooper and Company's trading post near Sacaton.

131. See Calendar of Mejoe Jackson, 1870–71, in chapter 5.

132. See note 119 above.

133. See Russell, *The Pima Indians*, pp. 148–51, on textiles.

134. David H. DeJong, "Good Samaritans of the Desert: The Pima-Maricopa Villages as Described in California Emigrant Journals, 1846–1852."

135. See note 54 above.

136. See note 124 above.

137. See note 53 above.

138. For the Santan Canal, see note 57 above. For the Blackwater/Santan battle, see note 50 above.

139. Construction on the Santan Floodwater Canal commenced in 1908 and was completed in 1913. It incorporated parts of the Santan Canal. The canal was 14.88 miles in length in 1914, with a capacity of 300 cfs. The U.S. Reclamation Service began construction on the canal in 1908. Due to political considerations (with a congressional investigation into the activities of the Reclamation Service in the Salt River Valley), the U.S. Indian Irrigation Service took over the work in 1911 and completed constructed two years later. *Report in the Matter of the Investigation of the Salt and Gila Rivers—Reservations and Reclamation Service,* pp. 134–35.

140. William Johnson was sixty-five years old at the time of the interview. He was born in Casa Blanca but later moved to Blackwater, where he owned and cultivated twenty-five acres of land. In 1872 he moved to Cottonwood, where he owned about fifty-five acres of land, fifteen acres of which he cultivated. He also owned about fifteen acres in the Santan settlement, six acres of which he cultivated. He did not speak English. His statement was given to his son Rudolph Johnson in May 1914.

141. George Webb, *A Pima Remembers*, pp. 64–67; Allison, *The White Man's Friend*, pp. 9–15.

142. See note 50 above.

143. Cos-chin was ninety years old at the time of the interview. At the age of fifty-six he left his home in the Sweetwater District and moved to Santan, where he had about twenty acres under cultivation in 1914. He did not speak English. His statement was given to John D. Enis in May 1914.

144. See note 57 above.

145. After Mexican independence from Spain in 1821, Mexican immigration to the north increased. Farmers, ranchers, and miners moved into Papago Country, using their watering holes and taking their land. The Papago resisted this intrusion with an armed conflict in May 1840. Hostilities continued until June 1843. Bernard L. Fontana, *Of Earth and Little Rain: The Papago Indians*, pp. 57–60. See Calendar of Mejoe Jackson, 1842–43, in chapter 5.

146. See DeJong, "Good Samaritans of the Desert."

147. See note 119 above.

148. This was in March 1862. See DeJong, "The Granary of Arizona."

149. See note 55 above.

150. *Ki* is the Pima word for "house." Pima homes were made from cottonwood frame poles attached to four supporting mesquite posts, completed with willow poles set in the

ground, bent over the roof, and tied down. The frame was then covered with brush or straw. The *ki* was 10 to 25 feet in diameter.

151. See note 57 above.

152. Tor White was sixty-five years old at the time of the interview. When he was forty he left his home in the Sweetwater District and moved to Santan, where he cultivated about twenty acres of land. He spoke English. His statement was obtained by John Enis in May 1914.

153. See note 57 above.

154. See note 60 above.

155. W. W. Hill, "Notes on Pima Land Law and Tenure," p. 586.

156. See note 57 above.

157. The length in 1914 was 14.88 miles.

158. Jose Enis was eighty-four years old at the time of the interview. He was born in the Sweetwater District and lived there until he was fifty years old. He then moved to Santan, where he had about ten acres under cultivation. He did not speak English. His statement was given to J. E. Enis in May 1914.

159. See DeJong, "The Granary of Arizona."

160. See note 57 above.

161. See note 139 above. This is the Santan Floodwater Canal.

162. Juan Jose was sixty-eight years old at the time of the interview. He was born in Sweetwater and moved to the Blackwater Island around 1861, farming there for about twenty years. He then moved to Santan, where he lived in 1914. He did not speak English. His statement was given to J. E. Enis in May 1914.

163. See DeJong, "The Granary of Arizona."

164. The Pima cut an estimated 100,000 acres of mesquite wood to sell as fuel in the surrounding off-reservation towns. See David H. DeJong, "Forced to Abandon Their Farms: Water Deprivation and Starvation among the Gila River Pima, 1892–1904," pp. 41–42.

165. Harvier was seventy-two years old at the time of the interview. He lived in the Sweetwater District until about the age of forty-seven and then moved to Santan, where he had about eight acres under cultivation. He did not speak English. His statement was given to J. E. Enis in May 1914.

166. See note 12 above.

167. See DeJong, "The Granary of Arizona."

168. See note 57 above.

169. Juna Osif was sixty-six years old at the time of the interview. He lived in Sweetwater from birth and had about sixteen acres under cultivation. He did not speak English. His statement was given to Lewis Nelson in June 1914.

170. See Russell, *The Pima Indians*, pp. 148–51.

171. See note 69 above.

172. See note 119 above.

173. This area described by Juna Osif was the traditional breadbasket of the Pima villages. Cave Couts, marching with Major Lawrence P. Graham (U.S. Army) through the Pima villages in 1848, described this area as eighteen miles of bottomlands along the river that "far surpass[ed] anything we have ever witnessed for fertility." It represented "a series of the finest fields" he had ever seen. Dobyns, *Hepah, California! The Journal of Cave Johnson Couts*, p. 66.

174. Juan Manuel (Chir-purtke) was sixty-seven years old at the time of the interview. He lived in Alkali Village all his life and had about seven acres under cultivation. He did not speak English. His statement was given to Lewis Nelson in June 1914.

175. See note 80 above.

176. The 1859 Act of Congress establishing the Pima Reservation included the following items for men as gifts for Pima friendship: 444 axes; 618 shovels; 31 handsaws; 706 butcher knives; 516 hoes; 240 sickles; 48 files; 270 harrow teeth; 48 mattocks; 72 whetstones; 15 grindstones and fixtures; 36 hay forks; 36 hammers; 48 iron rakes; 48 trowels; 12 screw drivers; 1 carpenter's shop, with a complete set of tools; 15 plows; 15 sets of plow harnesses; 1 forge, 1 anvil, and 1 vice; 1 set of sledges; 1 cast-steel hand-hammer; 3 pair tongs; 1 set of files; 12 file handles; 36 hatchets; 120 picks and handles; 7 kegs of nails; 9 gross of screws; 1,400 needles; and 1 box sheet tin (for repairing implements). Women received gifts of sewing needles and cloth. The federal government continued this policy of providing gifts of tools into the twentieth century. In 1870 the Pima "officially" had eleven to fifteen dozen axes, shovels, hoes, spades, sickles, and picks. They also had an undetermined number of government-provided steel plows.

177. See note 164 above and table 3.1.

178. Chief Thomas was one of the oldest men who remained in the Old Sranuka District. He was about sixty at the time of the interview and lived in Alkali Camp Village, a mile west of the Old Sranuka Village.

179. See note 80 above.

180. Juan Lagons was forty-eight years old at the time of the interview. He lived at Sacaton Siding District (Old Santa Cruz) until the age of twelve. He then moved to Gila Crossing. He did not speak English. His statement was given to Lewis Nelson in June 1914.

181. All the land under this ditch was irrigated and cultivated within four years. It irrigated 660 acres in 1914 with 8 cfs of water taken from the Gila River; it was 4.9 miles in length. Southworth, "History," p. 140.

182. The fields west of Sacaton Siding were under the Sranuka and Santa Cruz ditches. Both were abandoned in the 1870s due to water loss. The Pima cultivating these fields moved downstream in search of seepage water near Gila Crossing in the late 1870s and early 1880s.

183. James Hollen was fifty-three years of age at the time of the interview. At the age of seventeen he left his home in Sacaton Siding and moved to Gila Crossing, where he cultivated about twenty acres. He did not speak English. His statement was given to Lewis Nelson in June 1914.

184. See note 181 above.

185. Joseph Head was seventy years old at the time of the interview. After residing in the Casa Blanca District, he moved to Gila Crossing, where he lived for forty-one years. Joseph was a historian (calendar stick holder) for his village and irrigated an undetermined amount of land. He did not speak English. His statement was given to Lewis Nelson in June 1914.

186. The Hoover ditch was the first ditch constructed in the Gila Crossing area and was 7.07 miles in length. In 1914 it irrigated 954 acres and carried 12 cfs of water taken from the Gila River. Southworth, "History," p. 140.

187. The John Thomas ditch was on the south side of the Gila River and carried 15 cfs of water. It took two years to construct the ditch and three years to cultivate all the land under it.

Most of the cultivated land washed away with the floods of 1904–5. It still irrigated 587 acres in 1914, with at least 108 previously irrigated acres. The ditch was 4.65 miles long. The Lancisco ditch was a small branch off of the John Thomas. Southworth, "History," pp. 140–41.

188. After the 1904–5 flooding washed away some of the land under the John Thomas, the remaining land was irrigated by the Lancisco ditch. Southworth, "History," p. 141.

189. The Pima constructed the Joseph Head ditch in 1886. It was incorporated into the John Thomas Ditch after the 1904–5 floods. It irrigated 139 acres, with another 30 previously irrigated acres. The ditch had a capacity of 4 cfs of water and was 2.48 miles in length. Southworth, "History," p. 141.

190. Returned boarding school students constructed the Cooperative ditch in 1900 to take advantage of water in the lower Gila. It irrigated 594 acres in 1914, with 390 acres no longer irrigated due to insufficient water. The Cooperation ditch carried 10 cfs of water and was 5.33 miles long. Southworth, "History," pp. 141–42.

191. See note 164 above and table 3.1.

192. David H. DeJong, "Abandoned Little by Little: The 1914 Pima Indian Adjudication Survey, Water Deprivation and Farming on the Pima Reservation."

193. For the Stotonic, see note 69 above. For the Ancient Stotonic, see note 60 above.

194. John Rhodes was forty-nine years old at the time of the interview. He lived in Sranuka until the age of eight, when he and his family moved to Gila Crossing, where he lived and farmed. Rhodes had about twenty-five acres under cultivation. He spoke a little English. His statement was given to Lewis Nelson in May 1914.

195. See note 186 above.

196. See note 187 above.

197. See note 188 above.

198. See note 181 above.

199. See note 189 above.

200. See note 35 above.

201. See note 190 above.

202. Oliver Sanderson was fifty-one years old at the time of the interview. At the age of seventeen he left his home in Sho-nic and moved to Gila Crossing, where he lived and farmed, with about twenty-five acres under cultivation. He spoke a little English.

203. This was the Mass Acumult (clear river). This wetland about four or five miles above the Hollen ditch heading was fed by springs and the underflow in the Gila River, creating a series of lakes or sloughs about six feet deep. Lee, *The Underground Waters of Gila Valley, Arizona*, p. 24.

204. See note 164 above.

CHAPTER 4. FRIENDS OF THE PIMA SPEAK OUT

1. Cook, *Apostle to the Pima Indians*, p. 212.

2. Frederick Grossman served as Pima agent from October 1, 1869, until July 24, 1871. He replaced Levi Ruggles. Ulysses S. Grant appointed Grossman under the president's Peace Policy. Grossman constructed the first permanent government buildings at Sacaton.

3. *Jof quaatom* or *bav quaatom* refers to the Papago (Tohono O'odham) and may mean "dirt eaters" or more specifically "tepary bean eaters." I am indebted to Henrietta Lopez for these translations.

4. Kwahadk (or Kohadk) is a subgroup of the Tohono O'odham Nation. The Kohadk lived south of the Pima villages along Vekol Wash, a tributary of the Santa Cruz River. Historically, they had close ties with both the Pima (with whom they often lived during the winter months) and the Tohono O'odham (with whom they lived in the summer months). Today they reside within the Tohono O'odham Nation. Paul H. Ezell, "A History of the Pima," p. 149.

5. Cook is referring to the Santan Canal (#27), which he surveyed and the Pima constructed between 1877 and 1883.

6. The Roosevelt Reservoir is part of Roosevelt Dam and the Salt River Project. The Pima contributed $100,000 to this project but received no benefit other than excess electrical power. DeJong, "A Scheme to Rob Them of Their Land?"

7. Bigler, "Exploring and Analyzing Historical Native American Irrigated Agriculture Using Geographical Information Systems."

8. Yat-tupt-Autum (Hia-t-ab Autum) means people from the land of the dunes (the Santa Cruz River below the Sierra Estrella Mountains); *volk-est-a-bia* may refer to *vaika* (ditch). Wynkoop apparently uses the term to refer to the John Thomas Ditch; Com-madt-worcho-Autum refers to the people living below (or at the base of) the Sierra Estrella Mountains or those O'odham living at the base of the mountains in the Gila Crossing and *komatke* area; *boy-o-man* (or *wo'o man:* natural pond) means "get it," as in get the water from the ditch, and refers to the Joseph Head ditch. I am indebted to Henrietta Lopez for these translations.

9. This refers to the Old Santa Cruz village. This village moved downstream to the Santa Cruz River in 1875.

10. Herbert Martin was financial clerk for the Pima Agency. He was an outspoken advocate of Pima rights and played an important role in informing Congress about irrigation matters on the reservation.

CHAPTER 5. TWO PIMA CALENDAR STICKS

1. Statement of C. H. Southworth, p. 97.

2. [J. Ross] Brown[e], in his *Adventures in the Apache Country,* page 104, says that the fight between 75 Yuma and Pima took place near Maricopa Wells, in 1857[,] and was witnessed by R. W. Laine (C.H.S.) [Southworth's note].

3. Russell, *The Pima Indians,* pp. 172–73. These races could be up to 20 miles in length and were often intertribal in nature, usually Pima versus Papago. Sometimes two youths would engage in a long distance run by kicking the ball in the air as they ran. The balls were made of mesquite wood.

4. This is the second 1889–90 entry; all such duplicate dates are in the original.

5. Arizona Eastern Railway, now part of the Southern Pacific Railroad [now the Union Pacific Railroad] system [Southworth's note].

6. Edward B. Linnen arrived at Gila River in the winter of 1911 and conducted a series of investigations related to Pima Agency superintendent John B. Alexander. Linnen discovered

falsified payrolls, forged checks, withheld checks, and other evidence of embezzlement. A federal grand jury indicted Alexander and six agency employees on twelve counts of defrauding the United States government. The federal court in Phoenix acquitted Alexander and his associates of all charges. Alexander arrived as superintendent of the Pima Agency in October 1902 and resigned in March 1911. *Annual Report of the Board of Directors of the Indian Rights Association*, pp. 10–18, 19–23.

7. Carlos Montezuma became one of the first Native American physicians in the United States. He was an eminent Chicago doctor who also spent several years in the Dakota working on the Sioux Agencies. He died at Fort McDowell, Arizona, on January 31, 1923, of tuberculosis. Peter Iverson, *Carlos Montezuma and the Changing World of American Indians.*

CHAPTER 6. EPILOGUE

1. J. E. Morrison to U.S. Attorney General G. W. Wickersham, May 31, 1911, RG 75, Records of the Bureau of Indian Affairs, Central Classified Files, National Archives and Records Administration.

2. "An Appeal for Justice—The Pima Indians of Arizona Appeal to Congress and the People of the United States for Redress of Their Wrongs," in "Conserving the Rights of the Pima Indians of Arizona," p. 8.

3. John F. Truesdell, Department of Justice, to C. R. Olberg, Superintendent of Irrigation, Los Angeles, California, dated March 6, 1914, Washington, D.C., C. R. Olberg Letterbox, SCIP Archives.

4. U.S. House of Representatives, *Indians of the United States,* p. 1006; Charles R. Olberg, "Report on Water Rights of Gila River and Feasibility of San Carlos Project" (United States Indian Irrigation Service, 1915), SCIP Archives.

5. DeJong, "'Abandoned Little by Little.'"

6. *San Carlos Irrigation Project: House Report 618*, p. 1; *An Act for the Continuance of Construction Work on the San Carlos Federal Irrigation Project in Arizona and for Other Purposes*, 68 Stat. 475.

7. In 1932 Congress enacted the Leavitt Act (47 Stat. 564), which canceled all irrigation debt of the Pima and other tribes. Congress was made aware by the *Report of Advisors on Irrigation on Indian Reservations* that most Indian irrigation projects had actually benefited non-Indians rather than the Indians they were supposed to assist.

8. *United States v. Gila Valley Irrigation District*, Globe Equity 59 (June 29, 1935).

9. It must be recalled that non-Indian farmers could receive water for up to 160 acres of land per capita, while the Pima and Maricopa were limited to 10 acres. This discriminatory practice limited Indian farmers to a subsistence life, although non-Indian farmers were allowed and encouraged to increase their farmlands and expand their operations. For one argument favoring continued agricultural growth, see Paul H. Ezell with Bernard L. Fontana, "Plants without Water: The Pima-Maricopa Experience."

10. Shelley C. Dudley, "Pima Indians, Water Rights, and the Federal Government: *U.S. v. Gila Valley Irrigation District*," p. 107; Nathan Margold to Secretary of the Interior, dated February 19, 1935, RG 75, Records of the Bureau of Indian Affairs, Central Classified Files: Pima, National Archives and Records Administration.

11. *Gila Valley Irrigation District v. United States,* 118 F2d 507 (1941).
12. *San Carlos Irrigation Project: Annual Report, 1994.*
13. Testimony of George Truman Jones, secretary of the Pima Tribal Council, in U.S. Senate, *Bridge Canyon Project: Hearings before a Subcommittee of the Committee on Public Lands,* p. 196; U.S. Senate, *Bridge Canyon Project: Senate Report 832,* p. 5. Senator Ernest McFarland substantiated the Pima claim that only one of four acres on the reservation could be irrigated.
14. U.S. Senate, *Bridge Canyon Project: Hearings,* pp. 416–17.
15. Simon Rifkind, Special Master, *Arizona v. California Report,* Central Arizona Project Library, p. 256, added: "Furthermore, the claims of the United States to water from the Colorado River for the benefit of Indian reservations are of such great magnitude that failure to adjudicate them would leave a cloud on the legal availability of substantial amounts of mainstream water for use by non-Indian projects."
16. *Arizona Water Commission, First Annual Report, 1970–1971,* Central Arizona Project Library, p. 7. Water requests were as follows:

Entity	Irrigation	Municipal & Industrial	Recreation	Total
Ak-Chin	78,768	—	—	78,768
Fort McDowell	5,000	25,000	—	30,000
Gila River	436,000	—	—	436,000
Salt River	77,000	33,000	—	110,000
Tohono O'odham	394,400	50,000	—	444,400
San Carlos Project	120,000	—	—	120,000
Non-Indian	2,959,162	1,010,575	205,400	4,175,137
Totals	4,070,330	1,118,575	205,400	5,394,305

In addition to these tribes, non-Indian requests came from three individuals, thirteen utility and/or water companies, fifteen cities, nine governmental entities, and twenty-five irrigation districts.

17. *Central Arizona Project Indian Water Projects, Report of the Allocation of CAP Water for Five Applicant Tribes,* Central Arizona Project Library, pp. 3–6.
18. "Indians Convinced of Water Rights Plot," *Arizona Republic,* August 23, 1973.
19. *Federal Register* (40:76), April 18, 1975, p. 17299. The Indian response can be found in "Comments, Suggestions and Objectives regarding Proposed Allocation of Central Arizona Project Water for Indian Use," Central Arizona Project Library.
20. Alexander Lewis, Sr., to Rogers C. B. Morton, April 1, 1975, Central Arizona Project Library; "5 Tribes Weigh Legal Fight to CAP Allocations," *Arizona Republic* April 22, 1975.
21. U.S. Senate, *Indian Water Rights of the Five Central Tribes of Arizona: Hearings before the Committee on Interior and Insular Affairs,* p. 4.
22. Central Arizona Indian Water Resources Act of 1976, *Congressional Record,* April 13, 1976 (122:9), pp. 10644–45. Water would have been allocated for the following acres: Ak-Chin Indian Community, 19,000 acres; Fort McDowell Yavapai Nation, 3,300 acres; Tohono O'odham Nation, 29,500 acres; San Xavier District, 9,000 acres; Salt River Pima-Maricopa Indian Community, 30,500; and Gila River Indian Community, 118,000 acres. The Kennedy bill was designed to force a settlement of Indian water claims prior to a final allocation of

CAP water. The lands to be purchased were in the Wellton-Mohawk Irrigation District in southwestern Arizona. Kennedy targeted these lands under the assumption that it would be less expensive to purchase the land and transfer the water rights rather than construct a "$1 billion" taxpayer-assisted desalting plant to fulfill U.S. obligations to Mexico. *Congressional Record*, June 21, 1976 (122:16), p. 19446. The Pima's claims to the Salt River would not have been affected by the act.

23. "No Friend of Arizona," *Phoenix Gazette*, April 16, 1976, in *Congressional Record* (122:9), p. 11183. Senator Barry Goldwater (R-AZ) staunchly opposed the bill and Kennedy's efforts, going so far as to state that Kennedy deserved "the Golden Fleece Award of the Century" for his efforts. "Hearings Scheduled on Bill Allowing Transfer of Water Rights to 5 Arizona Tribes," *Arizona Republic*, May 22, 1977; and "$2 Billion Price Placed on Indian Water Transfer," *Phoenix Gazette*, May 23, 1977.

24. *Federal Register* (41:202), October 18, 1976, p. 45889.

25. *Gila River Indian Community v. United States*, U.S. District Court (1977), p. 1; "Indians File Suit Seeking 70% of State's CAP Water," *Arizona Republic*, January 5, 1977.

26. *Arizona v. San Carlos Apache Tribe* and *Montana v. Northern Cheyenne Tribe*, 103 Supreme Court 3201 (1983); "State Courts Can Try Indian Water Cases," *Arizona Republic*, July 7, 1983; "Historic Water Decision," *Arizona Republic*, July 7, 1983.

27. "Concern over CAP May Speed Indian Talks," *Arizona Republic*, July 25, 1979; Memo from Leo M. Krulitz to Secretary Cecil Andrus, n.d. file: Arizona Indian Water Rights, Central Arizona Project Library; Thomas W. Frederick, Associate Solicitor, to Leo M. Krulitz, Solicitor, June 15, 1979, file: Arizona Indian Water Rights, Central Arizona Project Library. The Department of the Interior was forcing local water users to come to the table by denying a $7.8 million loan to the Roosevelt Water Conservation District (RWCD) and investigating whether the Salt River Project should enlarge its borders to include part of the Gila River Indian Community. Associate interior solicitor Thomas Frederick concluded that non-CAP water would reduce the need for continued negotiations with the RWCD and Salt River Project to provide water to the Indians.

28. "U.S. Accused of Pressuring State on Indian Water Rights," *Arizona Republic*, July 14, 1979; "Concern over CAP May Speed Indian Talks," *Arizona Republic*, July 25, 1979.

29. "Interior Secretary Is Delaying Delivery of CAP Water, 4 Congressmen Charge," *Arizona Republic*, July 30, 1979. Arizona Republicans Barry Goldwater, John J. Rhodes, Eldon Rudd, and Bob Stump signed the letter to the secretary. Senator Dennis DeConcini (D-AZ) and Representative Morris Udall (D-AZ) did not, believing it would not help the situation.

30. The four AMAs were Prescott, Phoenix, Pinal, and Tucson. A fifth AMA was added in 1994 for Santa Cruz County.

31. "Evaluation of Sewage Effluent Usage on Arizona Indian Reservations under CAP Conditions," Central Arizona Project Library, pp. 1–11.

32. *Federal Register* (45:155), August 8, 1980, p. 52940; *Federal Register* (45:239), December 10, 1980, p. 81268. The Gila River Indian Community argued that all land with San Carlos Irrigation Project rights, whether developed or not, should be irrigated with CAP water.

33. *Federal Register* (45:239), December 10, 1980, p. 81272.

34. "Arizona Files Suit to Block Andrus on Water Shares," *Arizona Republic*, December 2, 1980. Senator Dennis DeConcini suggested that the lawsuit would be dropped if incoming secretary James Watt would remove the Indian priority and require tribes to accept effluent in times of shortages. "DeConcini Seeks CAP Compromise," *Arizona Republic*,

December 20, 1980. The lawsuit was dropped in March 1981, even though Watt made no concessions. Representative Morris Udall had much to do with this, because he believed the lawsuit to be "a mistake." Udall thought the Indians could be induced to accept effluent by offering money. "Udall Says Legislation Could Solve Indians' CAP Problems," *Tucson Daily Citizen*, January 13, 1981.

35. "Tribes Sign CAP Pacts before Judge Can Act," *Arizona Republic*, December 13, 1980.
36. "Draft Environmental Impact Statement, Water Allocation and Water Service Contracting, Central Arizona Project, Volume 1," Central Arizona Project Library, pp. 1–3.
37. "CAP Water Allotment 'Irrational,' Tribe Says," *Arizona Republic*, February 19, 1983. The tribe objected to the quantity, quality, cost, and poor monitoring of such water.
38. *Federal Register* (48:58), March 24, 1983, p. 12452. The Pima continued to meet with Salt River Valley cities to solicit their support in encouraging the Interior Department to drop its mandatory exchange clause. Chandler, Mesa, and Gilbert all agreed and sent letters in support of the tribe. This urban support largely grew from self-interest, as cities that exchanged effluent for Indian CAP water would have been forced to reduce their M & I CAP water supply by a like amount. In effect, the cities, which were finding urban uses for the water, would have given up such effluent without a tangible benefit. In November 1983 Arizona governor Rose Mofford informed interior secretary Donald Hodel that Arizona would agree to drop the mandatory exchange.
39. "Gila River Indian Community Master Plan Report for Land and Water Use," Central Arizona Project Library, pp. 5-9, 5-15, 5-52 to 5-57. The report set a lofty goal and was primarily intended to serve a political function of encouraging water settlement.
40. "Indian Water Rights Claims: Settlement Update." Central Arizona Project Library.
41. White had argued in March 1992 that no other "CAP contract had been held hostage to settlement of its rights." The Central Arizona Water Conservation District Board had opposed the provision because it feared that Pima-contracted water would not be credited to its Winters reserved rights. Dropping the mandatory effluent exchange would enable the Pima to effect any potential water exchange on more agreeable terms.
42. "Central Arizona Project Water Delivery Contract between the United States and the Gila River Indian Community," Central Arizona Project Library. Contracted water may only be used on lands deemed arable by the secretary. Furthermore, the tribe was required to accept CAP water in exchange for Gila River water that would be used in the upper Gila River system.
43. The CAWCD Board recognized that the Pima had legitimate claims to the waters of the Gila, Salt, and Verde rivers and feared that a court might order it to use CAP water to satisfy Indian claims or that the secretary of the interior might do it unilaterally. Grady Gammage, Jr., "Steiger's Rantings on Water Need a Dose of Reality," *Tribune Newspapers*, March 8, 1998.
44. "Draft Programmatic Environmental Impact Statement: Pima-Maricopa Irrigation Project." Central Arizona Project Library.
45. "CAP Cost, Shift to Tribes Discussed," *Casa Grande Dispatch*, April 15, 1998.
46. Rita Pearson, "Gila River Indian Community, Issues concerning Claimed Water Rights," Central Arizona Project Library. Cities in the Phoenix metropolitan area understood that if they joined in the negotiation process they could help frame a settlement that would be less injurious to their interests. George Britton, deputy city manager of the City of Phoenix, argued in 2004 that "virtually no congressional member is going to support a

settlement that is going to do damage to the existing domestic water supply." Anything else would result in the "iron fist" of the cities "causing tremendous political agitation." Quoted in Bonnie G. Colby, John E. Thorson, and Sarah Britton, *Negotiating Tribal Water Rights: Fulfilling Promises in the Arid West*, p. 47.

47. *Federal Register* (64:146), July 30, 1999, p. 41457. The reallocation to the Gila River Indian Community would be as follows: 102,000 acre-feet from the federal government; 17,800 acre-feet relinquished by the Harquahala Valley Irrigation District; 18,600 acre-feet from the Roosevelt Water Conservation District; and 17,000 acre-feet from ASARCO (American Smelting and Refining Company). All of these would be reallocated to the Gila River Indian Community as part of a comprehensive settlement of all claims.

48. *In re the General Adjudication of All Rights to Use Water in the Gila River System and Source*, Arizona Supreme Court Nos. WC-90-0001-IR through WC-90-0007-IR Consolidated and WC-79-0001 through WC-79-0004, Maricopa County Nos. W-1, W-2, W-3, and W-4 Consolidated (November 19, 1999). Seven months later John E. Thorson, special master in the Gila River General Stream Adjudication, recommended that the court limit Pima claims to the Gila River. Thorson argued that Indian allottees' water rights were settled in the 1935 Gila Decree. Case Nos. W1-203, Report of the Special Master, Appendix B, Proposed Order, Maricopa County Superior Court, Phoenix, Arizona, June 30, 2000, in ibid. Six months later Thorson issued a second recommendation, encouraging the court to reject Gila River Indian Community claims to Salt River water other than the 1,490 acres of reservation land that had rights under the Haggard Decree of 1904. Case Nos. W1-203, Second Report of the Special Master, Maricopa County Superior Court, Phoenix, Arizona, December 28, 2000, in ibid.

49. An Act Making Supplemental Appropriations for the Fiscal Year Ending September 30, 2001, 115 Stat. 155. Kyl politically tied the secretary's hands, because Babbitt refused to assure him that he would not reallocate water absent a water settlement for Gila River.

50. A Bill to Provide for Adjustments to the Central Arizona Project in Arizona and for Other Purposes, S. 3231, 106th Congress, 2nd Session, October 24, 2000.

51. *In re the General Adjudication of All Rights to Use Water in the Gila River System and Source* (W-1-203), March 7, 2003. The court relied on the special master in this ruling. In March 2005 the U.S. District Court in Tucson accepted the argument of the Gila River Indian Community that the subsurface flow and surface flow of a river are connected. For the first time the subflow of the Gila River was covered by the Gila Decree. *United States v. Gila Valley Irrigation District*, No. CV31-0059-TUC-SRB (March 29, 2005).

52. "Gila River Tribe Approves Water Settlement with US," *Arizona Republic*, February 6, 2003. The settlement agreement is more than 2,600 pages in length and includes thirty-five parties: the Gila River Indian Community, the United States, the State of Arizona, thirteen irrigation districts, sixteen cities, two corporations, and one water company. The bills were introduced in both houses on February 25, 2003.

53. The Arizona Water Settlements Act of 2004, Public Law 108-360, 118 Stat. 3479 (2004).

54. *Federal Register* (72:240), Friday, December 14, 2007, pp. 71143–45.

55. Sources of water include an average of 156,700 acre-feet of groundwater (existing), 125,000 acre-feet of Gila Decree water (existing), 5,900 acre-feet of Haggard Decree water (existing), 173,100 acre-feet of CAP Indian priority water (existing), 18,600 acre-feet of Roosevelt Water Conservation District (RWCD) non-Indian agriculture CAP water (new), 4,500 acre-feet of RWCD surface water (new), 18,100 acre-feet of Harquahala Valley

Irrigation District non-Indian agriculture CAP water (new), 17,000 acre-feet of ASARCO non Indian agriculture CAP water (new), 20,000 acre-feet of Salt River Project stored water (new), 4,500 acre-feet of Chandler reclaimed water (new), 2,230 acre-feet of Chandler premium exchange water (new), 5,870 acre-feet of Mesa reclaimed water (new), and 102,000 acre-feet of CAP non-Indian agricultural water (new), for a total of 653,500 acre-feet of water. The Gila River Indian Community then exchanged 8,960 acre-feet of its CAP water for 11,200 acre-feet of Chandler reclaimed water and 4,500 acre-feet of Chandler "contributed reclaimed water." In addition, the tribe exchanged 23,540 acre-feet of its CAP water with the City of Mesa for 29,400 acre-feet of Mesa reclaimed water.

BIBLIOGRAPHY

SECONDARY SOURCES

Allison, Lloyd. *The White Man's Friend*. Tucson: University of Arizona Special Collections, 1974.

August, Jack L., Jr. "Carl Hayden's Indian Card: Environmental Politics and the San Carlos Reclamation Project." *Journal of Arizona History* 33:4 (Winter 1992): 397–422.

Berkhofer, Robert F. *The White Man's Indian: Images of the American Indians from Columbus to the Present*. New York: Knopf, 1978.

Bigler, Wendy. "Exploring and Analyzing Historical Native American Irrigated Agriculture Using Geographical Information Systems." *Historical Geography* 33 (2005): 11–32.

Bloom, Lansing B., ed. "From Lewisburg to California in 1849: Notes from the Diary of William H. Chamberlin." *New Mexico Historical Quarterly* 2 (April 1945): 144–80.

Bolton, Herbert E. *Anza's California Expeditions*. 4 vols. Berkeley: University of California Press, 1930.

———, ed. *Father Eusebio Kino's Historical Memoir*. Vol. 1. Cleveland: Arthur H. Clark & Company, 1913.

———. *Rim of Christendom*. New York: MacMillan Company, 1936. Reprint. Tucson: University of Arizona Press, 1984.

Browne, J. Ross. *Adventures in the Apache Country*. Tucson: University of Arizona Press, 1974.

Carlson, Leonard A. *Indians, Bureaucrats, and Land*. Westport, Conn.: Greenwood Press, 1981.

Castetter, Edward, and Willis H. Bell. *Pima and Papago Indian Agriculture*. Albuquerque: University of New Mexico Press, 1942.

Castetter, Edward, Willis H. Bell, and A. R. Grove. *The Early Utilization and the Distribution of Agave in the American Southwest*. University of New Mexico Bulletin, Biological Series 5:4. Albuquerque: University of New Mexico Press, 1938.

Clarke, Dwight, ed. *The Original Journals of Henry Smith Turner with Stephen Watts Kearny to New Mexico and California, 1846–1847*. Norman: University of Oklahoma Press, 1966.

Colby, Bonnie G., John E. Thorson, and Sarah Britton. *Negotiating Tribal Water Rights: Fulfilling Promises in the Arid West*. Tucson: University of Arizona Press, 2005.

Cook, Minnie. *Apostle to the Pima Indians: The Story of Charles H. Cook, the First Missionary to the Pimas*. Tiburon, Calif.: Omega Books, 1976.

Coues, Elliot, ed. *On the Trail of a Spanish Pioneer: The Diary and Itinerary of Francisco Garcés in His Travels through Sonora, Arizona, and California, 1775–1776*. New York: F. P. Harper, 1900.

DeJong, David H. "'Abandoned Little by Little': The 1914 Pima Indian Adjudication Survey, Water Deprivation and Farming on the Pima Reservation." *Agricultural History* 81:1 (Winter 2007): 36–69.

———. "An Equal Chance?: The Pima Indians and the Florence–Casa Grande Project, 1916–1924." *Journal of Arizona History* 45:1 (Spring 2003): 63–102.

———. "Forced to Abandon Their Farms: Water Deprivation and Starvation among the Gila River Pima, 1892–1904." *American Indian Culture and Research Journal* 28:3 (Winter 2003): 29–56.

———. "Good Samaritans of the Desert: The Pima-Maricopa Villages as Described in California Emigrant Journals, 1846–1852." *Journal of the Southwest* 47:3 (Fall 2003): 457–96.

———. "The Granary of Arizona: Civil War, Settlers and Pima-Maricopa Agriculture: 1860–1869." *Journal of Arizona History* 48:3 (Fall 2007): 221–56.

———. "A Scheme to Rob Them of Their Land?: Water, Allotment and the Economic Integration of the Pima Reservation, 1902–1921." *Journal of Arizona History* 44:2 (Summer 2003): 99–132.

———. "See the New Country: The Removal Controversy and Pima-Maricopa Water Rights, 1869–1879." *Journal of Arizona History* 33:4 (Winter 1992): 367–96.

de Vattel, Emmerich. *The Law of Nations or Principles of the Law of Nature: Applied to the Conduct and Affairs of Nations, Book I.* Philadelphia: T. & J. W. Johnson & Company, 1883.

"Diary of Judge Benjamin Hayes' Journey Overland from Socorro to Warner's Ranch, from October 31, 1849, to January 14, 1850." MS 341, Arizona Historical Society, Tucson.

Dobyns, Henry F., ed. *Hepah, California! The Journal of Cave Johnson Couts from Monterey, Nuevo León, Mexico, to Los Angeles, California, during the Years 1848–49.* Tucson: Arizona Pioneers Historical Society, 1961.

———. "Who Killed the Gila?" *Journal of Arizona History* 19:4 (Winter 1978): 17–30.

Dudley, Shelley C. "Pima Indians, Water Rights, and the Federal Government: *U.S. v. Gila Valley Irrigation District.*" Master's thesis, Department of History, Arizona State University, 1996.

Dunbar, Robert G. *Forging New Rights in Western Water.* Lincoln: University of Nebraska Press, 1983.

Dunne, Peter Masten, ed. *Jacobo Sedelmayr, 1744–1751: Missionary, Frontiersman, Explorer in Arizona and Sonora, Four Original Manuscripts.* Tucson: Arizona Pioneer's Historical Society, 1955.

Ezell, Paul H. *The Hispanic Acculturation of the Gila River Pima.* American Anthropologist 63:5, Part 2 (1961). Menasha, Wisc.: American Anthropological Association.

———. "History of the Pima." In *Handbook of North American Indians,* vol. 10, ed. Alfonzo Ortiz, 149–60. Washington, D.C.: Smithsonian Institution, 1983.

Ezell, Paul H., with Bernard L. Fontana. "Plants without Water: The Pima-Maricopa Experience." *Journal of the Southwest* 36:4 (Winter 1994): 311–92.

Fontana, Bernard L. *Of Earth and Little Rain: The Papago Indians.* Flagstaff, Ariz.: Northland Press, 1982.

Goetzmann, William H. *Exploration and Empire: A History of the Exploration of the American West from 1805 to 1900 Which Reveals the Impact of the Great Adventure on the Whole American Culture.* Reprint. New York: Vintage Books, 1972.

Golder, Frank Alfred. *The March of the Mormon Battalion Taken from the Journal of Henry Standage.* New York: Century Company, 1928.

Goodman, Jake B., III., ed. *Personal Recollections of Harvey Wood.* Pasadena, Calif.: privately printed, 1955.

Guiteras, Eusebio, ed. and trans. *Rudo Ensayo.* Records 5:2. Philadelphia: American Catholic Historical Society, 1894. Reprint. Tucson: Arizona Silhouettes, 1951.

Hackenberg, Robert A. "Pima and Papago Ecological Adaptations." In *Handbook of North American Indians*, vol. 10, ed. Alfonzo Ortiz, 161–77. Washington, D.C.. Smithsonian Institution, 1983.

Hammond, George P., and Edward D. Howes, eds. *Overland to California on the Southwestern Trail, 1849: The Diary of Robert Eccleston*. Berkeley: University of California Press, 1950.

Hannan, Anna Raschall, ed. *The Adventures of Charles Edward Pancoast on the American Frontier: A Quaker Forty-Niner*. Philadelphia: University of Pennsylvania Press, 1930.

Hays, Samuel P. *Conservation and the Gospel of Efficiency: The Progressive Conservation Movement, 1890–1920* (1959). New York: Atheneum Press, 1980.

Hill, W. W. "Notes on Pima Land Law and Tenure." *American Anthropologist* 38 (1936): 586–89.

Hoxie, Frederick E. *A Final Promise: The Campaign to Assimilate the Indians, 1880–1920*. Cambridge: Cambridge University Press, 1992.

Hurt, R. Douglas. *Indian Agriculture in America: Prehistory to the Present*. Lawrence: University Press of Kansas, 1987.

Iverson, Peter. *Carlos Montezuma and the Changing World of American Indians*. Albuquerque: University of New Mexico Press, 1982.

Jefferson, Thomas. "Notes on the State of Virginia" and "Letters." In *Thomas Jefferson: Autobiography, Notes on the State of Virginia, Public and Private Papers, Addresses, Letters*, ed. Merrill D. Peterson. New York: Viking Press 1984.

Klyza, Christopher McGrory. *Who Controls Public Lands?: Mining, Forestry, and Grazing Policies, 1870–1990*. Chapel Hill: University of North Carolina Press, 1996.

Lewis, David Rich. *Neither Wolf Nor Dog: American Indians, Environment, and Agrarian Change*. New York: Oxford University Press, 1994.

Limerick, Patricia. *The Legacy of Conquest: The Unbroken Past of the American West*. New York: W. W. Norton & Company, 1987.

Lloyd, J. William. *Aw-aw-tam Indian Nights: Being the Myths and Legends of the Pimas of Arizona*. Westfield, N.J.: Lloyd Group, 1911.

Manje, Juan Mateo. *Unknown Arizona and Sonora, 1693–1721, from the Francisco Fernández del Castillo Version of Luz De Tierra Incognita*. Ed. Harry Karns and Associates. Tucson: Arizona Silhouettes, 1954.

McCool, Daniel. *Command of the Waters: Iron Triangles, Western Water Development, and Indian Water*. Tucson: University of Arizona Press, 1994.

McDonnell, Janet. *The Dispossession of the American Indians, 1887–1934*. Bloomington: University of Indiana Press, 1991.

Meeks, Eric V. "The Tohono O'odham, Wage Labor, and Resistant Adaptation, 1900–1930." *Western Historical Quarterly* 34:4 (2003): 468–89.

Morgan, Lewis Henry. *Ancient Society or Research in the Lines of Human Progress from Savagery through Barbarism to Civilization*. New York: Henry Holt & Company, 1877.

Myrick, David F. *Railroads of Arizona*. Berkeley: Howell-North Books, 1975.

Nash, Gerald D. *The Federal Landscape: An Economic History of the Twentieth-Century West*. Tucson: University of Arizona Press, 1999.

Nichols, Roger. "A Miniature Venice: Florence, Arizona, 1866–1910." *Journal of Arizona History* 16:4 (Winter 1975): 335–55.

Nicholson, John, ed. *The Arizona of Joseph Pratt Allyn*. Tucson: University of Arizona Press, 1974.

Otis, D. *The Dawes Act and the Allotment of Indian Lands*. Ed. Francis Prucha. Norman: University of Oklahoma Press, 1973.

Perry, Anna M., ed. *Travels in Mexico and California: Comprising a Journal of a Tour from Brazos Santiago, through Central Mexico, by Way of Monterey, Chihuahua, the Country of the Apaches, and the River Gila, to the Mining Districts of California.* College Station: Texas A&M University Press, 1988.

Pisani, Donald. *Water and American Government: The Reclamation Bureau, National Water Policy, and the West, 1902–1935.* Berkeley: University of California Press, 2002.

Powell, John Wesley. *Report on the Lands of the Arid West, with a More Detailed Account of the Lands of Utah.* Washington, D.C.: Government Printing Office, 1879.

Prucha, Francis Paul. *American Indian Treaties: The History of a Political Anomaly.* Berkeley: University of California Press, 1994.

———. *The Great White Father: The United States Government and the American Indians.* Lincoln: University of Nebraska Press, 1986.

Ravesloot, John. "The Anglo American Acculturation of the Gila River Pima, Arizona: The Mortuary Evidence." Paper presented at the 25th Annual Conference on Historical and Underwater Archaeology, 1992.

Rea, Amadeo M. *At the Desert's Green Edge: An Ethnobotany of the Gila River Pima.* Tucson: University of Arizona Press 1997.

Reisner, Marc. *Cadillac Desert: The American West and Its Disappearing Water.* New York: Penguin Books 1986.

Russell, Frank. *The Pima Indians.* U.S. Bureau of American Ethnology, Twenty-sixth Annual Report, 1904–5. Washington, D.C.: Government Printing Office, 1908.

Sauder, Robert A. *The Yuma Reclamation Project: Irrigation, Indian Allotment, and Settlement along the Lower Colorado River.* Reno: University of Nevada Press, 2009.

Schoolcraft, Henry Rowe. *The American Indians, Their History, Condition and Prospects, from Original Notes and Manuscripts.* Buffalo: George H. Derby & Company, 1853.

Southworth, Charles. "A Pima Calendar Stick." *Arizona Historical Review* 4:2 (July 1931) 44–51.

Smith, Karen L. "The Campaign for Water in Central Arizona: 1890–1903." *Arizona and the West* 23:2 (1981): 127–48.

Stegner, Wallace. *Beyond the Hundredth Meridian* (1953). Reprint. New York: Penguin Books, 1992.

Underwood, Lonnie E. *The First Arizona Volunteer Infantry, 1865–1866.* Tucson: Roan Horse Press, 1983.

Webb, George. *A Pima Remembers.* Tucson: University of Arizona Press, 1959.

White, Richard. *Roots of Dependency: Subsistence, Environment, and Social Change among the Choctaws, Pawnees, and Navajos.* Lincoln: University of Nebraska Press, 1983.

Wilkinson, Charles F. *Crossing the Next Meridian: Land, Water, and the Future of the West.* Washington, D.C.: Island Press, 1992.

Wilson, John P. "Peoples of the Middle Gila: A Documentary History of the Pimas and Maricopas, 1500s–1945." Report No. 77. Gila River Indian Community, 1997.

Wolcott, Marjorie Tisdale, ed. *Pioneer Notes from the Diaries of Judge Benjamin Hayes, 1849–1875.* Los Angeles: privately printed, n.d.

Woodson, M. Kyle. "A Research Design for the Study of Prehistoric and Historic Irrigation Systems in the Middle Gila Valley, Arizona." P-MIP Technical Report No. 203-10. Gila River Indian Community, Cultural Resource Management Program, Sacaton, Arizona, 2003.

Worster, Donald. *Rivers of Empire: Water and Aridity and the Growth of the American West.* New York: Pantheon Books, 1985.

Zarbin, Earl. "Desert Land Schemes: William J. Murphy and the Arizona Canal Company." *Journal of Arizona History* 42:2 (Summer 2001): 155–80.

ARCHIVAL SOURCES

Arizona State Museum Library Archives (Tucson)

Hackenberg, Robert A., to William H. Kelly, dated August 30, 1962, Tucson, Arizona. A-690.
Southworth, C. H. "Statements by Pima Indians Regarding Irrigation on the Gila River Indian Reservation." A-690.
Southworth, C. H., to Mr. Odd S. Halseth, dated March 9, 1931, San Carlos Irrigation and Drainage District, Florence, Arizona. A-690.

Central Arizona Project Library (Phoenix)

Arizona Water Commission, First Annual Report, 1970–1971. Phoenix: Arizona Water Commission, 1971.
Case Nos. W1-203, Report of the Special Master, Appendix B. Proposed Order, Maricopa County Superior Court, Phoenix, Arizona, June 30, 2000.
Case Nos. W1-203, Second Report of the Special Master. Maricopa County Superior Court, Phoenix, Arizona, December 28, 2000.
Central Arizona Project Indian Water Projects, Report of the Allocation of CAP Water for Five Applicant Tribes. Phoenix, Arizona, July 7, 1972.
"Central Arizona Project Water Delivery Contract between the United States and the Gila River Indian Community." Phoenix, Arizona, October 22, 1992.
"Comments, Suggestions and Objectives regarding Proposed Allocation of Central Arizona Project Water for Indian Use." In *Indian Water Rights of the Five Central Arizona Indian Tribes.* Phoenix: Five Central Arizona Indian Tribes, 1975.
"Draft Environmental Impact Statement, Water Allocation and Water Service Contracting, Central Arizona Project, Volume 1." U.S. Bureau of Reclamation, Lower Colorado Region in Cooperation with the Bureau of Indian Affairs, U.S. Department of Interior, December 1, 1981.
"Draft Programmatic Environmental Impact Statement: Pima-Maricopa Irrigation Project." Prepared for the U.S. Department of the Interior, Bureau of Reclamation—Lead Agency and Bureau of Indian Affairs—Cooperating Agency. Prepared by EcoPlan Associates, Inc., October 1996.
"Evaluation of Sewage Effluent Usage on Arizona Indian Reservations under CAP Conditions." Bureau of Indian Affairs, Phoenix Area Office, Trust Protection Office, October 1980.
File Folder "Arizona Indian Water Rights." Frederick, Thomas W., Associate Solicitor, to Leo M. Krulitz, Solicitor, dated June 15, 1979.
"Gila River Indian Community Master Plan Report for Land and Water Use." Prepared by Franzoy Corey Engineers and Architects, Phoenix, Arizona, November 1985.
"Indian Water Rights Claims: Settlement Update." Arizona Department of Water Resources, Phoenix, Arizona, May 12, 1994.
Lewis, Alexander, Sr., Sacaton, Arizona, to Rogers C. B. Morton, Secretary of the Interior, Washington, D.C., April 1, 1975.

Memo from Leo M. Krulitz to Secretary Cecil Andrus, n.d. File: Arizona Indian Water Rights.
Pearson, Rita. "Gila River Indian Community, Issues concerning Claimed Water Rights."
    October 1, 1998.
Rifkind, Simon. Special Master. *Arizona v. California Report*. December 5, 1960.

National Archives and Records Administration (Washington, D.C.)

RG 48, M1070. Reports of Inspections of the Field Jurisdiction of the Office of Indian Affairs,
    1873–1900. Rolls 35, 36.
RG 75, M234. Letters Received by the Office of Indian Affairs, 1824–81. Rolls 2, 3, 19.
RG 75, M734. Records of the Arizona Superintendency of Indian Affairs, 1863–73. Rolls 3, 4, 8.
RG 75, M1011. Superintendents Annual Narrative and Statistical Reports, 1907–38. Records of
    the Bureau of Indian Affairs. Rolls 104, 105.
RG 75, T21. Records of the New Mexico Superintendency, 1849–80 (Letters Received from
    the Agencies, 1859–60). Roll 4.
RG 75. Irrigation Division, General Correspondence, 1901–31.
RG 75. Letters Received, Indian Division, Office of Indian Affairs.
RG 75. Records of the Bureau of Indian Affairs, Central Classified Files, 1907–39. Pima.
RG 75. Records of the Bureau of Indian Affairs, Records of the Irrigation Division, Reports
    and Related Records, 1891–1946. Gila River Project.
RG 393. Records of the U.S. Army Continental Commands, 1821–1920. M1120 (Fort Mojave,
    Letters Sent and Received, 1859–90). Roll 6.

Pinal County Historical Society (Florence, Arizona)

File Folder "Irrigation in the Florence District." Handwritten report of C. H. Southworth on
    the San Carlos Water Supply, n.d. Florence, Arizona.

San Carlos Irrigation Project (SCIP) Archives (Coolidge, Arizona)

"Gila River Priority of Irrigated Acres, Charts #1–4." United States Indian Service, Irrigation,
    January 20, 1926.
Merritt, E.B. to Charles Curtis, dated March 24, 1916, Washington, D.C.
Olberg, C. R. Letterbox. From Central Office to Olberg, 1913–14.
Olberg, Charles R. "Report on Water Rights of Gila River and Feasibility of San Carlos Proj-
    ect." *Indians of the United States*. (United States Indian Irrigation Service 1915) 1006.
Southworth, C. H. Letterbox, Historical Correspondence, 1914–16.

Southworth Family Files (Courtesy of Robert Southworth, Scottsdale, Arizona,
originals in the Western History Research Center, Laramie, Wyoming)

"Appropriation Is Double for Fort Hall Project." *Pocatello Tribune*, September 15, 1918.
Clark, Fred C., Jr., to Mrs. Clay Southworth, dated February 11, 1963, Brigham City, Utah.
Clotts, Herbert W., to C. H. Southworth, dated December 8, 1936, Los Angeles, California.
Dietz, H. W., to the Commissioner of Indian Affairs, dated March 4, 1920, Salt Lake City.
Gressley, Gene M., Director of the Western History Research Center, to Mrs. Clay H.
    Southworth, dated May 26, 1966, Laramie, Wyoming.

Greesley, Gene M., Director of the Western History Research Center, to Mrs. Clay H.
Southworth, dated July 21, 1966, Laramie, Wyoming.
Lee, H. Rex, Acting Commissioner of Indian Affairs, to Clay H. Southworth, dated July 26,
1951, Washington, D.C.
Myers, Dillon S., to Ralph M. Gelvin, dated September 12, 1952, Washington, D.C.
Peel, Roy V., Director of the Bureau of the Census, to Clay H. Southworth, dated April 25,
1952, Department of Commerce, Bureau of the Census, Washington, D.C.
Southworth, C. H., to Commissioner of Indian Affairs through Major C. R. Olberg, dated
December 10, 1928, San Carlos, Arizona.
Southworth, C. H., to Major C. R. Olberg, dated April 14, 1924, Sacaton Diversion Dam.
Southworth, C. H., to Randall Henderson, editor of the *Desert Magazine*, dated May 2, 1942,
Washington, D.C.
Southworth, Clay H. Employment Biography.
Southworth, Robert H. Interview with author. Scottsdale, Arizona, November 13, 2007.

COURT RULINGS

Arizona v. San Carlos Apache Tribe. 103 Supreme Court 3201 (1983).
George Lobb v. Peter Avenente et al. Pinal County Superior Court (1916).
Gila River Indian Community v. United States. U.S. District Court (1977) (filed but no decision
rendered).
Gila Valley Irrigation District v. United States. 118 F2d 507 (1941).
In re the General Adjudication of All Rights to Use Water in the Gila River System and Source.
Arizona Supreme Court Nos. WC-90-0001-IR through WC-90-0007-IR Consolidated
and WC-79-0001 through WC-79-0004, Maricopa County Nos. W-1, W-2, W-3, and W-4
Consolidated (November 19, 1999).
Lone Wolf v. Hitchcock. 187 U.S. 553 (1903).
Montana v. Northern Cheyenne Tribe. 103 Supreme Court 3201 (1983).
*The United States of America as Guardian of Chief Charley Juan Saul and Cyrus Sam, Maricopa
Indians, and 400 Other Maricopa Indians Similarly Situated, v. Haggard et al.* Cause No. 19 in
District Court of the Third Judicial District of Arizona Territory, June 11, 1903.
United States v. Gila Valley Irrigation District. Globe Equity 59, U.S. District in and for the
District of Arizona (June 29, 1935).
United States v. Gila Valley Irrigation District. No. CV31-0059-TUC-SRB (March 29, 2005).
United States v. Rio Grande Dam and Irrigation Company. 174 U.S. 690 (1899).
United States v. Winans. 198 U.S. 371 (1904).
Winters v. United States. 207 U.S. 564 (1908).

NEWSPAPERS

Arizona Blade Tribune
Arizona Republic
Casa Grande Bulletin Print
Chicago Tribune
Florence Tribune

Phoenix Gazette
Tribune Newspapers
Tucson Daily Citizen
Weekly Arizona Miner

U.S. GOVERNMENT DOCUMENTS

Annual Report of the Attorney General, 1914. Washington, D.C.: Government Printing Office, 1915.

Annual Report of the Board of Directors of the Indian Rights Association. Philadelphia: Office of the Indian Rights Association, 1912.

Annual Report of the Commissioner of Indian Affairs. Washington, D.C.: Government Printing Office, 1866, 1867, 1869, 1872, 1878, 1880, 1887, 1890, 1895, 1896, 1898, 1900, 1903, 1904.

Annual Report of the United States Geological Survey, Part 4. Washington, D.C.: Government Printing Office, 1901.

"Annual Report of the United States Indian Irrigation Service, District 4." Fiscal year 1913, 1915. United States Indian Irrigation Service, Annual District and Project Records.

"Conditions of Reservation Indians, Letter from the Secretary of the Interior, dated February 21, 1902." In *House Document 406*, 1–15. 57th Congress, 1st session. Washington, D.C.: Government Printing Office, 1902.

Congressional Record. Washington, D.C.: Government Printing Office.

"Conserving the Rights of the Pima Indians of Arizona, Letters and Petitions with Reference to Conserving the Rights of the Pima Indians of Arizona to the Lands of Their Reservation and the Necessary Water Supply for Irrigation." In *House Document 521*, 1–81. 62nd Congress, 2nd Session. Washington, D.C.: Government Printing Office, 1912.

Cooke, Philip St. George. *Report of Lieutenant Colonel P. St. George Cooke of His March from Santa Fe, New Mexico, to San Diego, Upper California. House Executive Document 41*. 30th Congress, 1st Session. Washington, D.C.: Wendell and Van Benthuysen, 1848.

Diversion Dam on the Gila River at a Site above Florence, Arizona, Excerpts to Be Used by the Committee on Indian Affairs. 64th Congress, 2nd Session. Washington, D.C.: Government Printing Office, 1917.

Emory, William H. *Notes of a Military Reconnaissance from Fort Leavenworth, in Missouri, to San Diego, in California, Including Parts of the Arkansas, del Norte, and Gila Rivers Made in 1846–1847. House Executive Document 41*. 30th Congress, 1st Session. Washington, D.C.: Wendell and Van Benthuysen, 1848.

———. *Notes of a Military Reconnaissance from Fort Leavenworth, in Missouri, to San Diego, in California, Including Parts of the Arkansas, del Norte, and Gila Rivers Made in 1846–1847. Senate Executive Document 7*. 30th Congress, 1st Session. Washington, D.C.: Wendell and Van Benthuysen, 1848.

Federal Register. Washington, D.C.: Government Printing Office.

Fourteenth Census of the United States Taken in the Year 1920, Volume VII, Irrigation and Drainage. Washington, D.C.: Government Printing Office, 1922.

Hearings before the Committee on Expenditures in the Interior Department of the House of Representatives on House Resolution No. 103 to Investigate the Expenditures in the Interior Department, June 5, 1911. Washington, D.C.: Government Printing Office, 1911.

Jackson, Reverend Sheldon, and Reverend George L. Spining. "Our Red Reconcentrados—
Some Facts concerning the Pima and Papago Indians of Arizona." In *Congressional Record*,
1515. 56th Congress, 2nd Session, January 26, 1901, part 2.

Lee, Willis T. *The Underground Waters of Gila Valley, Arizona*. Water Supply and Irrigation
Paper No. 104, 58th Congress, 2nd Session. Washington, D.C.: Government Printing
Office, 1904.

Nicklason, Fred. "Report for the Gila River Pima and Maricopa Tribes." In *Indian Water
Rights of the Five Central Arizona Tribes of Arizona, Hearings before the Committee on Interior and Insular Affairs, United States Senate*, 603–97. 94th Congress, 1st session, October
1975. Washington, D.C.: Government Printing Office, 1975.

*The Pima Indians and the San Carlos Irrigation Project: Information Presented to the Committee
on Indian Affairs, House of Representatives in Connection with S. 966, an Act for the Continuance of Construction Work on the San Carlos Federal Irrigation Project in Arizona and for
Other Purposes*. Washington, D.C.: Government Printing Office, 1924.

Records of the Inspector General. Washington, D.C.: Government Printing Office, 1870.

*Report from the Secretary of War, Communicating a Copy of the Official Journal of Lieuten-
ant Colonel Philip St. George Cooke, from Santa Fe to San Diego, etc.* Senate Report No. 2.
30th Congress, 1st session. Washington, D.C.: Wendell and Van Benthuysen, 1849.

*Report in the Matter of the Investigation of the Salt and Gila Rivers—Reservations and Reclama-
tion Service*. House Report 1506. 62nd Congress, 3rd Session. Washington, D.C.: Government Printing Office, 1913.

Report of Advisors on Irrigation on Indian Reservations. Washington, D.C.: Department of the
Interior, June 1928.

San Carlos Irrigation Project: Annual Report, 1994. Washington, D.C.: Bureau of Indian Affairs,
U.S. Department of Interior, 1994.

San Carlos Irrigation Project: House Report 618. House of Representatives, 68th Congress,
1st Session, May 1, 1924. Washington, D.C.: Government Printing Office, 1924.

Southworth, C. H. "The History of Irrigation along the Gila River." In "Report on the
San Carlos Irrigation Project and the History of Irrigation along the Gila River, Appendix
A." In *Indians of the United States, Hearings before the Committee on Indian Affairs, House
of Representatives, on the Conditions of Various Tribes of Indians*, appendixes, 103–223.
66th Congress, 1st Session. Washington, D.C.: Government Printing Office, 1919.

Statutes at Large of the United States of America, 1789–1873. Vols. 2, 3, 7, 19, 47, 67, 115, and 118.
Washington, D.C.: Government Printing Office, 1875–1936.

Testimony of Wendell Reed. In U.S. House of Representatives, *Indians of the United States,
Hearings before the Committee of Indian Affairs on the Conditions of Various Tribes of Indians*,
vol. 1. Hearings, 66th Congress, 1st Session. Washington, D.C.: Government Printing
Office, 1919.

Thirteenth Census of the United States Taken in the Year 1910, Volume VI, Agriculture. Washington, D.C.: Government Printing Office, 1912.

U.S. House of Representatives. *Indians of the United States: Hearings before the Committee on
Indian Affairs*. 66th Congress, 1st Session. 1919. Vol. 2, Appendixes. Washington, D.C.:
Government Printing Office.

U.S. Senate. *Bridge Canyon Project: Hearings before a Subcommittee of the Committee on Public
Lands*. 80th Congress, 1st session, on S. 1175, June and July 1948. Washington, D.C.: Government Printing Office, 1948.

———. *Bridge Canyon Project: Senate Report 832.* 81st Congress, 1st session, August 3, 1949. Washington, D.C.: Government Printing Office, 1949.

———. *Indian Appropriation Bill: Hearings before the Committee on Indian Affairs, United States Senate, on H. R. 20150.* 63rd Congress, 3rd session. Washington, D.C.: Government Printing Office, 1915.

———. *Indian Water Rights of the Five Central Tribes of Arizona: Hearings before the Committee on Interior and Insular Affairs on Water Rights of Ak-Chin Indian Reservation, Ft. McDowell Reservation, Gila River Indian Reservation, Papago Indian Reservation, and Salt River Pima-Maricopa Indian Reservation.* 94th Congress, 1st Session, October 23 and 24, 1975. Washington, D.C.: Government Printing Office, 1976.

INDEX

Printed in the USA
CPSIA information can be obtained
at www.ICGtesting.com
LVHW101616290723
753153LV00002B/3